D

T   f

Pluto Irish Library
Series editor Mike Milotte

Already published

James Larkin
Irish Labour Leader 1876–1947
EMMET LARKIN

Forthcoming

Labour and Nationalism in Ireland
J. D. CLARKSON

Communism in Modern Ireland
MIKE MILOTTE

Was Ireland Conquered?
TONY CARTY

Labour and Partition in Ireland
The Belfast Working Class 1905–1923
AUSTEN MORGAN

The Politics of James Connolly

KIERAN ALLEN

PLUTO PRESS

London • Winchester, Mass

First published 1990 by Pluto Press
345 Archway Road, London N6 5AA
and 8 Winchester Place, Winchester MA 01890, USA

Bookmarx Club edition in conjunction with
Bookmarks, 265 Seven Sisters Road
Finsbury Park
London N4 2DE

British Library Cataloguing in Publication Data
Allen, Kieran
    The politics of James Connolly.
    1. Ireland. Marxist movements. Role Connolly, James, 1868–
    1916
    I. Title
    322.4'2'0924

    ISBN 0–7453–0394–3

Library of Congress Cataloging-in-Publication Data
    Allen, Kieran, 1954–
        The politics of James Connolly/Kieran Allen.
            p.   cm.
        Includes bibliographical references.
        ISBN 0–7453–0394–3
        ISBN 0–7453–0473–7 (pbk.)
        1. Connolly, James, 1868–1916.   2. Ireland—Politics and
    government—1901–1910.   3. Ireland—Politics and
    government—1910–1921.   I. Title.
    DA965.C7A62   1990
    335.4'092–dc20   89–48320
                                                          CIP

Typeset by BP Integraphics Ltd, Bath
Printed in Great Britain by Billing and Sons Ltd, Worcester

Contents

Abbreviations

AFL	American Federation of Labour
AOH	Ancient Order of Hibernians
CGT	Confédération Générale du Travail
CPI	Communist Party of Ireland
ICA	Irish Citizen Army
ILP	Independent Labour Party
ILP(I)	Independent Labour Party of Ireland
IRB	Irish Republican Brotherhood
IRA	Irish Republican Army
ITGWU	Irish Transport and General Workers Union
ITUC	Irish Trade Union Congress
ISRP	Irish Socialist Republican Party
IWW	Industrial Workers of the World
LEA	Labour Electoral Association
NUR	National Union of Railwaymen
NSFU	National Sailors' and Firemen's Union
SDF	Social Democratic Federation (Britain)
SPA	Socialist Party of America
SDKPiL	Social Democratic Party of Poland and Lithuania
SPI	Socialist Party of Ireland
SPD	Social Democratic Party of Germany
SLP	Socialist Labour Party (America)
SLP	Socialist Labour Party (Scotland)
SSF	Scottish Socialist Federation
STLA	Socialist Trade and Labour Alliance
UVF	Ulster Volunteer Force
TUC	Trade Union Congress

Chronology

1868: Connolly born in Edinburgh, Scotland.
1889: Connolly joins the socialist movement in Scotland.
      The Second International formed in Paris.
1894: Connolly stands as a socialist candidate in elections in Edinburgh.
      John Leslie's *The Irish Question* published.
      Irish Trade Union Congress formed.
1896: Connolly arrives in Dublin and founds the Irish Socialist Republican Party.
1897: Commemoration movement for United Irish Rebellion of 1798.
      Connolly forms 'Rank and File '98 Club'.
      Anti-Jubilee protest organised.
      Erin's Hope published.
1899: ISRP contest elections under local government franchise.
      Bernstein publishes his revisionist attack on Marxism.
      The French socialist Millerand joins a Coalition Ministry.
1900: ISRP delegates attend Fifth Congress of Second International.
1901: Connolly tours Scotland to organise revolutionary left.
      New Evangel published.
1903: Socialist Labour Party formed in Scotland with Connolly's support. Connolly departs for America as ISRP collapses.
1904: Polemics with De Leon on Wages, Marriage and Religion.
1905: Revolt in Russia.
      International Workers of the World formed in the USA.
1907: Connolly elected to National Executive of Socialist Labour Party but leaves party shortly afterwards.
      Connolly appointed organiser for IWW.
      Belfast dock strike.
      Stuttgart Congress of the Second International debates colonialism and war.
1908: Connolly issues the Irish American paper, *The Harp*.
      Socialism Made Easy published.
      Connolly joins Socialist Party of America.

1909:   Connolly becomes a National Organiser for the SPA.
1910:   Connolly returns to Ireland.
        Labour in Irish History and *Labour, Nationality and Religion*
        published.
1911:   Connolly appointed Belfast organiser of the Irish Transport and
        General Workers Union. Debates with William Walker, an ILP
        supporter.
1912:   Connolly proposes resolution to found the Irish Labour Party.
        Third Home Rule Bill moved. Pro-Home Rule workers driven
        out of their workplaces in Belfast.
        Second International meets at Basel to pledge itself to oppose
        war.
1913:   Lock out of Dublin working class.
        Connolly becomes General Secretary of the ITGWU.
        Irish Citizen Army formed.
1914:   World War I declared. Connolly opposes war.
        Irish Trade Union Congress demonstrates against proposals to
        partition Ireland.
1915:   *The Re-conquest of Ireland* published.
        Zimmerwald conference of socialists against the war.
1916:   Easter Rising.
        Connolly executed in its aftermath.

Acknowledgements

This book could not have been written without the assistance of a number of people who devoted many hours of their time to redrafting original manuscripts. Particular thanks is due to Mike Milotte, whose careful editing and discussion of a number of points was most helpful. I also owe a particular debt to Marnie Holborow for suggesting many changes and for offering encouragement over the four years it took to write the book. My thanks also to Willie Cummings, Mike Thompson and Kevin Wingfield, who made useful comments and helped prepare the final draft. Finally, the book is written from within the general framework of the theory and perspectives of the Socialist Workers Movement and it is from that organisation as a whole that I have drawn the ideas which have shaped this book.

Introduction

James Connolly was the founder of the Marxist movement in Ireland. For two decades he strove tirelessly, and mostly in desperate poverty, to build Ireland's first socialist parties. These followed each other with bewildering speed. First, there was the Irish Socialist Republican Party (ISRP), then the Socialist Party of Ireland (SPI), and, latterly, the Independent Labour Party of Ireland (ILP(I)). None of them managed to break out of the margins of Irish society. All of them contained fewer than 100 members. Yet it was to the building of this Marxist political movement that Connolly dedicated his life.

This singular fact has been buried beneath the legend. Today Connolly has joined the pantheon of nationalist heroes. Eamonn De Valera, when he was about to become the first Fianna Fail prime minister in 1932, asked himself rhetorically which statement of Irish policy would most coincide with his views. He replied that he would 'stand side by side with James Connolly'.[1] Since then the political establishment have named hospitals, train stations, and streets after Connolly. Branches of both the dominant party, Fianna Fail, and its republican opponents, Sinn Fein, are called the 'Connolly Cumainn'. Yet his ideas are rarely discussed, and still less understood.

Instead there has been a splintering of his politics that is best expressed by two ballads dedicated to his name. In one he appears as 'the brave son of Ireland', in the other as the 'hero of the working man'. The connections between his fight for the working class and his battle against the British Empire are rarely drawn. Rather he is portrayed as a man who 'belonged to, and worked in two worlds: the world of international socialism and the world of militant nationalism'.[2] It is as if he were pulled by two mutually contradictory passions; uncertain, wavering, and torn by conflicting emotions; moving ceaselessly from one to the other until the ultimate sacrifice of 1916 resolves his terrible dilemma.

The contention of this book is otherwise. It is that Connolly must be viewed as a revolutionary socialist who was trapped inside the decaying traditions of the Second International – the international socialist movement of his day. He tried to seize every opportunity and foment every struggle that would lead to a break with capitalism. His involvement in the fight for Irish freedom arose from this intention. The Second International proved incapable of developing a strategy for socialists in the colonies and the manner in which Connolly sought to link the struggle for national independence and socialism was unique at the time.

With little assistance from any other quarter, Connolly pursued a distinct strategy from his arrival in Ireland in 1896 to his execution in 1916. It was based on tremendous insights into Irish history and into the dynamic of the Irish revolution. But it was also ultimately flawed and was unlikely to be otherwise, given the state of the working class movement. Pretending that this was not the case and that Connolly is the font of all wisdom on the Irish Question is a recipe for the continued weakness of the Irish left. This book focusses on Connolly's revolutionary strategy and its legacy for the Irish left. It makes no attempt to claim Connolly for a particular tradition but, rather, subjects his ideas to considerable criticism. It does so, however, from a Marxist, and therefore a revolutionary socialist, position.

Biographies

Connolly's stature meant that any serious left-wing organisation in Ireland had to come to terms with him. One can almost trace the history of the Irish left and its lines of division through the commentaries it has produced on Connolly. It therefore behoves any new book on Connolly to situate itself in relation to the vast bulk of literature that has been written on him.

Biographies and assessments of Connolly have traditionally fallen into three categories. The first has sought to produce a sanitised version of Connolly that fitted in with the conservatism of Irish society. The second has idealised Connolly as an Irish Lenin who developed the proper synthesis between nationalism and socialism. The third and most recent brand has sought to dismiss Connolly as a misguided nationalist.

The sanitised version of Connolly made its appearance shortly after his death. The Irish bourgeoisie faced the acute embarrassment of finding a self-proclaimed Marxist among the heroes of 1916. Moreover, between 1918 and 1923 there was a tremendous wave of militancy among Irish workers. A Sinn Fein commentator at the time wrote that Catholic communities are

> generally hostile to socialism and so the socialistic enthusiasm which ran over Ireland during 1919 puzzled many. But there the fact was. Never was Ireland more devoutly Catholic than to-day ... yet nowhere was the Bolshevik revolution more sympathetically saluted.[3]

There existed a real danger of a generation of militant workers making a connection between the writings of Connolly and the Bolshevik tradition. In response to this threat a number of articles and pamphlets appeared after Connolly's death which were to leave an abiding image for decades to come. The first major assessment of Connolly was undertaken by a Reverend Coffey in the *Catholic Bulletin* of 1920.[4] A series of five articles appeared, bristling with attacks on capitalism, virtually justifying revolution, and arguing that, contrary to previous beliefs, the Catholic Church was not opposed to socialism. Their ultimate aim, however, was to reclaim Connolly for the Church. They were followed by a pamphlet, *The Social Teaching of James Connolly* by the Reverend McKenna, published by the Catholic Truth Society. More critical of Connolly than Revd Coffey's, this nevertheless started out from a proclaimed anti-capitalist position.

The Revd McKenna stated that 'Connolly's patronage has given to Marx's philosophy a vogue among Irish men which it would never otherwise have enjoyed.'[5] His pamphlet aimed to rectify this. In 1925, when reaction had finally begun to triumph, Connolly's comrade in the Irish Citizen Army, Countess Markievicz, lent her considerable credibility to the new image of Connolly by producing a pamphlet, *James Connolly's Policy and Catholic Doctrine*. This supported the points previously made by the learned priests.

There were two central themes that ran through the sanitised version of Connolly. The first argued quite simply that because he was a Catholic and an Irishman, he could not have been a Marxist. Countess Markievicz remarked that he merely studied Marx as he studied all social reformers. A provincial Connolly that had no connection with socialist tradition was presented: 'Socialism was what he stood for but it was the socialism of James Connolly and of nobody else.'[6] With the sophistication of a good Jesuit, the Revd McKenna informed his readers that Connolly's problem was that he tended to use Marxist formulae for what were genuinely orthodox Catholic and nationalist ideals. 'Connolly's voice', he claimed, 'is ever the voice of Tone or Lalor though his words are often the words of Marx.'[7]

The second theme was that Connolly was a type of 'guild socialist', as distinct from the 'state socialists' who had made the revolution in Russia. The Revd Coffey took up Connolly's marvellous articles against the dangers of middle-class reformers advocating 'state capitalism' under the guise of socialism.[8] Connolly's attacks on those who identified socialism with state ownership were compared with the positions of Catholic intellectuals such as Belloc and Chesterton. These had railed against capitalism from the vantage point of extolling the virtues of feudalism with its narrow-minded and repressive co-operation that was expressed in the guilds. In Coffey's view Connolly stood simply for co-operative ownership rather than workers' exercising their class rule over the whole of society by means of *their* state.

These themes were tremendously influential. For decades socialists protected themselves against Catholic reaction by pointing to the fact that Connolly was relatively safe to read because he had nothing to do with Marxism. Connolly's union, the Irish Transport and General Workers Union, constantly used the phrase 'Co-operative Commonwealth' in place of the more militant-sounding phrase, 'the Workers' Republic'. As late as 1968, when the revolutionary wave in Western Europe was at its height, the Irish Congress of Trade Unions invited Owen Dudley Edwards to give a lecture to commemorate Connolly's birth. This was later published as the book *The Mind of an Activist – James Connolly*. It made the extraordinary claim that Connolly perceived an 'essential inter-dependence of Catholicism and Socialism' and that he was, in fact, 'one of the best and most enlightened apologists the Catholic Church has seen since the industrial revolution'.[9]

This sanitised image of Connolly as a non-Marxist socialist who could have no sympathy with the Bolshevik revolution could only be produced by ignoring the facts, for Connolly had spent most of his life in openly Marxist parties. Before arriving in Ireland he was a member of the Scottish Socialist Federation, an openly Marxist body, as distinct from the Independent Labour Party. In 1900 he had his own ISRP affiliate to the Second International, a self-proclaimed world Marxist organisation. In America he was an active member of the Marxist Socialist Labour Party until internal factionalism disillusioned him with its regime.

In his pamphlet *Labour, Nationality and Religion* Connolly quite explicitly set out to defend the Marxist notions of the 'materialist conception of history' and the 'labour theory of value'.[10] Moreover, it was precisely revolutionary Marxists such as Connolly who, impressed by syndicalist criticisms of reformism, were to be most impressed by the Bolshevik revolution. The building of a workers' state based on the soviets embodied their twin ideals of public ownership and workers' control. That, at least, was the view of Connolly's first biographer, Desmond Ryan, whose book appeared in 1924 before the myth-making machine in both Ireland and Russia had begun to work. Ryan claimed that, 'broadly speaking, James Connolly must be classified as a Workers' Republican and Communist' and that in much of his rhetoric 'he foreshadows many a trenchant outburst of Trotsky.'[11]

There was undoubtedly a weakness in Connolly's application of the Marxist method. His syndicalism eventually led him to downplay the importance of openly Marxist organisations. There was also a caution about taking on the power of the Catholic Church (although he had nothing to do with the versions of 'Christian socialism' attributed to him after his death). But the notion of Connolly as an innocent who had fallen among Marxists or as a socialist concerned to retail exclusively his own unique brand could only have been dreamt up in the deeply conservative society that Southern Ireland became.

The merit of the second type of biography, typified by Greaves' *The*

Life and Times of James Connolly was that it destroyed this fiction.[12] Greaves's book, which was first published in 1961, was a detailed and scholarly study of Connolly's political development. Several pamphlets and articles followed in its wake accepting its general analysis which was informed by the politics of the Communist Party.

Desmond Greaves had been an active member of the Connolly Association in Britain. Its paper, the *Irish Democrat*, reached some of the 400,000 Irish workers who had been forced to emigrate in the 1950s. Freed involuntarily from the vicious anti-communist hysteria at home, a minority of these workers made their first contact with socialist politics through the Connolly Association. When some of these returned to Ireland in the 1960s, they were to become the backbone of a revived left. They played a considerable role in influencing sections of the republican movement who were later to form Official Sinn Fein (the Workers Party today).

The Connolly Association held a strict 'stages' view of the national question in Ireland. During the first stage the working class would unite with progressive sections of the national bourgeoisie to fight for national liberation. This would demand a certain 'discipline' on the part of workers to maintain this unity. The raising of demands that might frighten off the national bourgeoisie from the alliance was classified as 'ultra-left'. Only after the first stage of national liberation had been won could socialist demands be raised.

In order to implement such a strategy Marxism was reinterpreted in nationalist terms. Thus, the Communist Party historian, T.A. Jackson, argued, in an introduction to a pamphlet on Connolly, that 'internationalism rightly understood is the completion and growth of nationalism.'[13] The Connolly Association itself put the matter simply and crudely when it claimed that Connolly's merit was that he was distinguished from other socialists by his saying, 'Get Ireland free first and we can talk of the social system afterwards.'[14]

This perspective influenced Greaves's biography of Connolly in two ways. First, the importance of *Labour in Irish History*, Connolly's major contribution to Irish Marxism, was played down. Greaves claims that the book 'smacked of syndicalism'; that 'it was inclined to discount the value of "legislative independence"'; that Connolly oversimplified under the influence of the American Marxist, De Leon. This despite the fact that the sections in *Labour in Irish History* to which Greaves most objects were written *before* Connolly met De Leon or encountered syndicalism. The real problem with the book for Greaves is that it tended 'to deny any progressive significance to the capitalist class'.[15]

These criticisms are occasioned by the fact that *Labour and Irish History* most clearly expresses one of the central tenets of Connolly's politics: namely that Ireland could not be freed from imperialism without the achievement of a workers' republic. As we shall see, there were problems in the manner in which Connolly arrived at, and argued for, this insight.

Nevertheless, it was a source of embarrassment to all those who wished to support a stages theory. It blew the elaborate enterprise apart by stating baldly and simply that the 'first stage' could not be achieved without the most determined fight by a socialist working class. It pointed to the cowardice of the national bourgeoisie and the ties that bound them to imperialism.

Second, and in sharp contrast to the criticism of *Labour in Irish History*, every concession Connolly made to nationalist politics is praised by Greaves as the height of wisdom. Such criticisms are described as a growth to maturity. The slippage from socialism to republicanism is recognised, but no analysis is presented as to why this might have occurred. After a while, the book ceases to be an assessment of Connolly's politics and becomes a hagiography. Every tactical step that Connolly takes in relation to the nationalists, once his supposed early ultra-leftism is overcome, is praised. This is particularly so when it comes to Connolly's role in 1916.

Socialists today are left with the obvious question: why, if Connolly's tactics and strategy were totally correct, was the left so weak for decades afterwards? The standard answer is that after 1916 Connolly's heirs did not follow the road he charted. The leaders of Irish Labour who followed Connolly, principally William O'Brien and Tom Johnson, played an appalling role. But it is also the case that these worked closely with Connolly in the years beforehand and were rarely subjected to any criticism from him. Any assessment of why the nationalist forces won out so totally over the left must therefore look closely at the type of concessions Connolly made in his own day.

The stages theory has led to countless disasters on the Irish left, mirroring as it did De Valera's dictum that 'Labour must wait.' Its concrete application to Northern Ireland in the late 1960s led to a call for reform of the Northern state as a preliminary even to the first stage of fighting to end partition. In the South it has led the Communist Party to call on workers to give their second preference votes under the proportional representation electoral system to Fianna Fail. The idea that Fianna Fail personifies the progressive national sections of the bourgeoisie has a currency far beyond the tiny Communist Party. Therefore, as part of the struggle to develop left-wing politics in Ireland, it is necessary to reassess the image of Connolly left by Desmond Greaves.

The most recent writing on Connolly has come from an altogether different source and stems from the deadlock in the struggle in Northern Ireland. In this context Connolly has been attacked for providing intellectual sustenance to those on the left who hold a 'Troops Out' position and seek an end to partition. Conor Cruise O'Brien began this form of criticism by charging that Connolly had written the Protestant working class out of Irish history.[16] More recently, Austen Morgan has produced a comprehensive biography to show that Connolly ceased to be a socialist in 1914 and became a national revolutionary instead.[17] But the clearest theoretical attack on Connolly's legacy has come from a number of intellectuals who are members and supporters of the Workers Party.

Bew, Patterson and Gibbon devote a major essay in their book *The State in Northern Ireland* to the arguments raised by Connolly's anti-imperialism.[18] They charge Connolly with sliding from a correct (Leninist) position – namely that the working class must play a leading role in the fight for national freedom – to the (Trotskyist) position that there could be no national freedom without the victory of the working class. Connolly's teachings have led the left to seek 'completion' of the national question when, in fact, the matter has been solved. Indeed any attempt to proceed in the direction of ending partition would mean that instead of half a million Catholics' being denied their democratic rights within Northern Ireland, the whole population would be denied democracy in a united Ireland that forcibly included one million Protestants.

This argument is conducted with considerable theoretical sophistication (one is tempted to claim sophistry). Connolly is charged with economism; of having a pre-Althusserian view of ideology; of not understanding the class basis of opposition to Home Rule. But in essentials it is a plea to the contemporary Irish left to break with Connolly's anti-imperialism. The authors arrive at the startling conclusion that, 'in 1969, when large-scale British military involvement in Ireland was resumed, the effects of imperialism in the classical sense upon Irish affairs was slight.'[19]

There has been considerable mysticism on the Irish left about 'completing' the bourgeois revolution. The impression has been created that any country which has not experienced events like those of France in 1789, still has a bourgeois revolution to complete. This has gone along with the notion that the South of Ireland, being an 'incomplete' entity, must perforce be a neo-colony of Britain. All of these ideas need to be challenged – although it is doubtful if Connolly can be held responsible for all of them.

But Bew, Patterson and Gibbon want to go a good deal further and deny there is *any* national problem in Ireland. However, the existence of a state structured around discrimination and violence against Northern Catholics suggests otherwise. The fight against partition today is primarily a fight for the democratic rights of this large community. All the failed efforts at reforming the North – including more than a decade of direct rule from Britain – show that there is no way of winning those rights other than through the destruction of the state of Northern Ireland. The fact that a united bourgeois Ireland could not be achieved without trampling on everyone's democratic rights – rather than an excuse for accepting the status quo – is precisely the reason for continuing Connolly's fight for a workers' republic

Bew, Paterson and Gibbon's learned definitions of imperialism amount to nothing other than claiming that since the specific nature of imperialism has changed since Lenin's day, imperialism itself has ceased to exist. On this basis America was not fighting an imperialist war in Vietnam because it had few direct economic interests there. To claim such would, of course, be nonsense. The division of the world among a hierarchy of states means that economic competition has grown over into military–political competition, primarily on a grand scale between the US and its allies and the USSR.

Britain remains a major player in the camp of Western imperialism. It cannot countenance defeat at the hands of a nationalist force in Ireland. To allow this would be to undermine the standing of the army and the strength of the British state in the eyes of British workers. Such a defeat would also contribute to undermining the military threat posed by the the NATO alliance against countless millions of oppressed people around the world. The British army will, therefore, have to be driven out of Ireland by mass working-class action throughout the island.

British imperialism remains the primary guarantor of partition in Ireland despite its pretence at reform. Today it is fighting a battle to underpin a bigoted and repressive state whose very existence is a source of division among Irish workers. Those who oppose the struggle against imperialism are not breaking just with Connolly – but with the whole Marxist tradition.

The Relevance of Connolly

Greaves has claimed that Connolly belonged to the middle ranks of the international labour movement. It is a fair assessment. He was not a major theoretician but primarily a propagandist and an activist. Nor did he manage to build a sizeable political organisation around his ideas. Connolly's contribution was far less specific than many of the giants of the international socialist movement. Nevertheless it was of immense importance. Connolly's whole political project rested on an anti-imperialist outlook. In this he was far ahead of many other socialists of his day. At its founding congress in 1896 the Second International had condemned colonialism, but this condemnation was couched in essentially liberal, humanitarian terms.

There was little understanding of how a blow struck against imperialism in the colonies might be of benefit to the international working class. The Second International was not able to move from a position of concern to an understanding that the fates of British and Indian workers were interdependent. They were highly pessimistic about the possibilities of the workers and peasantry of the colonies liberating themselves. Connolly's perspective was different. Anti-colonialism was not simply an article of faith – it was the basis of a socialist strategy. Therein lies his continued relevance today.

In many quarters the Third Worldism of the 1960s has given way to a disillusionment about anti-imperialism. The horrors of Kampuchea under Pol Pot, the war fought between 'socialist' Vietnam and 'socialist'

China, the new tendency for almost all nationalist regimes to accept a market economy are just some of the sources for that disillusionment. Moreover the leaders of the revolts against the imperial powers are no longer always left nationalists but sometimes right nationalists. Islamic fundamentalism, while it has suffered a blow after the Iran/Iraq war, still exercises an attraction for those who want to destroy American influence in the Middle East. The battles against imperialism today take place without raising hopes of ushering in 'people's communes'.

Connolly has the advantage of belonging to an age before 'anti-imperialism' was elevated into a distinct and separate creed. He held to the elementary notion that a victory over colonialism could only be achieved through the organised power of workers. There is no hint in Connolly's writing that countries which break from the world market could bestow liberation on their people by following a state-capitalist strategy. Instead he believed that anti-imperialism was simply an aspect of being a socialist.

This is of continuing relevance today. The US may not be in the same position as the British Empire in Connolly's day. Yet it is still the major imperialist power and has now recovered from the defeats inflicted on it in Vietnam. It has used the weakness of its main rival, the USSR, to reassume its role as the world's policeman. Peace on American terms today carries an immense cost for much of the world's population. Countries like Libya and Nicaragua are terrorised by the menace of US military strength. Nationalist movements like the PLO who try to come to terms with the US must first bow the knee to its humiliating demands. Connolly's argument for making anti-imperialism part of the ABC of the socialist alphabet could not be more relevant.

It is, however, in Ireland that his message can strike home most effectively. His name continues to haunt the two major parties of the Irish left – the Labour Party, which claims him as a founding father, and the Workers Party, which boasts of its Marxist positions. The parallels between Connolly's fight with the Empire and the struggle in the North of Ireland today are not immediate and direct. But they are sufficient to act as a source of embarrassment to these parties.

Both the Labour Party and the Workers Party have come to defend the institutions of partition against what they see as a 'terrorist threat'. Both have described the IRA as a 'fascist' organisation. This extraordinary description enables them to justify alliances with all manner of conservatives to defend the 'democratic institutions'. The result has been that they have managed to place themselves to the right of their own supporters. A number of examples will illustrate this.

In December 1987, the respective leaders of the Labour Party and the Workers Party, Dick Spring and Tomas McGiolla, sent a letter to Neil Kinnock, leader of the British Labour Party, complaining about the activities of the left-Labour MP, Ken Livingstone. Livingstone's crime was to complain in the House of Commons about the activities of the British army's undercover killer units of the Special Air Services (SAS), and to invite Sinn Fein representatives to Britain on a fact-finding mission. In their open letter, Spring and McGiolla argued that Ken Livingstone's activities were 'extremely offensive to Irish socialists'. They demanded that he be disciplined, as he shared 'part of the blame for future atrocities'.[20]

In 1988, when extradition dominated the Irish political agenda, the Labour Party and the Workers Party were among its most enthusiastic supporters. They repeatedly advised the Fianna Fail government to 'de-politicise' the issue. According to opinon polls, however, over 60 per cent of left voters opposed extradition.

Fighting the supposed 'fascist' threat has also meant turning a blind eye to terrible injustices. In 1984 a socialist republican, Nicky Kelly, was jailed for a train robbery. The trial before a juryless court was a complete fraud. The only evidence was a forced confession extracted after beatings by the Irish police. The campaign to win the release of Nicky Kelly had to overcome the opposition of the Labour Party and the Workers Party before it finally succeeded.

The position of both parties follows the same lines pursued by their predecessors in the 1920s who also supported the institutions of the Free State against its republican rivals. This position remains one of the main sources of the weakness of the Irish left. Today their collusion in repression forces the issue of 'security' and 'law and order' to the fore. It is precisely on these issues that parties of the right gain ground. Moreover, by taking a frankly pro-partition stance, they make it easier for Fianna Fail to engage in flourishes of nationalist rhetoric.

The writing off of the republican forces as 'fascist' is achieved by equating fascism with the cult of violence. On the basis of this loose definition, Padraig Pearse could be deemed to be a fascist because of his leadership of the 1916 rebellion. Connolly, fortunately, was far beyond these simplicities. His thoroughgoing anti-imperialism enabled him to understand who was the major enemy and whose violence was central. The prejudices and backward politics of the republicans were no reason to equate them with the militarism of the British Empire.

In a very real sense, then, the Irish left needs to recover the politics of James Connolly. His description of partition as a 'carnival of reaction' to be fought vigorously; his dismissal of 'gas and water' socialists such as William Walker, who put minor electoral gains above an opposition to Loyalism; his notion of a working-class leadership of the national struggle – all are of continued and direct relevance. They stand today as the basis for a revolutionary socialist position in Ireland.

This does not mean idealising Connolly. Quite the contrary. An honest assessment must look at both his strengths and weaknesses. In what follows there is much that is sharply critical of Connolly. But it takes as its starting point a shared position with Connolly: the continued relevance of anti-imperialism for the left.

1. The Formative Influences

Strenuous efforts have been made to remove any alien features from the image of James Connolly. To many he appeared first and foremost as a 'brave son of Ireland'. Ralph Fox, a socialist who came to support De Valera, epitomised this trend when he invented an Irish birthplace for Connolly, 'in a gloomy little cabin in Ballybay'.[1] The price paid for entering the pantheon of Irish nationalists was that his connections with the international socialist movement were neglected or played down.

Yet it was that involvement that holds the key to understanding his politics. Connolly joined the socialist movement in Scotland in 1889. In the same year the Second International was founded at a congress in Paris to link together socialist parties throughout the world. Connolly's own political activity coincided almost exactly with life of the Second International. Its collapse at the outbreak of World War I was a major influence propelling him towards the 1916 rebellion.

Connolly spent 14 years – just over half of his active political life – outside Ireland. Throughout this time he was involved with British and American socialist parties, which were among the smaller affiliates to the Second International. There he learnt the traditions and methods of the international socialist movement, which were heavily influenced by the experience of the German socialist party, the SPD. It is necessary, therefore, to examine briefly the background of the Second International as a major formative influence on Connolly's politics.

The Second International was based on mass workers' parties. This was a considerable advance from Marx's day when small socialist groups combined with English trade unionists to form the First International. The new pattern was set by the German SPD. It was truly a mass party. Founded in 1875, it was baptised in the fire of Bismarck's antisocialist laws when 1,500 party members had received prison sentences totalling 1,600 years. The party survived these obstacles and in 1890 was able to poll just under one and a half million votes. In France, although socialists were divided, they nevertheless could poll 440,000 votes by 1893. In Austria and Italy the socialist parties were formed in 1889 and 1892, respectively. Both were modelled on the German party.[2]

Moreover, these mass parties were explicitly Marxist. All previous competing ideologies in the workers' movement, ranging from Proudhon's artisan socialism to the anarchist movement, had been effectively vanquished. Anarchism, it is true, still maintained an influence in countries such as Spain where it could relate to previous radical peasant traditions of abstention from politics. Yet in the core of the system Marxism, with its stress on political action, reigned supreme.

There was a contradiction at the heart of this unprecedented growth. The impetus for the revival of the socialist movement had come from the great depression that capitalism experienced between 1873 and 1896. But the consolidation of the mass parties coincided with an era of unprecedented expansion of the system. By means of mergers and monopolies German and American capital had overcome the crisis. By 1897 there were 82 concerns in America with a capitalisation in excess of US$1,000 million.

Britain led the field in imperialist expansion. Its investment in foreign and colonial stock quadrupled between 1883 and 1889. Its exports increasingly went to the less developed world. Between 1860 and 1870, 52 per cent of Britain's capital investments went to the US and Europe. By 1911–13, only 25 per cent went to these areas.[3] Where Britain led, others followed. Virtually the whole of the globe was divided out among the major powers. Between 1870 and 1900 the whole of sub-Saharan Africa, with the exception of Liberia and Ethiopia, was partitioned into 23 colonial possessions of six European powers.[4] The period in which the Second International grew was one of monopoly capital and imperialism.

The expansion of the system made possible an era of reform. Many countries granted workers the vote: Britain and Ireland in 1884; the USA in 1870 for white males; Germany in 1871; Spain in 1890 and Belgium in 1893. Economic gains were also possible without large-scale struggle. In Britain, for example, real wages were 66 per cent higher in 1890 than 40 years previously.[5]

Despite these openings the socialist parties were either illegal or marginalised in terms of the wider political structures. But they still came to see the pursuit of reforms within capitalism as the major practical focus of their activity. The result was a combination of radical rhetoric with a cautious grasping for the reforms on offer. Hobsbawn noted of the British party, the Social Democratic Federation, that its tradition 'was not so much revolutionary but intransigent'.[6] Socialist party leaders typically took up positions of extreme verbal opposition to capitalism, while socialist trade union leaders made what practical gains they could.

The politics of the Second International was characterised by a blatant contradiction: its growing bureaucratic apparatus used splendid revolutionary rhetoric while ensuring a high degree of passivity from most workers. The leading party in the Second International, the German SPD, was able to build up considerable support for intransigent policies while still showing a low level of strike activity, refusing even to stop for the May Day protest for the eight-hour day.[7] Its leading theoretician, the 'Pope of Marxism', Karl Kautsky, produced a mechanical version of Marxism that served this purpose. Although Connolly never attended any of its congresses, there is little doubt that he shared its general theoretical outlook.

The Second International accepted as a dogma that socialism was inevitable. Capitalism would fall of its own accord, with socialist parties functioning as midwives in the birth of a new society. Kautsky explained that 'the capitalist system had run its course. Its dissolution is now only a question of time. Irresistible economic forces lead with the certainty of doom to the shipwreck of capitalist production'.[8] It was a theory that Connolly subscribed to. In his paper, the *Workers Republic*, he reported favourably that August Bebel, a German SPD leader, had predicted the downfall of the system after 1908 and added that 'I have always thought that the first decade of this century [20th] would behold the beginning of the end and am glad that such an acute thinker as Bebel has arrived at a somewhat similar conclusion'.[9]

This highly optimistic prophecy could arise only from a peculiar reading of Marxist theory. It was pure economic determinism. Indeed this was precisely the label that Connolly would apply to Marxism when he was defending it in *Labour, Nationality and Religion*.[10] The motor of history was no longer the conscious activity of human beings. The development of the forces of production led to changes in the relations of production and this, in turn, led to automatic changes in the whole superstructure. In this manner history was pushed down its predetermined path towards the inevitable goal of socialism.

The class struggle merely reflected laws of history that had already been set down. As the economic conditions changed, workers would move to a more conscious understanding of the inevitable. One sign of this would be the rise in the votes for socialist candidates. The process would culminate with the 'breakdown' of capitalism. Such certainty and blind faith in 'progress' were characteristic marks of the Second International.

If capitalism was fated to collapse of its own accord, then socialist parties had a relatively passive role. Alongside mobilising for elections, their primary function was to produce propaganda. The party was to educate its members about the laws of economic development and to inculcate a scientific world-view among its supporters which would serve as a basis for consolidating its electoral constituency. The notion of the party as a machine for intervention and leadership in day-to-day struggles would arrive only with Lenin's break from Second International fatalism.

The emphasis on propaganda, however, could coexist with the playing down of political and ideological questions. Electoral pressures often meant that nationalism, racism and sexism were not tackled. These questions simply belonged to the superstructure and would be swept aside as economic conditions matured in the direction of socialist transformation. Propaganda was concentrated on the realisation of the 'maximum' programme of social democracy – the final transformation into socialism – and the 'minimum' programme – the proposals for reform under capitalism.

Connolly took an extreme view within the Second International on the exclusion of key ideological issues from socialist argument. He thought that all questions pertaining to religion and sexual relationships should not be discussed inside socialist parties. Their intrusion blurred the focus on the maximum and minimum parts of the programme. Nevertheless, if Connolly's total exclusion of these questions was uncommon, it still sprung from the same theoretical source: namely that working-class consciousness would passively reflect economic conditions and move spontaneously to socialism.

The political hallmark of the Second International was parliamentarianism. As early as 1893, the Zürich Congress of the International excluded anarchists because of their rejection of political action. Connolly supported this position enthusiastically. The content of political action was, however, defined exclusively in parliamentary terms. Socialists worked towards winning a majority in parliament as the method for introducing socialism. This was a significant break from the conclusion Marx had arrived at after the Paris Commune. Then Marx had written that workers could not lay hold of the ready-made state machine but had to smash it as the workers in Paris had attempted to do.[11] Kautsky defined the new attitude as follows: 'The objective of our political struggle remains what it has been up to now: the conquest of state power through the conquest of a majority in parliament and the elevation of parliament to a commanding position in the state. Certainly not the destruction of state power.'[12]

This was also Connolly's view, at least up to his departure to America in 1903. He regarded the ballot box as the most advanced form of political struggle and far superior to the conspiratorial methods of Irish republicanism. Later he rebelled against the consequences of an electoralist policy, but he never fully broke with it. He regarded the state as the management committee for the capitalist class. But the membership of the committee and its functions could be changed by the ballot box – at least in normal times.

On one area, however, Connolly had a serious problem with the Second International. The dominant orthodoxy held to a rigid stages view of history. Kautsky wrote that his theory was 'intended to be nothing more than the application of Darwinism to social development'.[13] The notion of stages of development implied that underdeveloped countries were destined to pass through the stage of capitalism. They would have to wait for the full development of the productive forces under capitalism before a struggle for socialism became possible. In that sense, each country was destined to follow the path taken by the more advanced.

Connolly had the peculiar vantage point of being one of the few socialists to come from the colonies. Awaiting the full development of capitalism there would demand infinite patience. His singular achievement in his analysis of Ireland was to break from the stages view of history. In a backward and impoverished colony he had the audacity to raise the fight for a workers' republic. Nevertheless he regarded Ireland as an exception to the general rule and the break with the Second International's stages view of history was not generalised. In isolated cases the mechanical stagist approach led to some extraordinary twists in Connolly's arguments. Thus, he favoured the expansion of Russia into Asia in order to hasten capitalist development in the former and thus bring a revolution sooner.[14] In World War I, it led him, as we shall see in Chapter 7, to develop a number of convoluted arguments to explain why he favoured a German victory.

Connolly's brilliance, then, lay in being a rebel within the traditions of the Second International. But like many rebels he could never fully break from its ideas. One finds constantly that many of his insights are profound – but the specific explanations he advances to support them are shaped by the politics of Second International Marxism. But to understand, firstly, how Connolly became a rebel inside the socialist movement we need to look at his experiences in Edinburgh.

Edinburgh Days

Connolly's decision to join the socialist movement brought him into conflict with some aspects of the Irish community in Edinburgh. He had been raised by impoverished Irish immigrants in the Cowgate ghetto of Edinburgh.[15] His father was an itinerant seasonal labourer who had come by more secure work as a manure carter for Edinburgh Corporation. His mother had worked as a domestic servant. Like the thousands who could not raise the fare to America after the Great Famine, they crowded into ghettoes such as Cowgate.

Cowgate was among the worst slums in Edinburgh. It had an average of seven people to a room. Yet in this 'little Ireland' it was possible for the skilled labourer to rub shoulders with his middle-class counterpart. A small section of the Irish community had found an opening in the clothing trade. This particular grouping dominated the politics of the ghetto, trading Irish votes for petty favours from the Liberals. They were organised around the Irish National League, an offshoot from the Home Rule party in Ireland. Run by the local clergy, it championed its Catholic faith and had links with Gladstone's Liberals. Socialists were denounced as atheists and, worse, as splitters.

The organisation that Connolly joined in 1899 was the Scottish Socialist Federation, which had been founded only a few months previously. It brought together the two chief currents within British Marxism at the time – the Social Democratic Federation and the former members of the Socialist League. The SDF was the first group to introduce Marxist politics to Britain. H.M. Hyndman, its leading figure, was an extraordinary individual who combined dogmatism with the most crass opportunism and jingoism. The Socialist League, on the other hand, had been formed in 1884 by William Morris as a breakaway from the SDF. It was a break to the left in that it attacked the dictatorial style of Hyndman, his opportunist electioneering and his support for the Empire. The Socialist League survived for just a short period of time. Its tendency to engage in the most abstract propaganda combined with the fact that, as Engels put it, its leaders were the most 'unpractical' men in England, ensuring its early demise.[16]

The Scottish Socialist Federation (SSF) was a local attempt at restoring unity between the Marxists. Its nucleus had supported the Socialist League during the split with Hyndman and tended to be on the left, though with some peculiarities. Its leading figures included Andreas Scheu, an Austrian exile described as an anarchist by Hyndman; Leo Maillet, a veteran of the Paris Commune; and the Reverend John Glasse, a radical Christian socialist. Connolly had been attracted to the last named's educational classes before being recruited by John Leslie.

The routines of the Federation, based on the older Socialist League emphasis on education, left a lasting impression on Connolly's view of how a party should organise. The winter season revolved around indoor propaganda meetings and French and economics classes as well as separate business meetings. In summer, open-air public meetings were held on Sunday afternoons. After emigrating to Ireland, Connolly was to insist on similar routines for building the Irish Socialist Republican Party.

Soon after Connolly joined the socialist movement a major wave of strikes broke out in Britain where 'New Unionism' had taken the traditionally nonunion unskilled workers by storm. Following the London gasworkers' and dockers' strikes, unskilled workers began to organise themselves into large general unions. Between 1889 and 1891 these were at their most militant as they fought for higher wages and shorter hours. Connolly and his brother John joined the Associated Carters Society of Scotland, which also sought to organise the unskilled.

In 1890 a strike of printers and railway workers occurred in Edinburgh. The response of the Marxists in Britain to 'New Unionism' was confused. Both Hyndman and Morris dismissed the union struggles as futile. Morris dismissed all preliminary skirmishes short of a general strike as useless. He believed that the major task was to 'make socialists' rather than fight for reforms.[17] Hyndman claimed that trade unions were the bulwark of capitalism and deplored the London dock strike as 'a lowering of the flag, a departure from active propaganda and a waste of energy'.[18] In Edinburgh the SSF were, however, slightly more flexible. They sponsored a Labour Day march in May 1890 and used the occasion to build support for the striking printers. Despite their origins in the Socialist League they also gave full support to the demand for an eight-hour day.

But during the railway strike the following year they reverted to a position of abstract propaganda. A leaflet was issued arguing that trade unionism in its present form was powerless. What was required was One Big Union for all workers in order to organise a general strike. Socialism as distinct from going on strike was offered as the way foward.

This incident shows how the first organisation Connolly joined suffered from the principal defect of British Marxism: it was isolated from the working class like no other party in Europe. Britain's pre-eminent role as the workshop of the world had allowed for an era of 'possibilism' – the accommodation by the working class to its own national capital – decades before the open tendency to reformism became evident on the Continent. Moreover the slow evolutionary development of British capitalism created a conservative culture where all the prejudices of the past could accumulate on top of each other.[19]

Cut off from immediate influence within the organised working class, British Marxists turned all the more vigorously to a purely propagandist role. They saw their task as explaining the economic laws of capitalism and preparing workers for the inevitable victory of socialism. In the British case the weakness of the Second International's politics was magnified by socialist organisations that survived as sects.

Connolly Turns to Labour

The defeat of the first wave of New Unionism after 1891 brought a change of mood for militants and socialists. Having failed to win the industrial struggles, many now looked to the state and the local councils for assistance. Some years previously, Keir Hardie, a union official with the miners, had drawn similar conclusions from his union's defeat during industrial struggles. He declared that 'we want a new party – a Labour Party, pure and simple'.[20] In 1887 he stood in the Mid-Lanark bye-election as a Labour candidate, although he claimed that he was merely adding workers' demands onto the existing Liberal programme. A year later he founded the Scottish Labour Party.

The Scottish Labour Party was conceived as a party of practical social reform. Hardie vigorously rejected the word 'socialist' in the title, hoping to maintain a relationship with the Liberals and to win the votes of workers 'with no strong bias for or against socialism'.[21] In 1892, he was elected MP for West Ham. His fame as the 'first member for the unemployed' coincided with growing disillusionment with the tactic of direct action after the defeat of New Unionism. The Scottish Labour Party, and the Independent Labour Party (ILP), as it was known after 1893, began to grow rapidly.

Connolly's SSF responded to this development without a clear strategy. Its older cadre had come to a stages view of how working-class politics would develop: first there had to be a Labour Party and only later could a purely socialist organisation be formed. After a heated discussion they decided that 'the individual member should be free to work as he saw fit in the new party but that the work of the SSF was education in socialist principles'.[22] This division between a Labour Party geared to electioneering and a socialist organisation that would produce abstract propaganda would become a model again for Connolly when Home Rule seemed a likelihood for Ireland after 1910.

At this stage he was among the several working-class members of the SSF who drifted enthusiastically towards the ILP. His own union had been broken during the wave of struggle in the early 1890s. He became a prominent figure among the Edinburgh socialists. He chaired the first meeting of the ILP in the town, in which 38 members joined up. Connolly's brother John was elected to its management committee. However, other Marxists such as Leo Maillet, the veteran of the Paris Commune, refused to join the ILP.

Connolly quickly immersed himself in the Independent Labour Party. Its management committee met regularly in his house. He was one of the Edinburgh delegates to a party conference in Glasgow in 1893. In the same year he became secretary of the Edinburgh Central branch of the ILP in addition to holding the secretaryship of the SSF. This indicates a virtual fusion of the two organisations that was comparatively rare. The Marxists and the ILP tended to have cool relationships throughout the rest of Britain.

By the end of 1893 Connolly was made overall secretary of the Edinburgh ILP. He wrote the rules and constitution for the branch and drew up its programme for the municipal elections. This was a classic example of the minimum demands of the Second International as applied to local elections. It called for taxation of unlet houses, direct labour schemes, the eight-hour day, pension rights for corporation employees and, more unusually, the municipalisation of the drink trade.

It is often imagined that Connolly was a born revolutionary. Nothing could be further from the truth. The ILP, to which Connolly devoted most of his efforts, was quite a moderate organisation. Most of its members rejected Marxism and hoped for an electoral pact with the Liberals. Connolly's Edinburgh branch stood on the left of the party owing to the influence of the Marxists in the SSF.

Nevertheless, even here the ILP's approach to politics had an influence on Connolly.

In 1894 Connolly was appointed an election agent for the ILP candidate, William Small, a miners' official. He took up the ILP method of electioneering by trying everything possible to win endorsement for his candidate. As the Irish National League had virtual control over the important Irish vote, he entered into negotiations with them to secure their backing. They promised their support privately but would go no further. Connolly then sought to build up sufficient pressure to get a public endorsement from them.

Among the suggestions he put to Keir Hardie was that he should approach the Home Rule leader in Ireland, John Redmond. When this course of action failed, Connolly advised Hardie to organise a socialist meeting in Dublin. The primary purpose at first was not to build a socialist movement in Ireland but, rather, to increase the pressure on the Irish National League in Scotland to back the Labour candidate. Rather optimistically, Connolly thought that if Hardie could organise a meeting in Dublin with the sympathetic Home Rule MP, William Field, speaking and get a resolution passed expressing support for Labour, this might sway the nationalists in Edinburgh.[23] The Irish National League was too deeply attached to the coat-tails of British Liberalism to be moved by such petty manoeuvres. Connolly's youthful conspiracies came to naught.

Connolly Turns Left

The experience was not lost on Connolly. It led to a rapid disillusionment with the ILP's desire for alliances with the Liberal Party and the nationalists. After the electoral debacle, Connolly moved sharply to the left. He resigned all his positions in the ILP and effectively withdrew from the party. He devoted himself to the building of an independent Marxist organisation. Two principal factors explain his shift.

First, the coming of the Liberals to office in a period of high unemployment showed up the weakness of the ILP position of looking for alliances with them. It was only after his own electoral defeat in 1895 that Hardie was to brand the Liberal Party as an obstacle in the ILP's path. Until then it was possible to find ILP members canvassing for Liberal candidates.[24] The softness of the ILP and its political confusion led to the rejuvenation of the Social Democratic Federation, now the only major Marxist organisation throughout Britain. Connolly's own SSF group in Edinburgh decided to rejoin the SDF fully in 1894. His decision to resign all positions in the ILP had followed an all-Scotland Marxist conference that had decided to build up the SDF as an independent party.

The second event that pushed Connolly to the left was the publication of John Leslie's pamphlet, *The Irish Question*. It appeared in 1894 after Connolly's abortive attempt to win Irish National League backing for ILP candidates. Leslie's pamphlet was a frontal assault on any accommodation with Irish nationalists and was an attempt to undermine their influence within the Irish community.

Leslie argued that the Irish question was not a purely political one in the sense that it could be solved by the establishment of an Irish parliament. He favoured Irish independence but claimed that the real source of Ireland's difficulties was the economic conquest of the country by the landlord and the capitalist class. Most nationalists, with the exception of Fintan

Lalor, had ignored this fundamental fact. He wrote that, 'despite their patriotism [they] were from a working class point of view, not much better, if any, than those they rebelled against and it was as hopeless to expect from them a true definition of the rightful basis of property as from the English governing classes themselves.'[25]

The middle class had seized control of the Irish national movement; they had foisted on it a deadening worship of a mythical past; they had suffocated it with clericalism and sold it off to the Liberals. Leslie urged Irish workers to recognise that:

> The emancipation of their class from economic bondage means emancipation from all bondage; that the interests of their class are paramount and before the interests of all other classes in society; if they refuse to be any longer the mere pawns in the great chess-game of the lay and clerical State gamblers for power and place, then they will clasp hands with the workingmen's parties of all other countries ...[26]

Many of Leslie's arguments would be taken up later in Connolly's *Labour and Irish History*. In the immediate term it was to lead to a break with the ILP strategy of seeking alliances with groupings such as the Irish National League. This was to remain a significant point of difference between Connolly and the British left from this point on. Connolly regarded their pandering to the Home Rulers as damaging to the socialist cause among Irish workers. This charge was originally directed at Hardie's ILP but later the SDF itself was attacked on the same ground. Connolly was moving towards a position that launched a general attack on reformism.

Connolly's shift of direction became clear when he stood in the St Giles Ward for Edinburgh Corporation. He was now a 'socialist candidate' rather than a Labour candidate.[27] This brought him into some conflict with the ILP, who were in the field before him. They had already brought Hardie to Edinburgh for a mass meeting. Connolly's new turn also led to a different attitude to the Irish National League. Instead of any pandering to them, he now sought to counter their influence by an open appeal to class politics:

> The landlord who grinds his peasants on a Connemara estate and the landlord who racks them in a Cowgate slum are brethren in fact and deed. Perhaps they will realise that the Irish worker who starves in an Irish cabin and the Scots worker who is poisoned in an Edinburgh garret are brothers with one hope and destiny.[28]

The Irish National League was denounced publicly. Connolly in turn was vilified by the League. He was opposed by an Independent who stood as a 'Catholic and an Irishman'.[29] Connolly still managed to draw crowds of up to 500 and poll one-seventh of the vote. But his approach to the elections had differed fundamentally from the ILP's.

The elections were no longer purely about returning a Labour representative who could introduce practical reforms. They were a platform for agitation, for encouraging struggle and for issuing bold socialist propaganda. After the election Connolly explained his decision to stand as a socialist rather than an ILP candidate as follows:

> The return of a Socialist candidate does not mean the immediate realisation of even the programme of palliatives commonly set before the electors. Nay, such programmes are in themselves a mere secondary consideration of little weight, indeed, apart from the spirit in which they will be interpreted. The election of a Socialist to any public body is only valuable in so far as it is the return of a disturber of the political peace.[30]

Connolly's relationship with the ILP and Hardie remained friendly and a high degree of co-operation existed between them. But he was by now firmly committed to the Marxist camp. He threw himself into building the Social Democratic Federation in Edinburgh and became secretary of the branch the following year. During Connolly's last year in Edinburgh the Marxists had begun to register a degree of success in recruiting and building.

In order to step up socialist agitation in the town, they invited Eleanor Marx and Edward Aveling to speak. As many as 1,500 people turned up to hear them. Connolly also chaired a meeting where the SDF leader, Hyndman spoke. The Edinburgh SDF had grown to 140 fully paid-up members. Connolly's position in the party was extremely prominent. He was charged with running educational classes in Marxist economics.

The Edinburgh Marxists, however, were peculiar in one sense. They combined a left-wing stance with an extreme conservatism on sexual and religious matters. This left a legacy affecting Connolly's views for the rest of his political life. The branch contained a strong contingent of churchgoers and kirk elders from the Presbyterian tradition. Connolly's own introduction to politics had been by way of the educational classes of the Revd Glasse. Glasse was a Christian socialist who had written a short pamphlet on socialism and the Church. One of his main objectives was to convince fellow ministers that the spirit of Jesus demanded that they work alongside socialists.[31]

Glasse's argument that socialism was a practical way of realising the ideals of Christianity was one that Connolly had some sympathy with, although he rejected the label of Christian socialism. Certainly, the pressures of the Irish community and the manner in which socialists were put on the defensive by the religious question helped to explain the Edinburgh socialists' refusal to challenge religious beliefs.

Connolly was to the fore in attacking those brave souls who tried to raise the question of religion or marriage within the Edinburgh SDF. He won a reputation for waging a battle against the 'Bohemian crowd' in the SDF and 'fighting their filth and metaphysical atheism'.[32] A number of members had managed to hold a few meetings in Edinburgh on such audacious topics as 'marriage under socialism'. It produced a backlash from a number of the Christian socialists who characteristically claimed that such topics were given undue prominence. Connolly reflected some of this reaction when he chaired a meeting for the socialist feminist, Edith Lanchester. When she spoke about marriage Connolly interrupted her to claim that 'socialism had no connection with family life and was in no way responsible for the opinion of individual socialists on the question'.[33]

His experience in these polemics left him with a deep suspicion of all 'faddist' attempts to raise issues beyond the economic and national struggles. All critiques of religion or the family were held to come from a liberal-reform perspective and were to be opposed by placing an emphasis on the bread-and-butter struggles of the working class.

In all other respects, Connolly was moving to the left by the time he left Edinburgh. He had withdrawn from ILP politics and was actively looking for an alternative to reformism. He had come to regard any overtures to the Home Rule party with deep suspicion. Under the influence of Leslie he had begun an analysis of the Irish question that regarded the Home Rulers' unwillingness to pursue a consistent fight with the Empire as resulting from their support for capitalism and landlordism. He had immersed himself in the economic theories of Marx. While still in agreement with the general Second International conception of parliamentarianism, he had already come up against the worst excesses of electoral opportunism.

His movement towards a more openly revolutionary position would guarantee his survival as a socialist in the hostile conditions of Ireland in the 1890s.

2. Building the Irish Socialist Republican Party

In May 1896 Connolly arrived in Dublin.

Driven out of his job in Edinburgh Corporation and living in dire poverty, he had placed an advertisement in the SDF paper *Justice* seeking a post as a socialist organiser. It brought one reply: from the Dublin Socialist Club. They sought a full-time worker who would help to build up the group. It could hardly have been a more difficult task.

Ironically, Connolly disbanded the 'club' as soon as he arrived and founded a new party in its place, the Irish Socialist Republican Party. Its first meeting in the back room of a public house held the grand total of eight paid-up members.[1] From this tiny beginning Connolly was to carve out a tradition of politics that has had a major influence on the Irish left ever since.

Dublin in the 1890s was a city whose decay bore harsh testimony to the ravages of colonialism. It had the fifth highest recorded death rate in the world.[2] Although tuberculosis was rife the nationalist-dominated corporation eventually voted down proposals to build a sanitorium. Arthur Griffith, the leader of Sinn Fein, supported the decision on the grounds that a TB sanitorium would have 'conveyed the impression abroad that we dwell in an island reeking of T.B. .... [and that] its products are calculated to convey the germs of the fatal scourge to wherever they are distributed'.[3]

Griffith's worry about the fate of Dublin's manufacturing base was not unfounded. Since the mid-19th century it had entered a period of decline as the market in luxury goods for the landlord class dried up. Industries such as textiles failed to switch over to mass production. Only the food-and-drinks industry showed any signs of growth. Dublin lay at the centre of a nexus that connected the products of rural Ireland to the centres of manufacture in Britain and as a result only 20 per cent of its male workforce were engaged in manufacturing while 45 per cent found themselves in the predominantly unskilled categories of general labourer, building and transport. Forty per cent of women workers were domestic servants.[4]

The working-class movement, such as it was, was dominated by craft unions. In 1894 they had taken the step of setting up an Irish Trade Union Congress (ITUC) but they were careful to claim that it existed only to 'supplement' the work of the British TUC. Based in industries that supplied luxury goods to the administrators and supporters of the Empire, the craft unions lent the ITUC a peculiarly conservative character. In 1889, for example, speakers at the Dublin Trades Council denounced the Land League's agitation, with some claiming that it had led to a reduction in the landlords' incomes and so made the market for hunting goods very poor.[5]

The craft unions were primarily concerned with exclusivist rules that kept their wages on a par with those in English cities and were deeply hostile to any organisation of the unskilled that might endanger their more privileged position. They were also obsessed with protecting native industries by means of 'Buy Irish' campaigns. Despite their apolitical stance, their union organisations were placed at the disposal of the most corrupt elements of the Home Rule Party.

The vast numbers of unskilled workers made repeated attempts to organise. Between 1889 and 1891 the example of the dockers and gasworkers in Britain inspired a brief period of unprecedented labour unrest. The National Gasworkers and General Labourers Union grew and even established the Irish Labour League as a quasi-political organisation that demanded nationalisation of land and transport.[6] But the high levels of unemployment, estimated at 20 per cent of the workforce, and the pattern of casual labour defeated their efforts.

By the time Connolly arrived wage levels for the unskilled had fallen below those of the 1870s.[7] The general unions never experienced that slow and gradual growth that, for their British counterparts, led to eventual recognition from the state and the employers. Instead the few unskilled unions that did survive, such as the United Labourers, led a very precarious existence.

The position of the socialist elements in Dublin was even more unstable. In 1894, Keir Hardie had toured Ireland and founded branches of the Independent Labour Party in Dublin, Belfast and Waterford. Before that Michael Davitt had founded a Land and Labour League. This tended to court sympathetic Labour-Nationalist MPs. There also existed small pockets of Fabian supporters, who dared not offend the conservative instincts of the craft-union leaders.

Connolly's first task on arriving in Ireland was to weld together the disparate individual socialists into one organisation, the ISRP. This meant arguing with some of the existing currents of socialist thought. Among the foremost of these was the Fabian tradition, which Connolly described as a tendency that would :

emasculate the working class movement, by denying the philosophy of class struggle, weakening the belief of the workers in the political self-sufficiency of their own class, and by substituting the principle of municipal capitalism, and bureaucratic State control for the principle of revolutionary reconstruction involved in Social Democracy.[8]

Accordingly, Connolly lectured a group of Fabians on 'Why we are revolutionists'.[9] One ISRP member present claimed that he 'pulverised them in debate ... shattered their little organisations, and from the fragments he founded a small Irish Socialist Republican Party'.[10]

Rigorous debate and honesty in his politics ensured that Connolly soon pulled a small nucleus around him. Within two years 50 people had enrolled in the ISRP, although weekly attendance at meetings hovered around 20.[11] Small groups which led a temporary existence were established in Cork and Belfast. By August 1899, Connolly was producing the *Workers Republic*, the first Marxist paper in Ireland.

The routines of political organisation which Connolly had learnt in Edinburgh were used to build the tiny party. The emphasis was entirely on education and general propaganda. The 'winter season' saw educational classes held indoors at the party's premises, while the 'summer season' brought a series of outdoor public meetings on Sunday afternoons in Beresford Place. Attendance was often as high as 200 although Connolly's prime concern was always the amount of literature sold and number of new members enrolled. A high level of politics was set at these talks. Lectures were held on 'The Technical Terms of Scientific Socialism'; 'Socialism and State Capitalism'; 'Celticism and Democracy'; the 'Paris Commune'; and 'A Note on Democratic Drama', which dealt with the works of George Bernard Shaw. In addition to the public meetings there was a weekly branch meeting.[12]

In 1898, the party produced its programme of political demands. This was constructed around the classic lines of the Second International: a maximum objective (socialism) and a minimum set of demands for 'palliating the evils of our present system'.[13] In addition to the standard socialist demands for nationalisation of the banks and railways, free education and universal suffrage, and a progressive income tax, there were also two specific items relating to Ireland.

In a period when the warring churches were agreed on their rights to divide up the Irish national schools on a denominational basis, the ISRP demanded 'public control and management of the National schools by boards elected by popular ballot for that purpose alone'.[14] The programme also addressed the poverty of the Irish countryside by seeking the 'establishment at public expense of rural depots for the most improved agricultural machinery, to be lent out to the agricultural population at a rent covering the cost and management alone'.[15] Almost a century later these minimum 'palliatives' are considered far too radical to be granted in the independent state that officially honours Connolly.

The distinctive feature of the programme was the manner in which the demands for national freedom and independence were integrated into the overall set of demands. The subjection of Ireland by Britain was not only a barrier to the free political and economic development of Ireland but could 'only serve the interests of the exploiting classes of both nations'.[16] Complete separation, as against autonomy within the Empire, was sought.

The ISRP built itself around propaganda campaigns for this programme which was to be achieved by the ballot box. The general orthodoxy of the Second International was summed up in the claim that 'The conquest by Social Democracy of political power in Parliament and all public bodies in Ireland, is the readiest and most effective means whereby the revolutionary forces may be organised and disciplined to achieve that end.'[17]

The first opportunity the ISRP received for utilising the ballot box came in January 1899 when the first elections under the Local Government Act were held. This broadened the franchise to include the working class although a significant minority were still disenfranchised under the system of registration. The ISRP presented a separate programme of municipal demands similar to those drawn up by Connolly in Edinburgh. Their candidate, E.W. Stewart, was nominated for the North Dock Ward.

The ISRP was not the only labour group in the field. The introduction of the wider franchise led to the formation of the Labour Electoral Association (LEA) composed of prominent Trades Council representatives and labour figures who had previously supported the Home Rule party. Not surprisingly a certain friction developed between these conservative trade unionists and the openly revolutionary ISRP. When the ISRP sought endorsement for its candidate in the North Dock Ward the LEA refused to commit itself either way.

Despite this Connolly warmly welcomed the formation of the LEA. He claimed that it was perhaps 'the most important step yet taken by organised workers in Ireland'.[18] He predicted that despite their disavowal of socialism, they would be driven to seek the application of the minimum programme of the socialists provided they remained true to their class. The ISRP candidate polled well but failed to win a seat while the LEA returned several members to Dublin Corporation.

Some months after the election Connolly proclaimed that the LEA was indeed taking up the municipal programme of the ISRP and that 'their prophecy had been fulfilled'.[19] Connolly was clearly hoping for a broader labour organisation to which the ISRP could relate as the advance guard for socialist propaganda. This was a realistic strategy given the tremendous gap that existed between the tiny revolutionary forces and organised labour, dominated as it was by craft unionism.

However, Irish Labour was stillborn. The LEA candidates turned out to be no more than disguised supporters of the various Home Rule factions. By the end of the year, the *Workers Republic* was denouncing one of their number, a certain Chambers, for proposing that the inmates of a workhouse be put to 'breaking stones' to keep them from idleness. He now believed that their actions would prove to workers that 'there can be no good gained for Labour by the action of men who believe in the present property system'.[20]

The majority of workers did not draw the same conclusion. The betrayal of the LEA only helped to postpone the emergence of genuine workers' representatives. Their actions engendered a cynicism which was to affect all who claimed to stand for independent working-class politics. In the immediate future it would be Sinn Fein, with its anti-corruption image, that would be the main beneficiary in Dublin.

Isolation

The demise of the LEA left the ISRP isolated and forced to operate in a political desert. The prospect of a trade union-sponsored Labour Party such as Keir Hardie was trying to establish in Britain was no longer a possibility in the short term. Connolly therefore argued that the working-class cause 'could only be adequately represented or forwarded by men impregnated with the faith of Socialist Republicans'.[21]

A number of writers subsequently have viewed this turn as a departure from conventional British left politics to the wilder fringes of sectarianism.[22] This is grossly unfair. We have already seen that Connolly had begun to break from a conventional ILP position before he arrived in Ireland. His assessment of the LEA was now also correct. The conservative craft unions dominated by a Parnellite culture and involved in corrupt relationships with Home Rule MPs were in no position to launch a party of labour. It would take a period of intense class struggle before the nationalist monolith would crack and allow the formation of an Independent Labour Party. This would only occur after the revolt of the unskilled that began after the formation of the Irish Transport and General Workers Union (ITGWU) in 1909. In the meantime the prospect of building a Marxist cadre around the isolated and tiny ISRP was the only one on offer.

The ISRP's stress on elections survived the demise of the LEA. Between 1901 and 1903 the ISRP contested seven seats in the municipal elections. Their growing stature brought sponsorship from individual unions such as Connolly's own United Labourers and even from the craft-dominated Trades Council in 1901. Connolly regarded this particular sponsorship as a mixed blessing. It widened the base of ISRP support but it also, he believed, 'temporarily admitted into our councils many who ... were ever pressing on our party and its candidate the supposed necessity of temporising with the middle class in order to snatch electoral success'.[23]

The high level of intervention in the elections stretched the resources of the party. Invariably, the *Workers Republic* failed to appear when an election was in progress. But there were even more serious consequences for the ISRP. Their electoral battles brought them into competition with the Home Rulers on precisely the terrain in which the latter were strongest. The widening of the franchise had opened up a major battle to determine who would control the patronage dispensed by Dublin Corporation. Every election was turned into a referendum on whether the nationalists could oust the 'West British' faction from control over the council.

In addition the ISRP had to put up with the most scurrilous of tactics in a city that was still characterised by a low level of political awareness. Connolly described in one election how he had to counter bribery in the form of free drink for the voters, and charges that he was a middle-class journalist and an Orangemen.[24] Not surprisingly the ISRP polled extremely badly. In the last election in which Connolly stood, he polled a mere 200 votes to his opponent's 2,000. This was to lead to growing demoralisation in the party.

By contrast the area in which the ISRP was potentially far stronger was neglected. Throughout this period there were strikes by dockers, building labourers, bakers and tailors. In some cases ISRP members occupied prominent positions in their unions. Thus, one ISRP electoral candidate named McLoughlin was the Trades Council representative for the tailors and another ISRP member, William O'Brien, was also active in the union. But the tradition that Connolly had learnt in Edinburgh of either ignoring strikes or of issuing the most abstract propaganda prevailed. During the tailors' strike, the *Workers Republic* informed the workers that 'the only remedy is socialism' as it would rid them of their 'industrial troubles'. It told them that the goal of ending sweated labour was 'perhaps too Herculean a task for mere Trade Union effort to accomplish' and that it would require the 'spectacle of working class representatives in the House of Commons forcing ... their employers' to end sweating.[25]

When the dockers were on strike, the paper noted that 'strikes being barbarous, they are therefore the natural accomplishments of a barbarous social system'.[26] It reminded the dockers that they had voted against socialists in the last municipal election and that now 'they looked like whipped curs as they slunk back to work on the capitalists' terms'.[27] This was scarcely calculated to win influence among a group of workers who had previously been a bastion of Home Rule support.

The pessimistic approach that Connolly brought to strikes was succinctly expressed in the following piece of advice: 'At the ballot box, the master would only count as one against the workers; their force could, if properly used, ensure the triumph of Labour as certainly as on the industrial plane the power of the master's purse will nearly always win.'[28]

It was not until his involvement in America with the syndicalist movement that Connolly was to place a far higher value on workers' own activity. In the meantime, the ISRP was confined to routine work and intervention in elections. The exaggerated hopes placed on the electoral struggle combined with the bleakness of the objective conditions eventually sapped the morale of the party. The ISRP experienced little growth in its short life and was to split amid a welter of abuse in 1903.

On the surface the issue was Connolly's 'bossism'. He had insisted that certain simple routines such as distributing the paper to subscribers be maintained. But there were clearly other tensions involved. In a letter to his friend Matheson he noted that the 'whole fight is being fought out around the corner from the real issues' and that 'all the moderates are aligned against me'.[29] One of the major sources of disagreement was on the question of the unions. Connolly had come under the influence

of the American Socialist Labour Party (see Chapter 4) and was opposed
to working within the hierarchy of the existing unions. In May 1903,
the ISRP's first candidate, E.W. Stewart, had resigned because, as Connolly put it, 'he was too busy in the Trades Hall pursuing reformers'
and was not pushing socialist politics within the unions.[30] Stewart had
some support within the party for his approach to union work.

The main problem for the ISRP, however, stemmed from isolation.
Its perspective of building an electoral base was in tatters. Elements of
the party around Stewart responded by attempting to adapt to the conservative trade-union apparatus. Connolly, by contrast, looked to a harden-
ing of the politics and a more open break from the type of union leaders
who had produced the LEA. The tiny organisation was simply too small
to withstand these disagreements.

Before the split occurred Connolly was forced to confront a number
of issues which he had not encountered in Scotland and it was in this
period that he defined the general outlines of his politics. The foremost
of these issues was the Irish national question (dealt with in the next
chapter). He also began to develop an analysis on three other issues which
influenced many subsequent left-wingers in Ireland. These issues were
the land question, the movement for the revival of the Irish language,
and the attitude of socialists to religious belief. We shall look at Connolly's
position on each of these in turn.

Land

Connolly's first period of political activity in Ireland coincided with the
final stages in the battle over the Irish land question. Between 1881 and
1903 a series of Land Acts transferred ownership of the land from the
British landlord class to the small farmers.

The process was accompanied by a shift in the pattern of Irish agriculture. The famine had cleared the ground for the consolidation of holdings.
The rise in rents which followed and the Land Acts themselves further
encouraged the process. Between 1851 and 1910 the number of farm
labourers and cottiers declined by 40 per cent. The number of peasants
with holdings of less than 15 acres declined by 20 per cent.[31] However,
the removal of the surplus agricultural population, who had paid vast
sums in rent to British landlords, did not encourage the development
of capitalist agriculture. Instead the Irish countryside was dominated by
petty peasant proprietors, many of whom possessed no more than 30 to
50 acres.

The Land League which mobilised the Irish peasantry in the early 1880s
was a very mixed movement. The increase in the entry of US cattle to
the British market led to extreme frustration among the richer graziers
who, from the famine until that point, had prospered through their exports
to the UK. Their 'Farmers Clubs' turned to the Land League to remove
the burden of rent placed on them. By contrast, the Land League also

organised landless labourers to whom Parnell had promised access to 4 or 5 million acres of unproductive grazing land in a redivision of land that would follow victory.[32] One of the leaders of the Land League, Michael Davitt, was a socialist who advocated the nationalisation of land. But the clergy, after some initial brushes with the Land League, played an extremely influential role within it.

The manner in which the Land League achieved its victory resulted in an extreme conservatism. The difficulty was that the agitation of the peasantry did not coincide with an upsurge from the urban working class. The leadership remained firmly in the hands of the Catholic middle class who were determined to negotiate themselves a place in the structures of the Empire. The Empire could afford to make room for them, for Britain was at the height of its power as an imperialist state. It was able to partially solve the land question by buying out a landlord class that was already on the verge of economic ruin. The losers were the still numerous class of agricultural labourers who were no longer needed by the smaller farmers.

Connolly has been accused of a metropolitan bias in his political analysis for neglecting the revolutionary instincts of the Irish peasantry.[33] Yet he was unique in supporting the fight against landlordism while still seeing the conservative results of the struggle. His concern was always with the poorer peasants and the agricultural labourers. He therefore understood that the land settlement represented not just a victory for the Irish countryside over absentee landlords but also a victory of the tenant farmer over all others. He claimed that 'the system of petty farming conveys no hope to the minds of the working class' and that the agricultural labourer had 'continually to meet the opposition of the very class' who launched a struggle against the 'graziers'.[34]

He castigated Michael Davitt for failing to fight for his socialist principles within the Land League. Davitt's 'advanced views and democratic watchwords' merely gave a radical cover to the bigger farmers and the urban middle class. He had failed to understand that 'the 40,000 peasant farmers ... [who] became owners of their land are now as much opposed to national ownership as Lord Clanricarde himself.' He had done nothing to champion 'the men whose fathers were hunted off the agricultural lands by landlord tyranny in the past [who had] as much title to the land as the men whose fathers were not hunted therefrom'.[35]

The victory of the tenant farmer over the poorer peasants within the struggle against the landlords resulted in the ascendancy of constitutional nationalism over republicanism. Irish patriotism expressed the idealised concerns of the tenant farmer and the urban middle class who had succeeded in identifying the interests of the nation with the interests of their own class. There was a need for urban workers to recognise this and begin the process of separating out *their* own class interests:

Every farmers' grievance became an Irish national grievance, every farmer refusing to pay rent was idealised as a patriot battling not for his own purse but for his country ... Thus the tenant farmers dominated the thought of the country and made the fight of their own class for its rights identical with the idea of Irish patriotism.

Now we are not pointing to this fact in order to denounce it. On the contrary we consider that the farmers acted wisely in their own interests ... When the interests of the working class will be in the ascendant every man's patriotism will be gauged by his services and devotion to those interests.[36]

This clear recognition of the class interests involved in the land struggle did not prevent Connolly from supporting the struggles of both the tenant farmers and the agricultural labourers. When the Home Rule MP William O'Brien launched a populist campaign in the West of Ireland to demand the break-up of grazing land among small farmers, Connolly gave support, complaining only that O'Brien's disrespect for the rights of private property did not extend into the cities.[37]

In 1897 after he first arrived in Ireland a famine broke out in parts of Kerry and Mayo. Connolly toured the area with Maud Gonne, a militant republican. They produced a joint manifesto on 'The Rights of Property and the Rights of Life'. Their main worry was that the events of 1847 would be repeated when 'our people starved as every ship leaving an Irish port was laden with food in abundance'. Connolly collected quotations from the Catholic Church to motivate the peasants to seize the fruits of the earth. Thus Pope Gregory was pressed into service with his claim that: 'the earth from which they sprang and of which they are formed belongs to all men in common'.[38] Connolly spent a month in Kerry distributing the manifesto, agitating among the peasants and sending reports to an American socialist paper.

Connolly was an advocate of land nationalisation. The Irish peasantry were unfortunate in winning ownership of their land rather late in the day. The Land Acts had modified the rigour of landlord–peasant relations but the problem was that the island was not 'surrounded by a wall of brass' which could shut out competition from the world economy.[39] Irish farmers would have to compete with their far larger and better equipped counterparts. The tiny plots of land they held combined with the burden of mortgages that rose from the land settlements and the fall in food prices would force many of their number into bankruptcy. They had exchanged the tyranny of landlordism for the tyranny of capital. The only possibility of introducing the levels of technology and scientific planning required for efficiency lay in the nationalisation of land.

When agriculture ceases to be a private enterprise, when a free nation organises the production of its own food-stuffs as a public function, and intrusts the management of the function to the agricultural population, under popular boards of their own election, then the 'keen individualism of the Irish peasant' will find its expression in constant watchfulness over the common stock and supervision of each other's labour, and will form the best security against wastefulness, and the best incentive to honest toil.[40]

Connolly's predictions on the inefficiency, waste and misery of private small-farming have been confirmed by the more recent history of Irish agriculture and by the emigration of thousands from the Irish countryside.

The Gaelic Revival

The other major movement which Connolly had to examine was the Gaelic Revival. Most nationalist movements have grown alongside the rediscovery of a past culture, the production of newspapers in the native tongue, and pressures to open the school and university curricula to the teaching of a native language and culture. The Irish were no exception. In 1884 the Gaelic Athletic Association was formed to foster Irish games and soon won a mass following. In 1893, the Gaelic League was formed to promote the Irish language. Its growth was phenomenal. By 1906 it had 900 branches with 100,000 members drawn mainly from the lower middle class.[41] In 1890 the Abbey Theatre was established with the aim of promoting a Celtic literary revival.

The founders of these organisations were invariably conservative Home Rule supporters. The rising Catholic middle class sought to idealise its roots among the simple peasants. The romantic folklore and religious faith of the peasantry provided a cultural badge of distinction against both the 'West British' Ascendancy and the secular revolutionary republican tradition of Wolfe Tone. The Catholic middle class feared the consequences of industrialisation and celebrated the values of rural life. Douglas Hyde, the founder of the Gaelic League, expressed the attitude with this following piece of advice on dress. His listeners should disgard the English-made trousers and wear in their place 'the clean worsted stockings and knee breeches of the past'.[42]

Connolly sought to debunk the romanticism of the cultural and literary movements. 'You cannot teach starving men Gaelic', he warned the enthusiasts of the Gaelic League.[43] As long as capitalism and the poverty it created debased the cultural level of the worker, 'the most priceless manuscript of ancient Celtic lore would hold but a secondary place in their esteem beside a rasher of bacon'.[44] He also attacked the elitism and parochialism of the movement. Addressing himself to the mystical wanderings of W.B. Yeats, he wrote:

The mental traits on which our Celtic enthusiasts base their claim, or should I say *our* claims, are but the result of the impressions left upon the Celtic mind by the operation of the natural phenomena of his material surroundings ... most if not all races have had similar experiences at similar periods in their history; and that therefore there has been nothing unique in the intellectual equipment of the Celt and nothing that he needs to ... cherish lest he lose his individuality.[45]

But for Connolly the Gaelic Revival was primarily a political rather than a cultural issue. Behind the conservatism and yearning for a mystical past lay the inspiration for a new period of resistance to colonialism. Socialists were not neutral when oppressed nations set out to resist their conquest. Part of that resistance would inevitably involve a revival of pride in the culture of the past.

Connolly recognised that the suppression of the Irish language was a necessary part of breaking the spirit of resistance. Its suppression had been helped by politicians such as Daniel O'Connell, who sought to forge an alliance with the British Liberals. O'Connell had insisted on conducting his meetings in English even though 75 per cent of his listeners spoke only Irish. The destruction of the Irish language helped to bring with it a period of servility where people tried to 'ape the gentry'. 'It was the beginning of the reign of the toady and the crawler, the seoinin [lickspittle] and the slave.'[46]

Therefore no matter how romantic or even reactionary some of its expressions, the revival of an oppressed language and culture paved the way for a struggle against imperialism. Socialists had no reason to be hostile to the Gaelic League. In fact as long as the Gaelic Leaguers saw that it was not purely a cultural problem they would find that the ISRP were their natural allies in the fight with British capitalism. Taking this point of view Connolly wrote, 'I cannot conceive of a Socialist hesitating in his choice between a policy resulting in ... self-abasement and a policy of defiant self-reliance and confident trust in a people's own power of self-emancipation.'[47]

Religion

The ISRP came under immense pressure from the Catholic Church. Its public rallies were attacked by the Ancient Order of Hibernians (AOH), an organisation which Connolly called the 'Pope's Brass Band'. This was a Catholic-sectarian movement which grew first in the North, dispensing patronage to its members, and later spread throughout the whole island.

The socialists were also denounced from the pulpit whenever they stood for elections. Any attempt to organise outside Dublin was met with unbridled ferocity from the Catholic Church. In 1901 for example the ISRP was engaged in forming a branch in Cork. The Bishop of Cork sent a letter to all churches in his diocese to announce that socialism was contrary to the Church's teaching and therefore 'could not be from God'. The letter, according to one member, 'scattered the weaklings of the party'. Unfortunately this consisted of nine tenths of the membership![48]

At this time Irish Catholicism was entering a period of immense growth and confidence. The clearances that occurred after the famine and the subsequent Land Acts had for the first time created a more secure Catholic farming class. Savings and petty accumulation of capital rose considerably. Between 1890 and 1913 the value of bank deposits doubled.[49] In the cities the sons and daughters of the larger farmers entered the professions, bought public houses, speculated in property and became the 'gombeen-men'. The proportion of Catholic lawyers and doctors rose from one-third to one-half between 1861 and 1911.[50]

The expansion of the middle class created the basis for the growth of the organised Church. The number of priests rose by 150 per cent in this period although emigration had taken a huge toll on the population. In 1861 there was one priest for every 755 Catholics. By 1911 there was one for ever 210.[51] The fanatical lay organisations such as the AOH also showed a dramatic growth. In 1900 they claimed 5,000 members. Nine years later they had 64,000 members.[52]

The powerful institutional Church reflected the aspirations and concerns of the new Catholic middle class. Rigid sexual abstention was encouraged to conserve the limited wealth on the farms and in the cities. Republicanism was decreed a threat to the status quo. Immoderate trade unionism and socialism were the product of the devil himself.

If one issue symbolised the growing ascendency of the ultra-Catholic middle class, it was their demand for a separate Catholic University. Countless articles were written, speeches made, and council resolutions passed in its favour. Throughout Connolly saw it as a 'Clericalist-cum-capitalist dodge to divert attention whilst a bargain is struck at our expense'. It was a demand that arose exclusively from the real base of Catholic fundamentalism: 'the shopkeepers, the lawyers, gombeenmen, rackrenting landlords, patriot publicans, slum proprietors and other bright jewels in the crown of the Church militant'.[53]

Connolly, however, was attacked inside the ranks of the ISRP for the manner in which he approached the religious question. A Cork member, O'Lehane, referred to him as 'Catholic Connolly'. He charged that Connolly defended himself against clerical attacks by parading his Catholicism.[54] This was an exaggeration but it did contain a degree of truth. Connolly developed a defensive attitude to militant Catholicism which remained with him for the rest of his life. To understand this attitude therefore, we need to break from the chronological order we have followed up to now and make reference to later events and articles.

Connolly was not a Christian, still less a Catholic, socialist. Christian socialism left itself open to interference from the clergy who could assert that they had a more correct interpretation of scriptures or church teaching. In 1909 Connolly summed up his attitude to Christian socialism as follows:

> Every time we approach a Catholic worker with a talk about Christian socialism we make this a religious question and as such a question, his religion teaches him that the clergy say the final word ... Why, then, should we go out of our way to give the clergy the right to interfere

in our politics by giving a religious name to an economic and political movement?[55]

He also took a courageous stance against clerical attacks on socialism. When the Catholic intellectuals of Maynooth College launched attacks on socialism's theoretical foundations, it was usually Connolly who replied. His pamphlet, *Labour, Nationality and Religion*, which appeared in 1910, was a brilliant response to the sermons of one Fr. Kane. Connolly's standard method was to show up the inconsistency and hypocrisy of the Church. Its role in supporting the colonisation of Ireland and in attacking all forms of nationalist resistance was illustrated by detailed examples. Its attacks on the socialists were mocked by quotations from its own figures from the Middle Ages who denounced private property and capitalism.

In *Labour, Nationality and Religion* Connolly set out quite explicitly to defend Marx's theory of history. He described himself as a materialist. By this he meant that the case for socialism was based on the knowable facts of history. He was also a materialist in the sense that he believed that the economic conditions under which people lived was the primary factor in explaining their beliefs and the political structures of their society. This meant that the forms taken by particular religions as they developed in history could be related to the real material conditions of the believers.

But this was as far as Connolly went. In an early article in the *Workers Republic* he argued that socialists were 'not necessarily materialists in the ordinary anti-theological sense of the word'. Connolly distinguished between the forms of particular religion and the essence of religion itself. Religious belief, or religion in general, was 'based on "faith", in the occurrence in past ages of phenomena inexplicable by any process of mere human reasoning'.[56]

Marx's historical materialism was thus limited. It could explain the facts of history and the workings of the present day capitalist society. But there was also a realm beyond 'mere human reasoning' to which it could not apply. Connolly made this limitation clear in an article written after clerical attacks on socialism during the 1913 lockout. His plea was that the clergy should confine themselves to their sphere while the socialists agreed to stick to theirs. It was a new version of the adage 'Render to Caesar what is Caesar's and to God what is God's'. He wrote:

> Let it be understood that the strictures upon socialism and syndicalism embodied in the Pastorals leave us unmoved. As a complete system of thought these two principles do not exist, whatever some extremists may say or imagine. As lines of action they do exist, and their influence is wholly beneficial. It is only when taken as offering a completely worked out system of thought capable of dictating human conduct in all possible phases, and hence governing human morals accordingly, that either of them come under the strictures of the theologians with any justification.

But in their present stage in the labour movement, viz, as indicating lines of activity in the industrial and political world – the only stage in which they are likely to be popular or useful in Ireland – the most consistent socialist or syndicalist may be as Catholic as the Pope if he is so minded.[57]

Connolly's principal concern here was to distance socialism from the charge of atheism. He had already been subjected to this form of attack within the Catholic Irish ghetto in Edinburgh. Now in founding a Marxist movement in Ireland he was determined to avoid the charge at all costs. There was no necessary philosophical link between Marxism and atheism; conflict with organised religion was therefore unnecessary.

He advanced two weak arguments to justify this stance. First, he claimed that 'almost all prominent propagandists for free thought [atheism] in our generation have been and are the most determined enemies of socialism'.[58] Second, he asserted that the attempt to make atheism and socialism synonymous sprung from 'an interested attempt of the propertied classes to create such a prejudice against Socialism as might deter the working class from giving ear to its doctrines'.[59]

In a major article on 'Roman Catholicism and Socialism' in 1908 Connolly developed this analysis further. The professional free-thinkers were not products of modern socialism but were 'a survival from the obsolete philosophy of the days preceding the first French Revolution'. This tradition developed by the Encyclopaedists in France saw religion in terms of the 'systematised business of deception and trickery invented and perpetuated by men thoroughly aware of its falsehood and baseness'.[60]

These points were valid in the abstract. Voltaire, Holbach, Diderot and many of the Encyclopaedists took an elitist view of religion. Diderot claimed, for example, that 'the progress of ideas is limited: they cannot spread to the suburbs. The populace is too dull witted.'[61] The methods of the liberal freethinkers were not those of socialist revolutionaries who were concerned to alter the conditions that gave rise to religious beliefs.

But it was equally the case that free thought only emerged when the bourgeoisie was at its most revolutionary. The systematic attacks on religion were a necessary condition for undermining absolutism and the monarchy. Marx would later build on and develop this early understanding of materialism. However, once the rule of the bourgeoisie was consolidated it was in its interest to re-create tradition, to foster continuity, and to mask all genuine scientific investigation into the nature of society. Connolly therefore was being dishonest in showing up the limitations of the Encyclopaedists in order to evade the question of religion entirely.

Paradoxically though, while 'Roman Catholicism and Socialism' set out to distance itself from atheism, it went on to advance Connolly's closest approximation to a version of a materialist analysis of religion. He wrote that:

The different stages of development of the human mind in its attitude towards the forces of Nature created different priesthoods to interpret them, and the mental conceptions of mankind as interpreted by those priesthoods became, when systematised, Religion. Religions are simply expressions of the human conceptions of the natural world; these religions have created the priesthoods.[62]

It was, however, a highly mechanical form of materialism that asserted that religion arose solely as a passive product of the inability of the human mind to understand nature. This was certainly one element in the development of religion but Marx's own analysis also stressed how religion arose from the alienation human beings experienced as a result of their social relationships. Against the freethinkers, Marx argued that religion could only be abolished by a practical material criticism of what exists in society rather than a rationalist criticism of what does not exist. But this did not imply taking the passive attitude of waiting on history that Connolly suggests. Socialists had a duty to advance a scientific view of the world by defending the philosophical basis of materialism.

Connolly's failure to do so was connected with his view that the Catholic Church was not *necessarily* hostile to socialist revolution. Although he took a courageous stance against individual bishops and clerics, he did not see the Catholic Church as a defender of capitalism. Instead he predicted that it would make its peace with the socialist movement as soon as it believed that the socialists were about to achieve victory. Connolly put it like this:

> To use a homely adage the Church 'does not put all her eggs in one basket' and the man who imagines that in the supreme hour of proletarian struggle for victory the Church will definitely line up with the forces of capitalism, and pledge her very existence as a Church upon the hazardous chance of the capitalists winning, simply does not understand the first thing about the policy of the Church in the social or political revolutions of the past.[63]

In support of this view Connolly cited the example of the change in the Church's attitude towards the Irish nationalist movement. The Catholic Church had denounced the nationalists of 1789, 1848 and 1867 but had allowed its priests to praise them a generation afterwards. However, for a number of reasons this was a false analogy. Connolly overemphasised the antinationalist position of the Catholic Church in the past. It had, for example, rallied to the Land League when the larger tenant farmers got involved. It had always restricted its opposition to the more subversive elements within the national movement. Its interests were bound up with a particular class within the national movement – the growing Catholic middle class. More importantly, there was no comparison between a nationalist movement that guaranteed more power to the Catholic Church within a new state and a socialist movement that aimed to secularise society and tackle the conditions that had led to religious beliefs.

The upshot of Connolly's twofold analysis of religion, that religion belonged to the realm of the unknowable or was a product of our ignorance of nature, coupled with his view that the Catholic Church would not oppose a socialist movement that looked like winning, was that the whole question should be ignored by socialists. In so far as the clergy involved themselves in politics they should be attacked as politicians. Otherwise the question of religion should be avoided entirely. This is why Connolly stated that the ISRP 'prohibits the discussion of theological or anti-theological questions at meetings, public or private'.[64]

But how was this to be implemented in a country undergoing a militant Catholic revival? In practice it led to an ultra-sensibility and deference towards religious feelings. In 1899, the ISRP passed a resolution urging that 'no member use phrases that by any process of distortion could be made to appear hostile to any form of theological views'.[65] During an election campaign the ISRP candidate E.W. Stewart, claimed that he had been 'cursed by the Church'.[66] Connolly took extreme exception to the form of words and a resolution was passed censuring Stewart. Outlawing discussions on religious matters prevented the ISRP from developing a core of members who took a materialist view of the world.

The result was that the ISRP was always on the defensive. Its idealistic attempt to exclude religion from the realm of socialist debate collapsed time after time. It was dragged into making more concessions to Catholicism. During the local election campaign of 1900, Connolly proposed a resolution at the ISRP branch meeting instructing all members to attend Mass![67] In many of his arguments Connolly was forced to reply to Church attacks from within the field of Catholic theology. At a later stage Connolly developed this approach by stressing how an independent laity was the best guarantee for the health of Catholicism. In a debate in the *Catholic Times* he wrote that:

> The firm distinction in the minds of Irish Catholics between the *duties* of the Holy See and the *rights* of individual Catholics has been a necessary and saving element in keeping Ireland Catholic, and he, by whatever name he calls himself ... who would seek to destroy that distinction ... is an enemy of the faith and liberties of our people.[68]

This retreat into arguing on Catholic terms was not surprising. The limitations of Connolly's Marxism had led to an exclusion of religion from socialist discussion. Outside the ISRP religious sentiment was strengthening with the growth of the organised church. If the ISRP did not provide a clear materialist culture for its members then inevitably they would succumb to religious pressures. This meant in turn that Connolly had to drop his naive notion of a division of spheres of influence between the clergy and the left. On numerous occasions he would have to argue frankly as a lay Catholic trying to find room to manoeuvre within the area of Catholic theology.

Did Connolly have any alternative given the strong attachment of Southern Irish workers to the Catholic Church? A comparison with Rosa Luxemburg is instructive here. Luxemburg began her political activity in Poland, a country that rivalled Ireland in its Catholicism. She was a member of a small organisation, called the Social Democracy of the Kingdom of Poland and Lithuania (SDKPiL), which grew rapidly after the 1905 revolution in Russia from a few hundred members to 30,000. Most of them were Catholics. In response to this, Luxemburg wrote a pamphlet entitled *Socialism and the Churches*.

Insisting that socialists do not set out to 'provoke' arguments with the clergy, Luxemburg clearly shared Connolly's caution. 'Never', she wrote, 'do the social democrats drive workers to fight against the clergy or to try to interfere with religious beliefs: not at all. The social democrats, those of the whole world and those of our own country, regard conscience and personal opinions as being sacred.'[69] But Luxemburg also understood that the Catholic Church as an institution would inevitably choose the side of reaction. She therefore focussed her pamphlet on providing workers with a materialist analysis of the church.

She showed how it originated among the poor Romans who supported communal property. She described its transition to a powerful institution under feudalism, where its bureaucracy became integrated into the wider ruling class. She showed how it eventually made its peace with capitalism. Her purpose was to warn workers that 'in order to defend themselves against the antagonism of the clergy at the present time, during the revolution, and against their false friendship tomorrow, after the revolution, it is necessary for workers to organise themselves in the Social Democratic Party'.[70]

Thus, under conditions similar to those of Ireland, Luxemburg took an equally sensitive but far harder attitude to the Catholic Church. Connolly moved from a position of excluding religion from socialist discussion to one of expecting immense flexibility from the Catholic Church. Luxemburg, because she was a thoroughgoing materialist, had the confidence to wage a struggle to break Catholic workers from a political trust in their priests and bishops.

In the course of building the ISRP Connolly had to take up and analyse the issues of the day in a way that his immediate predecessors were incapable of. There was no retreat into a concern for purely economic struggles. During these early years, Connolly laid the basis for his political outlook by intervening on all the major questions of the day. In the case of religion, this was marked by an extreme caution which he never shook off. But on most other issues he advanced a bold class standpoint that cut against the grain of many nationalist arguments. It is necessary to turn now to the question of how he set about advancing a class analysis of the supreme issue of Irish politics: the national question.

3. A Socialist Republican

Connolly's decision to name his tiny party the ISRP brought the term 'socialist republican' into use for the first time. It signalled a determination to fight for the republican demand of complete separation from the British Empire. Neither Connolly nor the ISRP were the first socialists to champion this demand.

Originally Marx and Engels had believed that the mass of the Irish people would first have to unite with the English Chartists to achieve their liberation. But after the failure of the 1848 revolution they came to argue that Ireland needed both self-government and protective tariffs against British imports. In keeping with this Marx and Engels were to the fore in the First International in pressing for solidarity with the Irish struggle. Thus, they took a courageous stance in defence of prisoners belonging to the Fenian Brotherhood, a republican underground movement who were involved in bomb attacks in England. They were extremely enthusiastic when Irish members of the First International in London organised a giant demonstration in 1872 to demand the release of Fenian prisoners.[1]

Marx and Engels' support for the demand for Irish independence arose primarily out of their concern for the British situation. Marx wrote that for *English* workers the 'national emancipation of Ireland is no question of abstract justice or humanitarian sentiment, but the first condition of their own social emancipation'.[2]

There were two reasons for this. The landed aristocracy was still a powerful, reactionary force in England dragging the whole of society rightwards. They drew much of their economic sustenance from the colonisation of Ireland. The defeat of the landed aristocracy in Ireland would 'be an infinitely easier operation than in England herself'.[3] This was because the land question in Ireland fused with, and was inseparable from, national aspirations.

Second, Marx and Engels were writing in a period which saw mass emigration from Ireland to the industrial centres of England. They noted that workers were divided into two hostile camps, as the English worker 'in relation to the Irish worker ... feels himself a member of a ruling nation'.[4] This chauvinism weakened the British working class and made them prey to the Liberal and Tory ideas that had grown since the defeat of Chartism.

Marx and Engels' defence of Irish independence did not stem from the view that Ireland represented a weak point within the capitalist system. They had a low opinion of the politics of some of the Irish revolutionaries. Engels regarded the Fenian leaders as 'mostly asses and partly exploiters'.[5] In an interview in 1888 – just eight years before Connolly arrived in the country – Engels summed up their pessimistic attitude by stating that 'a purely socialist movement cannot be expected in Ireland for a considerable time. People there want first of all to become peasants owning a plot of land, and after they have achieved that mortgages will appear on the scene and they will be ruined once more.'[6] But precisely because their primary concern was for the political development of the *British* working class, the oldest and most powerful section of the world's working class at the time, none of this diminished their enthusiasm for Irish independence.

While Connolly stood in the tradition of Marx and Engels in supporting national independence, he had arrived at that conclusion from a radically different perspective. His immediate concern was the politicisation of the *Irish* working class. He was therefore the first socialist not only to support independence but to look at how the struggle for this goal could tie in with the fight against capitalism in Ireland. The programme of the ISRP was unique in stating:

> The subjection of one nation to another as of Ireland to the authority of the British crown is a barrier to the free political development of the subjected nation and can only serve the exploiting classes of both nations.
>
> That, therefore, the national and economic freedom of the Irish people must be sought in the same direction, viz., the establishment of an Irish socialist republic.[7]

As we have seen in Chapter 1 this represented a significant break from the politics of the Second International. The Stuttgart Congress in 1907 was to reveal two major positions taken by socialists on the colonial question. On the right stood those led by Eduard David of the German SPD, who favoured a 'positive colonial policy'. Colonisation was a force for civilisation and could be applied more humanely under a socialist government. Although this won the majority of votes from the delegates of countries involved in colonisation it was defeated overall.[8] The majority upheld previous past anticolonisation resolutions passed at Paris in 1900 and Amsterdam in 1904.

Kautsky, representing the centre, was to the fore in defending this traditional policy. He and his allies argued that colonisation was not a force making for progress as it relied on forced labour and primitive forms of accumulation. They saw the drive to colonisation as coming from one wing of the ruling class – finance capital, as Kautsky would later formulate it – rather than being a central drive of the system. For this reason they saw no necessary connection between the struggles of workers in the colonies and in the metropolis. The links were rather of a humanitarian or ethical nature.

Moreover, the orthodox adherents of the Second International viewed the working class in the colonised countries primarily as victims of oppression rather than agents of their own liberation. It was the task of socialists in the metropolitan countries to introduce legislation in their own countries' parliaments that would improve the lot of the citizens of the colonies and eventually grant them some form of autonomy. Kautsky put the matter like this:

> Our tasks in the colonies are fundamentally just the same as at home. They are to protect the people against capitalist exploitation and against the burden of bureaucracy and militarism; in other words, to advance policies for democracy and social welfare.[9]

Connolly broke from the analysis that assigned a passive role to the working class of colonised countries. It was no longer a question of waiting upon the good offices of socialists in the metropolitan countries; nor even a matter of waiting to follow the path of development traced by the more industrially advanced nations. Instead the working class of the colony was now presented as the only class capable of leading the struggle for national independence and they would do so by fighting for a Workers' Republic.

To understand how Connolly came to break with these basic traditions of the Second International we have to take account of what was, in effect, his rapid shift to the left. In Scotland he had broken with labourism to embrace an openly Marxist party. But he still found that this organisation, the SDF, suffered from an excess of moderation. He, thus, had begun to criticise all orthodoxies. Connolly's critique of both the ILP and the SDF was widened to include their perspective on Ireland.

Both these parties saw the fight for Irish freedom as an obstacle left over from a bygone age. The Irish national question had to be settled before the battle for socialism could commence. In their view the surest way of resolving the issue was by supporting the demand of the constitutional nationalists for Home Rule, which would be won eventually by applying pressure on a Liberal government. In the meantime Irish nationalism was a peculiarity that had to be patronised.

The Home Rule MPs were invited onto the platforms of the ILP, in particular. ILP members such as James Sexton, organiser of the National Union of Dock Labourers, used the union apparatus in Dublin to build support for Home Rule MPs. While waiting for Home Rule to be granted by a Liberal government dependent on Irish support, the ILP calculated cynically that the presence of 'prominent' Irish MPs on their platform would help swing the Irish vote in their favour.[10] Connolly was initially repelled by his own experience of this type of electoral opportunism. Once in Ireland he started to question the supposed ability of the Home Rulers to solve the national question. Gradually, under the influence of the American Socialist Labour Party (see Chapter 4) he came to oppose the concept of all-class alliances. Through this process of moving to the left he had made a major break with the traditions of the Second International.

Connolly's decision to take up the national question from a revolutionary socialist standpoint was crucial. Previous socialist groupings had followed the orthodoxy of their British counterparts in seeing the demand for independence as the exclusive preserve of the nationalists while they concentrated on the general economic deprivations that workers suffered.

Such abstentionism, however, meant that members of these groupings were pulled into taking a stance on the national issue by forces outside the socialist movement. Thus, the Belfast branch of the ILP collapsed under the impact of sectarian politics in the city; the Waterford ILP saw its leading member join the Home Rule party; the Dublin ILP was in a state of crisis when Connolly arrived.[11] Connolly's decision to break with the orthodoxy of the Second International provided the only sure foundation on which a socialist movement could be built in Ireland.

Connolly Returns to Fintan Lalor

It was one thing to assert that the socialist republic was the only way to achieve Irish freedom but quite another to develop a clear argument for this position. Connolly faced the task of drawing the exact links between two forms of struggle, the national and the social, which he regarded as 'not antagonistic but complementary'.[12]

There is a difficulty in interpreting Connolly's early work on the national question. Between 1896 and his departure from Ireland for America in 1903, Connolly never produced a clear comprehensive argument that justified his theoretical position. The vast bulk of his writings were short articles for newspapers. In his own paper, *Workers Republic*, these articles often appeared as short editorials on current topics or in the 'Home Truths' column which was a mixture of witty left-wing journalism and hard political argument. His two pamphlets issued in this period, *Erin's Hope* and the *New Evangel*, were collections of previously published newspaper articles.

An added difficulty arises from Connolly's general approach. Rather than polemicise or sharply distinguish his positions from those of other socialists and republicans in order to clarify his viewpoint Connolly sought progressive ideas in the political ideologies of his rivals. He tried to draw his readers towards him by emphasising how much socialism had in common with their own beliefs. Connolly, therefore, tended to bend his arguments to suit particular audiences. While this method has led to an abundance of quotations to justify all manner of political positions, it did not help produce clarity in his own politics. With this in mind we can begin to piece together Connolly's general position on the national question in this period.

In July 1896 Connolly attended a lecture by Fred Ryan on 'The Social Side of the Irish Question'. Ryan was a left-wing republican. He was later to join the ISRP as a peripheral member but significantly he also retained his connections with Arthur Griffith. The basis of Ryan's lecture was an appeal to republicans to return to the politics of James Fintan Lalor. It had a major influence on Connolly.

Lalor had taken part in the uprising of 1848–49. His fellow revolutionaries in the Young Irelanders had sought to win over sections of the big landowners by excluding the social question from the national movement. Lalor, by contrast, looked to the peasantry. He called for a boycott of rent so that the British state would be forced to intervene on the side of the landlords. By showing that the Empire was pro-landlord and by mobilising the peasantry on the issue of their right to land, the national movement would make progress. Restricting the struggle to purely political demands would lead to disaster. According to Lalor, 'the land question contains and the legislative question does not contain, the materials from which victory is manufactured.'[13] In his view, the Young Irelanders should proclaim that 'the entire soil of a country belongs to the entire people of that country and is the rightful property not of any one class but of the nation at large.'[14]

Connolly saw a parallel between Lalor's fight within the national movement against the majority of Young Irelanders and the ISRP's fight with the Home Rulers. Soon after the Ryan lecture, Connolly produced excerpts from Lalor's writings in what was the ISRP's first pamphlet. In the introduction Connolly stated that the ISRP was 'the only political party which accepts Fintan Lalor's teachings from his declaration of principles to his system of insurrection'.[15] This was to remain a constant theme for Connolly in this period. It represented a deliberate attempt to root the ISRP in an earlier tradition of Irish nationalism.

From Lalor, Connolly derived two major planks that formed the basis of his own platform on the national question. The first was a hostility to what he termed the 'false exaggeration of purely political forms which has clothed in Ireland the struggle for liberty'.[16] By this he meant the exclusive focus on the constitutional at the expense of the social side of the question. In the first public statement of the ISRP, he connected the neglect of the social side to the class nature of the leadership of the national movement. The middle-class and aristocratic leaders did not

understand the economic basis of oppression and so neglected the strongest weapon in their armoury, or understanding it, were selfish enough to see in the national movement little else than a means whereby, if successful, they might intercept and divert into the pockets of the Irish middle class a greater share of the plunder which at present, flows across the Channel.[17]

The second notion that Connolly took from Lalor was the view that the national question in Ireland was underscored by fundamentally different concepts of land ownership between Ireland and Britain. Lalor and the genuine Irish nationalists favoured a form of communal land ownership: the British demanded private ownership and landlordism.

Erin's Hope

Lalor's influence was apparent when Connolly published his first pamphlet, *Erin's Hope*, in 1897. It was addressed to the small but growing band of radical nationalists and it advanced two central arguments for socialism.

First, Lalor's argument about the differing ideas in Ireland and Britain on 'the vital question of property in land'[18] are reworked in Marxist terms. The distinctive feature of Ireland, Connolly claims, was that primitive communism survived there for far longer than elsewhere and in a more highly developed form.[19] This society, whose laws were codified under the Brehon system, was one where land was held in common. Private property existed only in minor areas of social life. The key unit was the tribe. The tribal chief did not hold hereditary positions but was rather the 'freely elected chief of a free community'.[20] Although land might technically be vested in the chief, real control lay with the tribe as a whole.

Connolly did not attempt to explain why this form of primitive communism survived longer in Ireland nor what it signified from the standpoint of a materialist view of history. In an unusual sleight of hand, the Marxist interpretation of this phenomenon is split between two alternative approaches. The cold 'ardent student of sociology' finds the 'Irish adherence to clan ownership at such a comparatively recent date as the 17th century as evidence of retarded economic development, and therefore a real hindrance to progress'. But his rival the 'sympathetic student of history', expresses admiration for the 'sagacity of his Celtic forefathers'.[21] Connolly clearly belongs to the latter category.

The critical point in Connolly's argument is that feudalism and capitalism came with the English.

'English rule and Dublin parliaments were alike identified as the introducers and upholders of the system of feudalism and private ownership of land, as opposed to the Celtic system of clan and common ownership,

which ... [was] regarded and, I think, rightly, as the pledge at once
of ... [the people's] political and social liberty.[22]

Undoing the conquest fully, he informed the Irish nationalist, could not
simply be a matter of changing the seat of government. It had to reinstate
the Irish land system of common ownership. But this in turn would mean
breaking with the Home Rule party who represented an Irish bourgeoisie
who had 'so compounded with the enemy as to accept the alien social
system'.[23]

How did this explanation of the origins of the conflict affect the struggles
almost three centuries later? In particular, how did it relate to the urban
working class that Connolly would put at the centre of the national struggle? Here Connolly was forced to revert to idealist and cultural forms
of explanation. There was a 'principle' that underlay both societies. The
principle that lay behind Gaelic civilisation was 'socialistic' while that
of English civilisation was 'individualistic'.[24] Connolly implies that elements of these cultures continue to survive.

Socialism not only offered freedom to workers from wage slavery. It
provided the only means for a return to the ancient traditions of the Irish
nation. Writing in the first issue of *Workers Republic*, Connolly expressed
the matter as follows: 'We are socialists because we see in socialism not
only the modern application of the social principle that underlay the Brehon laws of our ancestors but because we recognise in it the only principle
by means of which the working class can in their turn emerge to the
age of Freemen.'[25]

The second argument Connolly advanced for the socialist position had
a more modern ring. It was simply that Irish capitalism had become an
impossibility. Capitalism demanded a manufacturing base but it had
become too late for Ireland to establish manufacturing industries owing
to the glut on the world market. The system had expanded to its limits
and there were simply no extra customers to buy its produce.

She [Ireland] cannot create new markets. This world is only limited
after all, and the nations of Europe are pushing their way into the remote
corners so rapidly that in a few years' time, at most, the entire world
will have been exhausted as a market for their wares ...

Our chance of making Ireland a manufacturing country depends upon
us becoming the lowest blacklegs in Europe. Even then the efforts would
be doomed to failure, for the advent of the yellow man into the competitive arena, the sudden development of the capitalist system in China
and Japan, has rendered forever impossible the uprise of another industrial nation in Europe.[26]

Socialism offered the only way out. Connolly's vision of an Irish socialist republic was, however, one that again borrowed heavily from the agrarian traditions of Lalor. It would be one that avoided the horrors of industrialisation. It would remain an agricultural country whose surplus would be exchanged for manufactured goods produced in other parts of the world. The stage of capitalist development would thus be skipped in what would prove to be an exceptional case.

How are we to assess these arguments? More importantly, what political conclusions would they lead Connolly to? The main problem with Connolly's first argument (leaving aside for a moment the question of whether it was an accurate picture of preconquest Ireland) is its implication that Gaelic primitive communism was superior to feudalism and capitalism. This owed little to the Marxist view of history, which Connolly was at pains to defend elsewhere. Marx viewed the stage of primitive communism as one where the means of production were so underdeveloped that they were unable to create a surplus that could sustain a ruling class. Such a society had to give way to the emergence of a class society once productivity increased. Marx regarded the formation of private property as a wholly progressive development, despite its attendant evils, because it was the only means by which the productive forces could be expanded still further.

The other difficulty with Connolly's argument was that his picture of preconquest Ireland was in fact false. It was derived from an uncritical reading of the Brehon laws. This was a common method among historians of the Gaelic Revival movement such as Alice Stopford Green. The Brehon laws were written for the ruling elite in the seventh and eighth centuries. Even then they reflected an idealised view of that society from the point of view of its rulers. To believe that they still defined the features of Gaelic society as late as the sixteenth or seventeenth centuries, as Connolly did, is to break entirely with a materialist view of history. The political and social relations of Gaelic society were no more static and fixed by unchanging custom than those of other societies.

Most historical studies since Connolly's death have shown that he greatly exaggerated the extent and significance of common ownership in land. One historian has shown that for a long period Ireland was a pastoral society characterised by an abundance of land. Although estimates are difficult, roughly half a million people resided there before the Norman invasion. The key to the economy was not land ownership but the possession of cattle. A chieftain's real wealth lay 'in the farmers who lived under his protection and the cows they tended. To conquer more land could in itself bring him no profit if he had no surplus of followers to occupy it.'[27]

Although there was not the same emphasis on the legal forms of private ownership of land as elsewhere, it still effectively existed. The Brehon laws placed emphasis on the five generations of males in the sept who were entitled to a share of the land of the sept. In practice, the chief and his family constituted the unit of inheritance. The main source of variation arose from the strength of the chief's family. Thus, in Sligo, the O'Connors were able to pass on land to the relatives of their family with a large degree of continuity but, in Mayo, the Burkes split into unstable factions over the ownership of land.[28]

Connolly was also mistaken in arguing that Gaelic primitive communism was only destroyed by the importation of feudalism at the time of the English invasion. Gaelic society itself was becoming hierarchical long before the invasion. A dynastic overlordship by the chiefs of the stronger clans existed as early as the ninth century. The O'Neills, the McCartys and the O'Donnells all exacted tribute. Lesser clans were reduced to landless labourers. A brisk slave trade was in operation between parts of the East coast and Bristol. A class of tenants-at-will emerged from former slaves and defeated lesser clans. Some held their land through a form of metayage where they provided their own stock and gave one-quarter of their harvest to the chiefs. K.W. Nicholls has argued that they did not have the same peasant rights to occupy and cultivate the land on payment of the lord's dues as tenants in other countries. As a result they were 'totally dependent on the master they followed'.[29]

By the twelfth century Gaelic literature records the existence of a class of 'bothachs' and 'fuidhirs' who took stock from the chief and in return paid a tribute, sometimes in the form of labour services.[30] By the sixteenth century, when Connolly claims that primitive communism was still in existence, historians have noted the existence of demesne cultivation where Gaelic chiefs such as the O'Briens and the McCoughlins demanded labour services in ploughing, weeding and reaping.

The system of electing chiefs was also transformed. The pressures of the Viking invasions, the need for defence against cattle raids, and the desire to enforce claims of tribute led to the emergence of a more professional military ethos after the ninth century.[31] Hence while elections were open on theory to all male descendants of the clan, in practice it was decided between representatives of segments of the clan based on the warrior retinue.

Thus although there were differences between Gaelic and Norman society – primogeniture for example was uncommon in the former – they could not be characterised as differences between a class and a nonclass society. Irish society was at a lower level of development. It had not yet imposed a system of full military obligation on the lower strata and often relied on Scottish mercenaries. Exactions and tributes were not fixed and regular. All of this made it less able to develop the political and military structures to resist invasion. But it still remains the case that class divisions in Ireland cannot be viewed as a 'foreign' import. In brief, there was little that was 'socialistic' about Gaelic civilisation.

Connolly's second argument for a socialist solution to the national question may be dealt with more briefly, for Irish capitalism has clearly become a reality, however miserable it may be for the mass of its population.

Connolly's belief that the world was 'glutted with goods' had assumed that there were physical and geographical limits to the system.

Capitalism, however, does not depend exclusively for its expansion on the amount of consumer goods purchased. Where it faces a limit on consumer spending, capital can flow from this sector of the economy to the capital-goods sector. This in turn eases the overexpansion of consumer durables, creates greater profit opportunities for the remaining capital and restores equilibrium to the system. Marx's analysis of capitalist crisis was not based primarily on an underconsumptionist model. He argued that the problems for the system lay within the sphere of production itself. The drive to accumulate led to the growth in the proportion of capital over labour and thus caused a tendency for the rate of profit to fall. This however could be offset for long periods through mechanisms such as the export of capital to the colonies. The overall growth in the system would create niches for the expansion of capitalism in former colonies such as Ireland.

Connolly thus had asserted brilliantly the need for a socialist solution to the national question but his two specific arguments – based on an original 'principle' of Gaelic civilisation and the impossibility of Irish capitalist development – were wrong. A number of problems stemmed from this mistaken analysis in *Erin's Hope*.

His focus on the destruction of the Brehon system led Connolly away from an examination of the relationship between British imperialism and Ireland in his own day. His theory stayed static because it focussed on the original conquest. There is little emphasis in any of Connolly's writings on the changing nature of the economic relationship between Ireland and Britain. Yet these changes, as we shall see, were vital to an understanding of how the Irish bourgeoisie came eventually to support the cause of republicanism.

The notion that class society was an alien import and had weak roots in Irish tradition would lead to a highly optimistic view of the nature of Irish nationalism: in effect the nationalist tradition could be turned against capitalism. If 'earnest' Irish nationalists could be encouraged to examine their own traditions, there was little to stop them moving towards socialism; they were already travelling in that direction.

Connolly's prediction that there was little room for an Irish capitalist republic meant that he ignored those inside the republican milieu who argued for an openly capitalist road. In effect, Connolly believed that the logic of history rather than the counterforce of socialist propaganda would deal with these arguments. In the particular case of Arthur Griffith, a nationalist who developed a detailed strategy for reviving Irish capitalism, this would have disastrous consequences. The overall strategy that stemmed from *Erin's Hope* was therefore straightfoward: the ISRP would situate itself within the Irish nationalist tradition. It would try to point that tradition back to its roots and combat the influence of its false representatives, the Home Rulers. It is now necessary to look at how Connolly approached the republican movement to encourage them to make this break.

The Republicans

The republican camp to which Connolly directed his arguments was in a weak state. The membership of the main organisation, the Irish Republican Brotherhood (IRB), was down to less than 2,000 members. It was unable to maintain any form of district organisation but was concentrated in handfuls grouped around strong individuals in the towns. Leading members such as John MacBride emigrated because of disillusionment. Those who remained lapsed into inactivity. According to Richard Mulchahy meetings consisted purely of a roll call.[32] Even the police in Dublin Castle considered the organisation virtually defunct.

However the audience for 'advanced nationalist' ideas was far wider than those directly involved in republican organisations. We have already seen that the cultural organisations were growing in this period and drawing their adherents from the lower middle class. Many of these had come to occupy the teaching and administrative jobs in the colonial machine but were still considered inferior 'natives'. While the focus of these organisations was on the language and the myths and culture of the 'simple' peasant, there soon developed a radical wing who moved to revolutionary republican politics. Symbolised by Padraig Pearse, these individuals at this stage were still outside the IRB, but their sympathies with that organisation were growing.

From 1896, when he first arrived in Ireland until 1898, when for a brief period he became disillusioned with the strategy, Connolly concentrated on winning the republican camp to a socialist position. He did this in several ways. Many of the articles in the *Workers Republic* were directed at them. So too was his collection of Lalor's writings and a later ISRP collection entitled *'98 Readings*, which drew on the radical writings of Wolfe Tone and the United Irishmen. He also carried the arguments directly into their own publications.

Two newspapers gave Connolly direct access to his chosen audience. Both were edited by women, although ironically the IRB refused to admit women as members. The first was the only surviving Fenian paper, *Shan Van Vocht*. This was essentially a legal front for the IRB and was edited by Alice Milligan in Belfast. The second was *Irlande Libre* edited in Paris by Maud Gonne, with whom Connolly worked closely.

Connolly prefaced his arguments by situating himself *within* the camp of the republicans. His concern was primarily to devise a strategy to make 'Irish republicanism no longer the "politics of despair", but a Science of Revolution'.[33] To do this it would have to cease comforting itself with its glorious tradition of martyrs and heroes.

It [the national movement] must demonstrate to the people of Ireland that our nationalism is not merely a morbid idealising of the past, but is also capable of formulating a distinct and definite answer to the problems of the present and a political and economic creed capable of adjustment to the wants of the future.[34]

This required taking on a threefold argument. First, he advised the republicans to form an open political party, and concentrate on elections.[35] Connolly's argument was derived from the standard view of the Second International which saw electoral activity as superior to the politics of conspiracy. He claimed that republicanism, as it stood, was both too narrowly and too broadly organised. It was too narrow in that the rejection of politics and open organisation confined its appeal to a tiny minority. These in turn failed to challenge the political influence of the compromisers. Every attempt at insurrection had failed in the past because the mass of people continued to support the constitutional nationalists. This was why both the Young Irelanders (in 1848) and the Fenians (in 1867) lost.

But republicans were also too broadly organised. Anyone who agreed with the need for physical force was welcome. Thus the republicans never knew what type of republic they were fighting for. Nor could they advance a clear programme to awaken the mass of people.

By forming an open political party the republicans would be forced to define their politics. They could challenge the Home Rulers and 'drive them from political life'. They could also use the ballot to ascertain when the majority of the Irish people were ready for revolution. His opposition to 'insurrectionism' arose not from pacifism but from tactical considerations. He asserted that 'a revolution can only succeed in any country when it has the moral sanction of the people. It is so even in an independent country; it is doubly so in a country subject, like Ireland, to the rule of another. Within this century, no Irish revolutionist had obtained this sanction before he took the field.'[36]

Connolly's second point was that those who sought a purely political republic without any social changes could be divided by sham concessions. 'A party aiming at a merely political Republic and proceeding along such lines, would always be menaced by the danger that some astute English statesman might, by enacting a sham measure of Home Rule, disorganise the Republican forces by an appearance of concessions, until the critical moment had passed.'[37] It is worth noting that Connolly's prophecy on nationalist splits was made a quarter of a century before the Anglo-Irish Treaty was signed with that 'astute English statesman' Lloyd George. Connolly argued that the only real immunity against this danger was a struggle that linked the national and social questions. The republicans should oppose the social system 'of which the British empire is the most aggressive type and resolute defender'.[38]

Connolly's third point was one which even the more radical republicans of today have difficulty with. If they were to link together the national aspirations with the hopes of the men and women who fought against the system of capitalism and landlordism they would have to adopt the goal of a socialist republic. The argument here was elegantly simple. Workers did not simply revolt for ideals drawn from the past. Nor did they compartmentalise the forms of oppression they had to fight. Once in struggle their consciousness tended to widen to look for the full liberation of their class. In an article in the second issue of *Workers Republic* he stated that it is ridiculous to 'talk of revolting against British rule and refuse to recognise the fact that our way to freedom can only be hewn by the strong hand of *labour*, and that labour revolts against oppression *of all kinds*, not merely the peculiarly British brand.'[39] In 'Patriotism and Labour', published in *Shan van Vocht* in August 1897, he warned that 'no amount of protestations should convince intelligent workers that the class which grinds them down to industrial slavery can, at the same moment, be leading them forward to national liberty.'[40]

The Irish Republican Brotherhood had few industrialists in its ranks. But this was not the decisive fact. Its nationalist politics meant that it aspired to represent all classes of Irish people – industrialists included. It could argue therefore that to struggle for a socialist republic would only frighten away potential support. To this Connolly made a devastating reply that deserves to be quoted at length:

It may be pleaded that the ideal of a Socialist Republic, implying, as it does, a complete political and economic revolution would be sure to alienate all our middle class and aristocratic supporters, who dread the loss of their property and privileges.

What does this objection mean? That we must conciliate the privileged classes in Ireland!

But you can only disarm their hostility by assuring them that in a *free* Ireland their 'privileges' will not be interfered with. That is to say, you must guarantee that when Ireland is free from foreign domination, the green-coated Irish soldiers will guard the fraudulent gains of capitalist and landlord from the 'thin hands of the poor' just as remorselessly and just as effectually as the scarlet-coated emissary of England does today.

On no other basis will the classes unite with you. Do you expect the masses to fight for this ideal?[41]

Connolly's points went straight to the heart of republican politics. But there was a problem. Here was Connolly advising adherents of a political tradition that rivalled his own. Unfortunately, it was a position that many Irish Marxists would subsequently aspire to. Yet the very thing he was advising them to do – break from a 'union of classes' – was central to republican politics. Republicanism was founded on the belief that all classes of Irishmen and women were potential allies in the fight for national independence. Even today when Irish republicanism uses the most left-wing rhetoric in its history, it still looks for a 'pan-nationalist' alliance to defeat British imperialism. Connolly discovered a similar phenomenon during the commemorations for the 1798 rebellion.

The '98 Commemoration

In 1897 a commemoration movement began to develop in preparation for the hundredth anniversary of Wolfe Tone's rising, which fell in the following year. Groups known as '98 Committees began to spring up around the country. The initiative came from the underground IRB. In the main, the Home Rule politicians boycotted the commemoration movement, believing it to be associated with unconstitutional activities. Despite this the movement grew in popularity and became intertwined with the demand for amnesty for republican prisoners.

The ISRP participated fully in the movement. It set up its own '98 Committee known as the 'Rank and File '98 Club'.[42] This operated as a loose front organisation for the party but it nevertheless affiliated with the main movement. It saw its primary function as that of uncovering the revolutionary message in Wolfe Tone's teachings. It produced a series of pamphlets on the writings of the United Irishmen of 1798. The aim of these *'98 Readings* was to show that the term 'United Irishmen' did not signify a unity of all classes. It referred rather to the unity of creeds. Connolly insisted that this unity was only forged by the willingness of Tone to fight a form of class war to win Irish independence. Writing later in the *Workers Republic* he spelt out the key to the propaganda of the Rank and File '98 Club. The year 1798 'was an Irish edition of the French Revolution – despite the lying twaddle of the present about the Society of United Irishmen being a "Union of all Classes", there is not in history any record of a movement, except the Paris Commune, in which the classes and the masses were so sharply divided.'[43]

To the more simple-minded nationalist he pointed out that 'Wolfe Tone and his comrades were overwhelmed by the treachery of their own countrymen more than the force of the foreign enemy'.[44] The clear message here was that the forces of constitutional nationalism represented the greatest threat to both Wolfe Tone and the movement in Connolly's day.

In June of that year official Dublin was being decked out for Queen Victoria's Diamond Jubilee. Connolly sought to involve the '98 Committees and the republicans in an anti-Jubilee protest. They refused to organise a mass demonstration and instead decided to hold the Convention of the '98 Commemoration Committee on Jubilee Day, 22 June. Connolly and the ISRP decided, however, to press ahead on their own with a call for a demonstration. In this they won the support of Maud Gonne.

On Monday, 21 June, the eve of Jubilee Day, the ISRP organised an anti-Jubilee meeting in College Green, Dublin. Connolly and Maud Gonne spoke from the platform. Black flags embroidered with details of famines and evictions in Victoria's reign were handed out. An audience of between five and six thousand people supported the resolution passed at the meeting calling for real republican freedom. A number of students tried to disrupt the meeting but were set upon by the crowd. After the meeting the crowd formed up into a procession and marched to the headquarters of the ISRP.

On Jubilee Day itself, the ISRP again took the initiative. They organised a demonstration behind a handcart that carried a symbolic coffin. This time, for a mixture of political reasons (not least of which was sheer embarrassment), the '98 Commemoration Convention was suspended by the leading ex-Fenian, John O'Leary, so that delegates could join the demonstration. On this occasion the police showed no patience with the assembled crowd. As soon as the demonstration reached O'Connell Bridge they were met by baton-wielding policemen. Connolly in a flash of inspiration, ordered the coffin to be thrown into the Liffey as the crowd shouted, 'Here goes the coffin of the British Empire' and 'To hell with the British Empire'.

Connolly was arrested for his efforts. But the rumours and excitement of the day's events brought an even larger crowd onto Sackville Street at night. Baton charges and riots ensued. One old woman was killed. The angry crowd turned on shop windows with Jubilee decorations. The damage ran into thousands of pounds. The myth of Dublin as a loyal city had been shattered.

The ISRP's stature now grew within the commemoration movement. Their policy of seeking mass protest as distinct from dignified gestures had worked. Two months later, when the Duke and Duchess of York visited Dublin, they again organised a major protest and invited the '98 Committees to participate. Again the republicans refused to join in. Connolly now broadened the 'Rank and File '98 Club' and began holding meetings such as 'Wolfe Tone and the Irish Social Revolution' under its auspices.

At this point, a major division arose between Connolly and the republicans. Around October 1897, the Home Rule party began to change their attitude to the '98 Committees. They sensed that the movement was growing in popularity and could provide an alternative focus of leadership. Maud Gonne records how supporters of the Home Rule MPs within some of the Committees 'began constant wrangling to get them elected as orators at public meetings'.[45] The Home Rule MPs now sought admittance to the executive committee of the movement as a first step towards bringing it under their sway.

At first a number of hard-line republicans held firm against their admittance. But by April 1898 the pressure for nationalist unity grew stronger and at last they gave way. The victory of the parliamentarians was soon complete. The platforms of the '98 movement were decorated with such luminaries as Joe Devlin, leader of the arch-sectarian Ancient Order of Hibernians; William Martin Murphy, the leading Catholic businessman of Dublin; and a variety of clerics. The commemoration itself was set for 15 August, a Catholic holiday. It was, as Connolly pointed out, a mockery of the revolutionary nonsectarianism of the United Irishmen.[46] On the day itself 100,000 people took part in the procession as nationalist businessmen closed their premises and encouraged their employees join in.

The '98 commemoration movement had begun under the initiative of the republicans, yet it ended up playing a major role in the revival of the Home Rule party. The Home Rule party showed that it could turn on the green rhetoric and associate itself with the nationalist heroes of the past. This coincided with a move by the Home Rulers in the West of Ireland, under the leadership of William O'Brien, to renew land agitation against the larger graziers. Both strategies were adopted with an eye to winning full control of the local councils – and the patronage that went with it – in the first mass suffrage elections to be held in 1899.

Connolly Draws the Lessons

Connolly had sufficient insight to be appalled at these events. His Rank and File '98 Club mounted a major protest against the admittance of the Home Rule MPs onto platforms of the movement. When these protests went unheard the Rank and File Club disaffiliated.[47] For the first time Connolly began to turn directly on the republicans for their fondness for a 'Union of all Classes'.

Connolly had believed that if the republicans could break their ties with the openly bourgeois Home Rule party, there was nothing to stop them moving in a socialist direction. This is why he concentrated his fire on the politics of constitutional nationalism rather than on republicanism itself. But now he found that his arguments were defeated by calls from the republicans for a 'broad platform'. He now described his feelings towards the republicans:

They will have no exclusiveness they tell us and open their ranks to all who like to enter, no questions asked ... As a result they get what they want, a 'broad platform'; so broad is it you can neither discover where it begins or ends.

For our part we are for a narrow platform – a platform so narrow that there will not be any place where anyone not an uncompromising enemy of tyranny can rest the soles of his feet.[48]

In the issue of the *Workers Republic* that came out just after the great commemoration march, Connolly analysed why the republicans and the Home Rulers found it so easy to unite. His answer lay in their common middle-class interests and common fear of the working class.

> The mixed character of all speeches in connection with the '98 Banquet and elsewhere prove conclusively that our middle class leaders are afraid to trust democracy. In the midst of their most fervent vituperations against the British government, there arises before their minds' eye the spectacle of the Irish working class demanding Freedom for their class from the economic slavery today.
>
> And struck with fright the middle class politician buttons up *his* trouser pocket and shoving his hand deep into the pockets of his working class compatriots cries as his fingers close upon the plunder: 'No class questions in Irish politics.'[49]

Almost a year later he returned to the same theme of the unity between republicans and Home Rulers against a risen working class: 'When the working class of Ireland begin to manifest a desire for real freedom and a determination to possess it, then you will see "Unity" for you will see all those warring kites and crows flocking together for mutual support against that danger.'[50]

Connolly's solution now lay in building the Irish Republican Socialist Party. 'It served to make me more and more convinced', he wrote, 'that in the uncompromising spirit, the rigid intolerance and stern exclusiveness shown by the Socialist Republican Party are to be found the only true methods whereby an effective revolutionary movement may be built up.'[51]

These were extremely harsh criticisms of the republicans. But were they merely a temporary outburst – the result of a bitter disappointment with the behaviour of his chosen allies? Partly, and partly not. Despite these outbursts Connolly never broke from the theoretical positions outlined in *Erin's Hope* where he set himself the project of seeking out 'earnest nationalists' and convincing them that consistency with their republican politics meant becoming socialists. Connolly's remarks reflected the bitterness of one whose high hopes had been shattered.

It must be remembered also that the particular target of his remarks was the old guard of the IRB and specifically John O'Leary. The old guard pretended to be 'all for Ireland' and completely above politics. Despite their lofty pretensions, they had shown a willingness since the Parnell era, not only to work behind the scenes with the constitutional nationalists but also to cede the leadership to them.

However, it is also clear that the actual experience of working with republicans in 1898 introduced a tension into Connolly's politics that he never resolved. Until his departure to America in 1903, his writings in the *Workers Republic* contained ever sharper criticisms of republican strategy and in particular of their aversion to political activity. Paradoxically this in turn led him to see virtue in those republicans, principally Arthur Griffith, who took to the political road.

The Boer War

Despite his differences with the republicans, Connolly soon found himself working with them again. The occasion was the Boer War. In 1899, the British imperial adventurer, Cecil Rhodes, managed to provoke a war with the independent Afrikaner republics of the Transvaal and the Orange Free State. The British Empire was determined to win control of the diamond and gold mines of South Africa.

Connolly's attitude to the war was clear. He wrote that he welcomed 'the humiliation of the British army in any one of the conflicts in which it is at present engaged, or with which it has lately been menaced'.[52] The ISRP was among the first organisations in Ireland to mount a protest against the war. A meeting in College Green drew 2,000 people. In his articles in the *Workers Republic* Connolly argued that the British government felt confident in transferring troops from Ireland to South Africa because they knew they could rely on the Home Rule party to assist the police in keeping order.

The republicans did not share this sharp insight. A loosely based 'Irish Transvaal Committee' was formed to mobilise the huge pro-Boer sentiment in Ireland, but while the republicans took the initiative in forming it, they again invited Home Rule MPs onto the committee. Connolly was furious at this latest alliance between the revolutionary nationalists and the Home Rule moderates.

The cowardice of the Home Rule MPs was soon demonstrated. A meeting called by the Irish Transvaal Committee, with John Redmond and Michael Davitt listed as speakers, was banned. The two Home Rulers complied with the ban. However Connolly, Maud Gonne, Arthur Griffith and John O'Leary spoke at the meeting. Afterwards they marched to Trinity College where Joseph Chamberlain, the main jingoist Tory, was accepting an honorary degree.

The mobilisation during the Boer War was almost a rerun of the '98 Commemoration movement: what began as a protest movement of socialists and republicans was absorbed by the Home Rule nationalists. Despite the latter's cowardice, the republicans sought to keep them as allies in a 'broad front'. Writing in *Workers Republic* after a successful antiwar meeting in November 1899, Connolly argued that 'The Nationalist anti-war meeting was a magnificent success – for the Home Rulers. It resuscitated their party in the minds of the people and taught them to look to Home Rule politicians for light and leading.'[53]

Again he set out to analyse why republicans could make such disastrous tactical alliances that helped to give the constitutional nationalists an opportunity to indulge in green rhetoric. His primary emphasis was on the republican abstention from politics, an abstention which resulted from a fear of splitting their movement on class lines. In the *Workers Republic* in December Connolly wrote:

> Perhaps our republican friends who have, or profess, such a dread of political action will now see the value of it, see how much stronger and aggressive they could be if ... they had taken our advice and captured representative positions in the revolutionaries' interest ...
>
> But of course such representation could only be secured by linking the political revolutionary cause to the cause of social emancipation of the workers, and perhaps that is why our friends are so afraid of it.[54]

Simultaneously, Connolly launched his most direct attack on the 'physical force' tradition of Irish republicanism. In an article entitled 'Physical force in Irish Politics', he insisted on a tactical approach to the question. 'We neither exalt it into a principle nor repudiate it as something not to be thought of.'[55] Rather his concern was to show that despite its militant image there was a parallel between physical-force methods and constitutional methods. He claimed that the Irish people had swung between 'constitutionalism' and 'insurrectionism' but ended in political despair. The problem was that when they switched from one tactic to another,

> their conception of what constitutes freedom was, in no sense changed or revolutionised; they still believed in the political form of freedom which had been their ideal in their constitutional days; but no longer hoping for it from the acts of the British parliament, they swung over to the ranks of the 'physical force' men as the only means of attaining it.[56]

The lack of politics – or rather the belief in conventional bourgeois politics – meant that militant physical-force advocates were also likely to compromise their principles. Their twists and turns in the '98 Commemoration movement was evidence of this. The difference between the republicans and the socialists was that between a 'mob in revolt' and an 'army in preparation'.

> The mob who cheer the speaker referring to the hopes of a physical force movement would, in the very hour of apparent success, be utterly disorganised and divided by the passage through the British legislature of any trumpery Home Rule Bill.
>
> The army of class conscious workers organising under the banner of the Socialist Republican Party ... would remain unaffected by any such manoeuvre and, knowing it would not change their position as a subject class, would still press forward, resolute and undivided, with their faces set towards their only hope of emancipation – the complete

control by the working class democracy of *all the powers of National Government.*[57]

These criticisms were harsh but there was a limit to them. Connolly was criticising the republicans at a strategic level – their elevation of 'physical-force methods' or, in present-day terms, the armed struggle into a principle; their abstention from elections; their failure to build a political party. This was not a full criticism of republican*ism* from a Marxist point of view, in the manner, say, of Lenin and Plekanov's criticism of the politics of the Narodnicks where they set out to supersede this particular radical tradition by rigorous polemics.

Connolly focussed on the 'union of classes' strategy and criticised it vigorously:

The cry for a 'union of classes' is in reality an insidious move on the part of our Irish master class to have the powers of government transferred from the hands of the English capitalist government into the hands of an Irish capitalist government and to pave the way for this change by inducing the Irish worker to abandon all hopes of bettering his own position.[58]

But while Connolly charged that republicans were prone to adopt this strategy, he never explicitly criticised the desire for class alliances as something which arose from the very nature of republican politics. Yet this was – and is – precisely the case. If the republican movement did not put workers at the centre of its strategy there was no alternative available to it other than to seek allies among the rich and powerful in society while encouraging workers to moderate their demands to make such an alliance work. Connolly's failure to deepen his criticism of republicanism arose from the theoretical framework of *Erin's Hope*. This left open the possibility that if republicans broke from the false strain of Home Rule nationalism, they could be won *en bloc* to socialism. As a result Connolly never tried to locate the class roots of the republican ideology among the lower-middle class.

In Connolly's defence it has to be argued that no other socialist in the colonies had come near to grappling with the difficult problem of the relationship between socialists and the revolutionary nationalist movement. It was Connolly's misfortune that before these theoretical issues could be resolved, the relationship between socialists and revolutionary nationalists became sharply focussed in Ireland as it embarked on one of the first major national liberation struggles of the twentieth century. There was little experience to go on and the general traditions of the Second International paid little attention to the role of socialists in the colonies.

Through bitter experience in Ireland and other countries revolutionary socialists have learnt that while it is absolutely necessary to fight alongside revolutionary nationalists against imperialism, it is also critically important to maintain an independent political project. Instead of operating as advisers to the nationalists, socialists have to challenge their politics as being incapable of fully uprooting imperialism. For Connolly this would have meant polemicising sharply with republicanism in order to draw as many of its adherents as possible to Marxism as the only politics that put the working class at the centre of the fight for national independence.

This gap in understanding the nature of republicanism was to cause tremendous confusion for Connolly, as became evident in his relationship with the most important ideologue of the modern Sinn Fein movement, Arthur Griffith. Griffith was virulently opposed to the Home Rule party and shared Connolly's perception of the need to destroy it by attacking hard at every possible opportunity. He was also in favour of a break with the conspiratorial methods of the old IRB. He favoured the development of a clear-cut republican party that would fight elections and challenge the Home Rulers. But he was also totally opposed to the socialist cause.

Connolly and Griffith

Connolly came to work closely with Griffith during the protests against the Boer War. Griffith had just returned from South Africa where he had worked as a machine supervisor in a gold mine in Johannesburg. He opposed the Boer War on grounds very different from Connolly's.

Griffith was both an anti-imperialist and a racist. His quarrel with Britain was over who had a right to exploit the blacks of South Africa. Griffith favoured the Afrikaners. Like some other opponents of the Boer War, he saw the roots of Britain's involvement as a Jewish conspiracy. Griffith was to run anti-Semitic campaigns throughout his life, and he gave full backing to the pogrom against the Jews in Limerick in 1904.[59]

Nevertheless Griffith at this point was a member of the IRB. Indeed he was one of the few members looking for a more active political stance. In order to advance this course of action he founded the *United Irishman* in 1899. This publication attacked the cowardice of the Home Rule party by contrasting their behaviour with the words and deeds of nationalist heroes of the past – John Mitchell, Thomas Davis and Fintan Lalor. This method of attack was also used by Connolly when he produced an edition of Lalor's writings and the *'98 Readings*. Indeed, with the exception of Thomas Davies, both the procapitalist Griffith and the revolutionary socialist Connolly often cited the same nationalist heroes.

Although Griffith changed his position after Connolly departed for America in 1903, the early issues of the *United Irishman* held the high ground of republican politics. It demanded, 'not a local legislature – not a return to our "ancient constitution" – not a golden link but: an Irish Republic, One and Indivisible'.[60]

The paper did not deny the importance of physical-force methods and in fact advocated that patriotic citizens practise route marching and drill. But at the same time it prepared the ground for a major shift in republican politics by calling for an open republican party (as Connolly had previously done). In 1903 Griffith took the first step in setting up the organisation that eventually became Sinn Fein.

Griffith's other major contribution at this time was to formulate an economic doctrine that would also have a major influence on republican thought. This put the demand for economic self-sufficiency alongside the republican demand for political independence. This objective would be achieved through the application of protectionist policies advocated by the German economist, Frederick List. Griffith also broke from the rural bias of previous nationalists by proposing extensive industrialisation. To this end he advocated an Irish Stock Exchange, the establishment of an Irish merchant marine and even the acquisition of Irish colonies. In line with these views Griffith campaigned vigorously against the 'socialist menace' that he saw threatening the nationalist instincts of Irish workers. Moreover from an early stage Griffith began to cultivate links with Irish businessmen. One of his main sponsors was Edward Shackleton, the Dublin paper-mill merchant.

One might have expected Connolly to have attacked Griffith's procapitalist ideology. Griffith's paper, the *United Irishman,* had a considerable circulation and had become the main republican organ. For a period it was funded by the IRB and was read by the very audience that Connolly wished to reach. Nevertheless there was not a word of criticism of Griffith's politics in the pages of the *Workers Republic* during this time. Quite the contrary: not only was there a friendly relationship but even, on occasion, an aspiration to unity.

The feeling was by no means mutual, however. In September 1899 Griffith launched a vitriolic attack on the socialists. Connolly's reply was mild-mannered in the extreme. He wrote:

I have a great respect for the above paper [*United Irishman*]. It is fresh, breezy, readable and interesting ... Always pretty straight on the national question the writers provide nationalist reading matter far above the high water mark of the Home Rule journals.

Of course there are a great number of subjects upon which there is no point of agreement whatever between the *United Irishman* and the *Workers Republic* but for the sake of the many points upon which we do agree I have hitherto refrained from adverting to any of the points upon which we disagree.[61]

What followed was not an attack on Griffith's politics but only a criticism of particular republican tactics: they had refused to organise an anti-Jubilee demonstration in 1898; they did nothing when the Duke of York arrived in Dublin; they sent a greeting to the Tsar of Russia; they had attacked the 'parliamentary republic of France'.

This set the tone of Connolly's general approach to Griffith. He would 'refrain' from taking up issues upon which they disgreed. Indeed Connolly asserted that the attacks on socialism in the pages of the *United Irishman* came from the pen of a particular individual, one Frank Hugh O'Donnell. When he left the paper, Connolly was extremely optimistic.

> Our honest and uncompromising nationalist friends may not choose to own the fact but they are nevertheless rapidly being forced to adopt the line of action we have all along advocated as the only possible one for a revolutionary party that means business. That line of action spells uncompromising hostility to half-way men and measures.[62]

Connolly now sought the support of Griffith and the *United Irishman* in the ISRP election campaign for a seat on Dublin Corporation. When this was not forthcoming he wrote an open letter to the paper and claimed later that 'Mr Griffith's attitude is unworthy of him – though it may be characteristic of some of his backers.'[63] Again there was no criticism of Griffith's politics, only a regret that he had mistakenly supported an opportunist candidate.

In 1902 when Griffith finally supported an ISRP candidate for Dublin Corporation, Connolly saw it as confirmation of his theory that all genuine nationalists would move towards the socialist camp. His enthusiasm for Griffith's backing was extraordinary:

> We have always maintained that every honest friend of freedom would sooner or later find themselves in accord with us. The support now spoken proves this.
>   Ere long our banner will be the natural rallying centre for all the forces in favour of clean and virile politics in Ireland.[64]

To explain this mysterious friendship we have to return to the theoretical positions that Connolly had developed in this period. His view in *Erin's Hope* was that militant republicanism was not only concerned with the political relationships between Ireland and the British Empire but was, in some fashion, also obliged to undo the conquest and the social system it had brought to Ireland. In other words, Connolly made the mistake that many socialists were to make afterwards: he imputed an anticapitalist dynamic to a movement that was simply anti-imperialist.

Griffith, however, openly paraded his support for an Irish capitalist republic. This caused a dilemma for Connolly which he resolved by ignoring. Griffith's capitalist project was just not taken seriously. The fact that

Griffith shared Connolly's opposition to the false nationalists in the Home Rule party was regarded as paramount. Griffith's right-wing views would simply melt away once he saw that Irish capitalism was an impossibility. Connolly thus avoided a direct challenge to Griffith's right-wing stance.

The Changing Needs of Imperialism

In this Connolly made a fundamental error. The focus in *Erin's Hope* on the original conquest meant that he ignored contemporary economic developments. This was both unfortunate and untimely. The onset of the twentieth century had seen a major shift in the needs of British imperialism in Ireland. This in turn underlay a change in the political attitudes of the Irish bourgeoisie.

By the end of the nineteenth century, Britain was engaged in an unprecedented imperial expansion. As a result the importance of Ireland diminished. The very attributes that had once made Ireland attractive were beginning to wane as exploitable material resources simply dried up. This was evident in three main areas.

The extraction of rent in vast quantities from the Irish countryside had played an important role in the initial accumulation of British capital. Through their reliance on the potato, vast numbers of Irish peasants were kept on the land, paying rent at exorbitant rates. Between 1660 and 1820 the rent from Irish land increased tenfold, from an estimated £800,000, or one-fifth of the national income, to £8 milion.[65] Most of this rent flowed out of the country to the banks and stock exchanges of London. Despite its impoverishment, Ireland had a highly elaborate banking network to facilitate the transfer. A list compiled in 1962 of the hundred oldest banks in the world showed that Ireland came third with six banks in this category.[66] However the mobilisation of the Land League, and the Land Acts that followed, led to the withdrawal of the landlords and a great reduction in this source of revenue.

Wealth was also extracted from Ireland in the form of tax. A commission at the end of the nineteenth century showed that Ireland had been over-taxed since the Act of Union in 1800. By 1913, however, this had changed. The poverty of the country and its ageing population (one consequence of high emigration) meant that it would benefit disproportionately from some of the welfare measures then being introduced. Expenditure on Irish old age pensions reached £2,400,000 a year by 1910. Between 1895 and 1910 British expenditure on public provision in Ireland rose by 90 per cent.[67]

The third area where Ireland had contributed to the Empire was in the supply of cheap food. Fresh beef, mutton, butter and eggs at reasonable prices were vital for the growing British working class after the Industrial Revolution. Yet at the beginning of the twentieth century a report from the Primrose Committee showed that the sources of these foodstuffs had changed dramatically. Frozen mutton and chilled beef were being imported from Australia and Argentina. Denmark was rivalling Ireland in the supply of butter and bacon. Refrigerated chambers on ocean steamers and cold stores at ports had rendered the English market independent of Irish suppliers.

These changes did not mean that the British ruling class wished to leave its oldest colony voluntarily. Its jingoist faction understood that any retreat in Ireland would be taken as a sign of weakness elsewhere. The Gladstonian Liberals merely contemplated a rearrangement of the political structures within the Empire. Ireland would be held onto even as a poverty-stricken backwater.

Nevertheless these changes underlay a subtle but decisive shift in the attitude of the Irish bourgeoisie that culminated in their acceptance of republicanism after the 1916 rebellion. The Irish bourgeoisie had begun to emerge more clearly after the land clearances that affected the Irish countryside. Wealth accumulated in the countryside found its way into the petty capitalist enterprises in the towns. The misery of this class was celebrated in Yeats's description of them as those who 'fumble in the greasy till and add the halfpence to the pence and prayer to shivering prayer'.[68] Their whole culture affected to despise the cities, one of the leading Home Rule party members, Jasper Tully, describing Dublin as 'the moral cesspool of Ireland'.[69]

Yet despite their own sentiments the Irish bourgeoisie was interested in promoting some form of industrial development. Their more astute representatives sensed that the Empire represented a blockage on their chances of doing so. They were offered the humiliating fate of native provincials who serviced a particular and declining segment of the British economy. Hence their more vociferous demands for some form of autonomy.

On the other hand, as a late bourgeoisie, and an extremely weak one at that, they also felt a need to stay with the Empire. It was still the largest and most powerful force in the world. It offered wider markets, military security, and, above all, stability. Caught within an Empire that had crushed their aspirations and yet still offered them some future, the Irish bourgeoisie vacilliated between a brand of Catholic nationalism and loyalty to British liberalism. Above all it was characterised by an extreme caution and conservatism.

The logjam in Irish political development was broken in the early twentieth century by the intervention of a new grouping: the urban intelligentsia drawn from the ranks of the teachers and civil servants who had found positions in the the colonial apparatus in Dublin. They increasingly took on the leadership of the national movement. The peasantry had traditionally provided the base of the national movement, but the exodus of the landlords after the Land Acts dissipated their militancy and most relapsed into passivity. The Home Rule party with its agrarian roots and its feeble-minded appeasement of the Empire also suffered from the declining rural base of the national movement.

The urban intelligentsia is a grouping that has played an increasingly important part in the national-liberation movements in the twentieth century. Like their subsequent counterparts, the Irish urban intelligentsia of the early decades of the century resented the backwardness imposed on their country; they yearned for a modern industrial economy; they saw no future for Ireland as a discarded backwater of the Empire. Many individuals from this stratum joined cultural organisations during Connolly's lifetime, discovering there a pride in being Irish before embarking on the harder task of developing a new political and economic programme for liberation.

Griffith's importance was that he had begun to fashion just such a programme. His aim was the revival of Irish capitalism. But this did not mean that his immediate appeal was to Irish capitalists. In the words of Emile Strauss, Griffith had to initially 'appeal to social groups who shared [the bourgeoisie's] aims but not its inhibitions'.[70] These were predominantly the intelligentsia to be found in the cultural organisations.

But Griffith's appeal would go far beyond the confines of these cultural organisations eventually. The argument between the Home Rulers and the Sinn Feiners was precisely about whether Irish private enterprise could prosper and grow more inside or outside the Empire. It took Griffith some time to convince the bourgeoisie of the correctness of his politics. The base he won for his politics in the urban intelligentsia in Dublin was decisive in the survival of these politics.

Griffith was the ideal figure to persuade the bourgeoisie of the new course. He expressed their contradictory position by vacilliating in his political career between a republican position and one that settled for a 'dual monarchy' giving Ireland independence under the crown. His support for small Irish businessmen and his attacks on the left showed that he was a reliable figure. He could provide a useful point of contact for the bourgeoisie as they became converted to republicanism after the war when they would face a weakened Empire which offered few opportunities for capital expansion.

Connolly could not have been expected to foresee all these developments but a number of points in his analysis in *Erin's Hope* meant that he was totally unable to appreciate how republicanism could offer an alternative road for Irish capitalism. He viewed the Irish bourgeoisie as a class absolutely wedded to an 'alien' social system and therefore to the Empire. His failure to engage in a contemporary analysis of the changing relationship between Ireland and Britain meant that he was unable to appreciate the bourgeoisie's contradictory position. His belief that an independent Irish capitalism was a complete nonstarter – based as it was on a faulty analysis – meant that he was unable to take seriously the way Griffith's project could meet with the aspirations of the Irish bourgeoisie.

Long before this occurred republicanism and with it the more specific ideas of Griffith won mass support among workers. Connolly unfortunately had ruled out the need to take those arguments on theoretically. This would make it far harder for the left after Connolly to point up the class nature of Griffith's Sinn Fein and Irish republicanism generally.

4. Connolly in America

While Connolly was building the ISRP in Ireland, the American socialist movement came under the influence of the former law lecturer, Daniel De Leon. De Leon joined the Socialist Labor Party (SLP) in 1890 and became editor of its paper, the *Weekly People*, two years later. From this influential position he campaigned tirelessly for a hard-left position. He described the leaders of nonsocialist trade unions, as 'lieutenants of the capitalist class' and argued for a policy of establishing socialist trade unions.[1] During the Spanish-American War over Cuba in 1898, he denounced colonialism and would have welcomed the defeat of his own rulers.

These positions provoked a response from the right wing of the SLP and in 1899 a large grouping split away to form eventually the Socialist Party of America. For the next decade two rival currents existed inside the socialist movement in America. The 'clear-cuts' around De Leon and the SLP fought for a 'revolution', by which they meant a majority in congress ushering in socialism at one fell swoop. The 'kangaroos' in the Socialist Party of America took the opposite view, equating socialism with the gradual achievement of reform. Every victory for municipal ownership or labour legislation was seen as a piece of socialism achieved.

De Leon was among the first to recognise the growing tendency towards reformism inside the socialist movement and to argue for an independent organisation of revolutionaries. This recognition, and the fact that his publications were readily available in English, earned him the sympathy and respect of Connolly. The *Weekly People* was distributed inside the ranks of the ISRP from 1898 onwards. Connolly's links with the SLP were cemented after a debate in the Second International on the question of coalition with capitalist parties. In 1899 the French socialist Millerand took office in a cabinet that included Gallifet, the butcher of the Paris Commune, as war minister. The response throughout the International was one of horror. But a subsequent congress, while condemning the specific instance, appeared to leave open the possibility of future coalitions. Only the ISRP, the SLP and Force Ouvrier opposed coalition on principle.

Connolly developed a close relationship with the SLP mainly as a result of his disgust at the politics of the Marxist party in Britain, the Social Democratic Federation. A number of incidents exposed the weakness of the SDF for Connolly. During the Boer War the SDF took an antiwar stance but debased this by racist attacks on Jews. According to Connolly, *Justice*, the paper of the SDF, used 'all the stock phrases of the lowest anti-semite papers until [it] ... became unreadable to any fair-minded man who recognised the truth, viz., that the war was the child of capitalist greed and inspired by men with whom race or religion were matters of no moment'.[2] In 1902 *Justice* refused to print a manifesto from the ISRP because it called on English socialists not to support the Irish Home Rule party. To compound all this, the SDF welcomed the coronation of King Edward by declaring that the 'great and growing popularity of the King is not undeserved'.[3]

In response to this political weakness Connolly tried to build an SLP-influenced revolutionary current in Britain. In 1901 he toured Scotland in order to pull together revolutionaries inside the SDF. At all his meetings he argued for members to take out subscriptions to the *Weekly People*, the paper of the SLP. As a result of his efforts, revolutionaries in Scotland came together to produce their own paper, *The Socialist*, in 1902. Connolly printed it in Ireland on his press and sent it over. After the left were finally expelled from the SDF in 1903, Connolly moved to Scotland for a brief period to become the organiser for the new party, named naturally the Socialist Labour Party (SLP).

Connolly drew up the platform and constitution of the new party. Two aspects of this constitution reflected the influence of De Leon. First, on the trade-union question, Connolly included a clause in the constitution which stated that 'no official of a trade union shall be eligible for membership'.[4] It also charged the executive of the new party with establishing the 'Socialist Trade Union'.[5]

Second, in contrast to the reformist currents, the Scottish SLP's platform included only a very short list of immediate demands. Moreover the draft platform stressed that 'these measures are in themselves economically insufficient and are temporary expedients of the passing moment. As the struggle between workers and employers develops all programmes will tend to become superfluous.'[6]

The British SLP was tiny. It had a grand total of 80 members to start with. Its paper had a circulation of a mere 1,400 copies. Its geographical base was confined to central Scotland. But for Connolly the key was that the party was built on revolutionary principles. He stated the general argument for an independent revolutionary organisation in the following terms: 'I believe firmly that the revolutionary socialist movement will always be numerically weak until the hour of revolution arrives and then it will be as easy to get adherents by the thousands as it is now to get single individuals.'[7]

In the short term, though, there was one unfortunate consequence for

Connolly. After three months, he discovered that the tiny party could not support him as an organiser. He decided to emigrate permanently to America in 1903. This time Connolly was hoping to work in a large established revolutionary organisation after years of isolation in Dublin.

Polemics

Connolly had previously toured the US in 1902. His purpose then had been to help the SLP election campaign for Congress. It was thought that he could make inroads into the Irish vote by attacking the pro-Home Rule politicians who were aligned with the Democratic Party. Connolly conducted the propaganda tour then without the slightest concession to Irish-American sentimentality. When asked by a Chicago newspaper the typical question of who were his ancestors, he replied that he had none – they were poor like himself. He claimed that as the Irish people like all others were divided into a working class and a master class, he could not 'represent the entire Irish people on account of the antagonistic interests of these classes – no more than the wolf could represent the lamb or the fisherman the fish'.[8]

His return to America a year later was not particularly welcome to the SLP. In America he was just another competent organiser and propagandist in a reasonably large party. In Ireland or Scotland, he could be central to building an SLP tradition. Despite his own expectations Connolly also experienced some difficulties in adapting to the 'style' of the SLP. But the roots of his difficulties were entirely political. Closer contact with the SLP revealed a deep-rooted sectarianism that stemmed from the flawed theories of its leading figure, Daniel De Leon.

De Leon advanced a highly mechanical interpretaion of Marxism. A crude materialist reading of Marx led him to believe that socialism was entirely dependent on the 'laws of science'. De Leon wrote that 'socialism takes science by the hand, asks her to lead and goes wheresoever she points'.[9] The role of the political party was simply to illuminate these laws. Human intervention played little role in history. 'The laws that rule sociology', he claimed, 'are an exact counterpart of those that the natural sciences have established in biology.'[10]

This simplistic philosophy could have led in many directions but in De Leon's case it led to a form of sectarian passivity. It suggested that the fate of capitalism had already been sealed by laws that operated behind the back of the mass of workers. The task of revolutionaries was reduced to pointing out the 'foolishness' of trying to tamper with the system. For De Leon the question of strategy – the connection between the party's principles and the consciousness of workers – was nonexistent.

In practice, this led to abstention from workers' struggles. De Leon believed that the fight for reforms would only produce 'concessions [which] were only banana peelings under the feet of the proletariat'.[11] There was not the slightest notion that in the course of *fighting* for reforms workers might gain confidence and possibly draw revolutionary conclusions. As a result of its failure to intervene in day-to-day struggles for limited objectives, the SLP became isolated.

The growing isolation of the SLP was matched by an increasingly authoritarian internal regime. Connolly came into conflict with this authoritarianism at an early stage. Six months after he arrived Connolly sent a letter to the *Weekly People* on the subject of 'Wages, Marriage and the Church'. He had approached the issue at the outset with the intention of a friendly debate and had already discussed it privately with De Leon. He now sought to raise some points of emphasis with the entire membership and the party paper was the main vehicle for so doing. The response was totally unexpected. It was to lead to a violent public controversy with De Leon and Connolly eventually being witch-hunted from the party. The controversy throws some light on Connolly's later break with the SLP.

Wages

Connolly had found a tendency among SLP members to argue that workers could not benefit even temporarily from a wage increase because 'every rise in wages was offset by a rise in prices'.[12] In his view this was both untrue and politically dangerous. Its logical outcome would be to reduce the Socialist Trade and Labour Alliance, the revolutionary union founded by the SLP, to passivity. At this point Connolly believed that he was dealing with a slight deviation from the party's line. The vehemence of De Leon's reply showed otherwise.

De Leon defended the position completely, adding only that the unions could prevent 'wages from dropping to the point that they inevitably would be in the absence of organisation'. 'Wages', he informed Connolly, 'are declining on the whole, relatively and absolutely, but long ago would we have reached the coolie stage if the union did not act as a brake on the decline.'[13] He ruled out any possibility of gains even of a temporary nature. De Leon argued this because he partially agreed with a theory devised by the German socialist Ferdinand Lassalle on the 'iron law of wages' which claimed that wages were always kept to a minimum.[14]

Connolly's rejoinder was not published in the paper. It was only discussed in his own section of the party. Nevertheless it was a defence of the classic Marxist stance. Marx had argued that the capitalist does not purchase a unit of labour but of labour *power*. The value of this commodity is determined by two elements. The physical limits have to be recognised so that labour is replenished. But beside this mere physical element:

the value of labour in every country is determined by a traditional standard of life. It is not mere physical life, but it is the satisfaction of certain wants springing from social conditions in which people are placed and reared up ... The historical or social elements, entering into the value of labour, may be expanded, or contracted, or altogether extinguished so that nothing remains but the physical limit.[15]

The trade unions, therefore, played a crucial role in influencing this factor.

Connolly took up and developed these points of Marx. But his intention was not to underpin theoretically the claims of many trade union officials that the labour movement was on a gradual ascent. Because the capitalist purchased labour *power* he had scope to allow for *both* wage increases and intensification in the rate of exploitation. Connolly wrote:

Yes we know that a rise in wages is a benefit to the worker, but we also know that other circumstances will not allow him to *retain* that rise or reap for long the benefit. We know that his employer will speed up his machinery, or intensify his labour so that he will have to produce more for his higher wages and that as a result he will receive absolutely more yet relative to the total product of his toil he will receive less than before his rise.[16]

But by granting that workers could make temporary gains Connolly was trying to free the SLP-sponsored unions from a sectarian dogma and make them 'take a real live part in the struggles of workers'.[17] Connolly's aim was to hold onto a clear revolutionary position – but still relate to the experience of workers. He had sensed the sectarian outlook that was implicit in the SLP's position but he still had not generalised.

His main concern in this debate was the future of the revolutionary union, the Socialist Trade and Labour Alliance (STLA). Founded in 1895, the STLA grew to 30,000 members as workers joined it in preference to the right-wing business union methods of the American Federation of Labour. A decade later, however, it shrank to 3,000 members. One of the major reasons for the decline was the reluctance of the STLA to fight for 'sops and concessions'.[18] For De Leon it was sufficient that the union declared for a revolutionary position. Its actual record in leading struggles was irrelevant. Connolly's aim was to broaden the base of the STLA beyond that of 'ward-heeling club for the SLP'.[19] This could only be done by taking part in struggle on day-to-day issues.

It is clear from the debate on wages that Connolly did not see revolutionary socialism as a set of politics that condemned one to passivity. He was looking for a revolutionary strategy that allowed revolutionaries to intervene in industrial struggles and agitate. In this quest his politics was superior to that of De Leon. The same could not, however, be said for the other two issues he raised in the debate.

Marriage and Religion

The second issue in the Connolly–De Leon correspondence was the position of socialists on marriage. Here the argument looked at first more unclear. Connolly held that there was a tendency in modern civilisation towards the 'perfection and completion' of marriage and monogamy. Yet he was surprised to find that other SLP members disputed this. However, De Leon happened to agree with Connolly on this point. Their argument therefore centred on the SLP's publication of the German socialist August Bebel's book, *Women and Socialism*. Connolly believed that its very publication gave ammunition to the right wing. It would allow them to throw the charge of sexual deviancy at an otherwise sound proletarian organisation. He suspected that the only purpose of the publication was to 'raise up for the proletariat friends in the camp of the enemy'.[20]

Many of the details of the argument are unimportant. But it once again threw light on the limitations of Connolly's Marxism. His conservative objections to the publication of Bebel's book was a continuation of the early positions he had developed in Edinburgh. In the course of the debate Connolly implied that socialism was concerned primarily with economic issues and other matters were beyond its scope. He wrote, 'I personally reject any attempt, no matter by whom made, to identify socialism with any theory of marriage or sexual relations.'[21]

A number of problems arose from this approach. Connolly was correct to argue that socialists do not advocate particular forms of personal relationships. Nevertheless the Marxist critique of society was not limited to purely economic questions. Engels' major work *The Origins of the Family, Private Property and the State* had set out to show how the family had emerged with class society. In the long run, relationships in society are affected by changes in the mode of production. Forms of marriage or sexual relationship were not excluded. As De Leon pointed put, albeit in his mechanical fashion, Connolly was denying 'the controlling influence of material conditions upon any and all social institutions'.[22]

Moreover, if marriage and sexual relationships were totally unrelated to the particular forms of society were not other spheres of life equally freely floating? In particular, religious practice and national sentiment. In effect, Connolly showed a tendency towards a two-track outlook – Marxism as an analytic tool for economic conditions, but different philosophies for other spheres of human activity. In practice, this would mean leaving vast areas of working-class experience uncontested by socialists.

In Connolly's own case, it also meant that prejudices learnt from a Catholic background could still pervade parts of his politics. In the course of the debate he wrote that, 'the question of marriage, of divorce, of paternity, of equality of men with women are physical and sexual questions, or questions of temperamental affiliation as in marriage, and were we living in a Socialist Republic would still be as hotly contested as they are today.'[23] The notion that, for example, the 'equality of men with women' would still be hotly contested under socialism seems surprising even when the particular experience of Connolly and other socialists at the time is taken into account. The quotation also implies that divorce was not an issue which socialists defended in principle. This would remain a consistent position for Connolly. Replying to later clerical attacks, he wrote in *Labour, Nationality and Religion*:

> Who, then, are the chief supporters of divorce? The capitalists. And who can come fresh from divorce courts, reeking with uncleanness and immorality, to consummate another marriage, and yet know that he can confidently rely upon Catholic prelates and priests to command the workers to 'order themselves reverently before their superiors', with him as a type? The capitalist.
>
> The divorce evil of to-day arises not from Socialist teaching but out of that capitalist system, whose morals and philosophy are based upon the idea of individualism, and the cash nexus as the sole bond in society.[24]

These views were not unusual in Connolly's time. The British SLP, for example, expelled members for living in unconventional relationships.[25] But the restrictions that Connolly placed even on discussing the issue meant that he and other Irish socialists were prey to the pressures of the Catholic environment. The incredible spectacle of Jim Larkin refusing to talk on a solidarity platform in 1913 because one of those present was a divorcee is an example of the price paid for this silence.[26]

The third issue raised for debate in the Connolly–De Leon correspondence was the question of religion. The *Weekly People* had published an article from the Belgian socialist Vanderville about the Catholic Church. This was unusual as Vanderville stood on the extreme right of the socialist movement and was a supporter of Millerand's participation in government. It seems that the sole reason for publication was that the article carried the very 'radical' argument that the most important remaining struggle was that between the Black International and the Red International – between the Catholic Church as the principal agent for reaction and the international socialist movement.

The anti-Catholic thrust of Vanderville's article pandered to a certain racism in America. Catholics made up the largest proportion of recent immigrants at the time and were often attacked on a religious basis, in a manner to some extent comparable with contemporary attacks on 'fanatical' Muslims. For example, after the assassination of President McKinley in 1901, great play was made on the killer's previous affiliation to the Catholic Church. Connolly exposed a tendency of De Leon to pander to some of these prejudices.

Nevertheless, Connolly's letter was also informed by some of his more general views on religion that we have discussed in Chapter 2. He denied that the Catholic Church presented a barrier to socialism and argued that it should not be fought as a church. He insisted that 'Socialism is a political and economic question and has nothing to do with religion.'[27] He understood his claim that religion was a private matter to be in line with the practice of socialists since the Erfurt programme of the German Socialist Party. In fact, Engels had insisted that while religion was a private matter in relations between the citizen and the state, it could not be so inside the socialist movement. Despite being a revolutionary in most other respects, Connolly consciously posed as a Catholic. Some years after the debate with De Leon, he wrote to his friend Matheson in 1908 that,

> though I have usually posed as a Catholic, I have not done my duty for 15 years, and have not the slightest tincture of faith left. I only assumed the Catholic pose in order to quiz the raw freethinkers whose ridiculous dogmatism did and does dismay me, as much as the dogmatism of the Orthodox.[28]

It is doubtful if this was the sole reason for posing as a Catholic. It is more probable that Connolly's overall view that the Catholic Church would not present a barrier to socialism led him directly to pose as a Catholic in order not to add difficulties to his propaganda inside the Irish Catholic community.

The SLP in Crisis

The manner in which the Connolly–De Leon debate was conducted showed that there were problems in the SLP. Connolly was denied the right to reply to De Leon's attacks. Almost 20 letters appeared in the *Weekly People* on the controversy and most of them attacked Connolly. Yet he was refused the right to answer or comment on them. His own branch in Troy, New York, decided to put him on trial for breaking party policy. To add insult to injury they wrote to De Leon to establish how such a trial might be conducted. The matter was finally raised at the SLP convention in July 1904 where Connolly was not a delegate. De Leon handled the controversy in a most dishonest way with all the skill of a trained lawyer.

The leadership of the SLP was behaving like a frightened sect. It was precisely what they had become. It was Connolly's misfortune to have raised issues for debate just at a time when the party's perspectives were in crisis.

De Leon and the SLP had argued that America was more ripe for revolution than any other country. They arrived at this conclusion partly through a peculiar form of chauvinism and partly from weak politics. De Leon wrote that 'the moment feudalism is swept aside and capitalism wields the scepter untrammeled, as here in America – from that moment the ground is ready for revolution to step on; what is more, from that moment reform becomes a snare and a delusion.'[29] Commenting on Germany, which had the largest socialist party in the world, the SPD, De Leon claimed that country 'was almost half a revolutionary cycle behind the USA'.[30]

This optimistic scenario for America was translated into more practical perspectives. At the 1900 convention of the SLP he claimed that because the economic and political developments were so advanced in America, there would soon emerge a situation where the SLP alone would be confronting the two major capitalist parties. After the coal strike of 1902, De Leon claimed that the revolution would have been accomplished in 1903 but for the fact that the movement was captained by the lieutenants of the capitalist class.[31]

This perspective was completely at variance with reality. The SLP's union organisation, the STLA, had shrunk to a tiny group that consisted of its own members with changed hats. Instead of becoming a major rival to the capitalist parties, the SLP found itself marginalised by the Socialist Party of America (SPA). This openly reformist organisation had received double the vote of the SLP in the 1900 presidential election. By 1904 the SPA was polling an impressive 408,000 votes. Yet they in turn faced a new challenge with the re-emergence of the populist movement after the democratic movement had turned rightwards.

Connolly like many other members was affected by the crisis in the party. He occasionally touched on some elements of the problem. He debunked the American chauvinism common in SLP ranks at every opportunity. He was sharply critical of De Leon's behaviour at the Dresden Conference of the Second International where De Leon, the extreme left-winger, had praised the most right-wing leader of the German SPD, Vollmar, as an intelligent leader who had adapted his conduct to local conditions. Connolly pointed out that De Leon was allowing for compromise because of his view of Germany as 'backward' compared to America.[32]

However, despite these criticisms, Connolly could not break fully from the theoretical framework set up by De Leon. Indeed despite his personal hostility to De Leon and his dissident stance within the SLP he agreed with the economic determinist outlook that had led De Leon to super-optimistic conclusions. Because he could not understand the depth of the crisis in the SLP, he tended to see De Leon's attacks on him in personal terms. Unfortunately the failure to face up to the theoretical roots of the crisis would eventually lead Connolly to a hostility to independent revolutionary organisation. But for the moment the birth of the International Workers of the World (IWW) was to offer a way out of Connolly's growing unease with the SLP.

The International Workers of the World

In June 1905 the International Workers of the World, known as the Wobblies, burst onto the stage of American labour. For the next ten years they were to blaze a trail of heroic class struggle that has remained a high-water mark. The roots of the IWW lay in the militancy of the miners in the western states. For ten years between 1894 and 1904 the miners had waged war on an employing class that resorted to the mass importation of scabs, regular victimisation, deportation of union members and even the use of martial law. The Western Federation of Miners organised the skilled and the unskilled; it did away with exclusivist apprenticeship rules and pinned its faith on the unity and solidarity of all sections of workers. During the climax of its organising efforts it entered into a major fight at Cripple Creek in the heart of the Colorado goldfields in 1903. It found that the American Federation of Labor (AFL), of which it was part, refused to help. The executive board of the miners concluded that there was a need for a different type of union from the AFL – one that would 'plan for the amalgamation of the entire working class into one general organisation'.[33]

The event which was to have a decisive impact on the formation of the IWW was the Russian revolution of 1905. At the opening of the first convention of the IWW one of its leaders, Lucy Parsons, told delegates, 'You men and women should be imbued with the spirit that is now displayed in far-off Russia and Siberia where we thought that the spark of manhood and womanhood had been crushed out of them.'[34] The 1905 revolution was to galvanise the revolutionary movement across the world. In Germany Rosa Luxemburg wrote her pamphlet *The Mass Strike, the Political Party and the Trade Unions* to hit out at the conservatism of the SPD leadership and their willingness to separate political and industrial activity, while in America the Wobblies saw 1905 as a confirmation of the power of the general strike.

The opening for the Wobblies had been created by the business union methods of the AFL, which demanded a high initiation fee and high dues. The AFL prided itself on its benefit funds rather than on its ability to fight. It had become a byword for scabbing and corruption. The 'American Separation of Labor' the Wobblies nicknamed it. The AFL made no effort to organise the unskilled, new immigrants, women or black workers. But while the AFL demanded immigration controls against the 'yellow peril', the IWW boldly told American workers that if they 'were but half as class-conscious as the average Japanese workers, there would be better conditions ... than the wretched ones they are now forced to submit to'.[35] They produced special leaflets in Japanese and Chinese to win workers over to the IWW. They set out to unite all nationalities in a common struggle.

The AFL also took an openly racist position on blacks and was silent on discrimination and lynchings. Its few black members were organised into separate branches in the Southern states. In contrast, the IWW made an open appeal to the black worker, telling him that 'the Negro has no chance in the old-line unions [where] they admit him only under compulsion and treat him with contempt'.[36]

Unskilled women were not wanted in the AFL. They were virtually excluded by the long apprenticeship requirements and the special examinations set for women. They were kept out of the best-paid branches in the belief that they would not earn half as much as men. But the IWW had considerable success in organising women textile workers on the east coast. The IWW did so by repeatedly pointing out that women 'cannot be driven back to the home ... they are part of the army of labor'.[37] They opposed as ghettoes separate trade-union branches for women and constantly praised the fighting spirit of women workers, appointing many women organisers such as Elizabeth Gurley Flynn.

The Wobblies banded together the most oppressed elements of the working class around a militant form of class struggle. They sought to make gains principally through direct action rather than negotiation. They rejected the idea of strike action as a 'passive siege' and relied instead on mass picketing, parades and demonstrations. Instead of long strikes where workers held out through a well-endowed strike fund, the IWW favoured the short strike that involved the maximum of solidarity. This philosophy was summed up in *The Industrial Worker*, an IWW paper: 'being a fighting organisation we place but little faith in well-filled treasuries. They invariably lead the workers to rely upon money rather than their own efforts and demoralisation results. The most conservative unions are always those with the largest treasuries.'[38]

The IWW would later have a major influence on Connolly and Larkin's leadership of the Irish Transport and General Workers Union. Both the Wobblies and the the ITGWU promoted industrial organisation as the only way to combat the growing concentration of capital; both aimed at the establishment of One Big Union (which later became the logo for the ITGWU badge); both combined the objective of overthrowing capitalism with a fight on day-to-day issues. Specific Wobbly tactics were also copied by the ITGWU. During a strike at Massachusetts in Lawrence, 1912, the Wobblies took the unusual step of removing the strikers' children from the hunger and misery, sending them to socialist houses in New York. Larkin and Connolly would apply the same tactic one year later in Dublin – but with less successful results.

The IWW and Syndicalism

The IWW brought Connolly to syndicalism. Syndicalist politics varied from country to country but the common thread lay in the emphasis on the industrial struggle and the forms of trade-union organisation.

Syndicalism sought to shift the focus from the ballot box to the day-to-day activity of workers in revolutionary or militant unions. At its most basic, syndicalism was a movement committed to destroying capitalism through revolutionary industrial struggles.

The heyday of syndicalist politics was in the early years of the twentieth century. Syndicalism emerged then as an international movement. The experience of the IWW was mirrored in the formation of the French General Confederation of Labour (CGT) which was committed to the ideas of Georges Sorel. In Britain Tom Mann's Syndicalist Education League was a propagandist body but it was very influential in the period of industrial unrest in 1911. Even in Germany, anarcho-syndicalist ideas gained a new lease of life after the 1905 Russian revolution.

The attraction of syndicalism for revolutionaries such as Connolly was obvious. They had recognised the drift to reformism in the international socialist movement. They had identified the major problem as the passivity among the rank and file of socialist parties which resulted from the exclusive focus on electoral activity. Moreover, the sheer opportunism through which socialist parties sought to win votes was repugnant. In America Connolly saw an extreme example of this opportunism in the behaviour of the Socialist Party of America which had become the main party.

The SPA defined socialism in terms of an opposition to the monopolies. It called for a moderate level of state control as a remedy. It prided itself on the high proportion of doctors, church ministers, lawyers and dentists in its ranks. It claimed for example that, 'the rich owed a duty to their wives and children to join the SPA and help prevent violence by working for the gradual inauguration of socialism'.[39] Its compromising policies were justified by a most touching faith in the ballot box. It claimed that 'when ten million American citizens will quietly drop a demand for the means of production into the ballot box, the capitalist army will have no foe but themselves and their riot bullets will be as harmless as children's marbles'.[40]

Many SPA militants who were dismayed by the practical implications of these politics turned to the IWW. However the IWW was also to offer a new method of struggle to existing revolutionaries such as Connolly and De Leon. By 1904 they had found themselves marginalised by the rise of the SPA. The sectarian traditions of the SLP had forced them into a corner where the choice seemed to be one of either holding on to revolutionary principles or winning mass support. Syndicalism now offered a way out. It showed a way of relating to the daily activity of workers that was linked to a revolutionary perspective.

Socialism Made Easy

Connolly wrote a number of articles and one major pamphlet in this period to outline his new attachment to syndicalist politics. *Socialism Made Easy* was the major theoretical work in which he advanced the case for syndicalism. It was his first successful publication, being sold throughout America by IWW supporters and also widely distributed in Britain and Australia. In the pamphlet Connolly used the term 'industrialism' rather than syndicalism but this made no material difference to the politics as the following summary of the arguments shows.

The pamphlet began by stressing the importance of industrial unions for a socialist strategy. He advances two reasons why workers should organise along these lines. First, the growth of reformist politics and the general political confusion among workers were directly attributable to divisions on the industrial field. Industrial unionism, therefore, would bring a new political clarity:

> As political parties are the reflex of economic conditions, it follows that industrial unity once established will create the political unity of the working class. I feel we cannot too strongly insist on this point. *Political division is born of industrial division. Political scabbery is born of industrial craft scabbery. Political weakness keeps even step with industrial weakness.*[41]

Second, industrial unionism performs an even higher function than simply overcoming political problems within capitalism. One of the purposes of the pamphlet was to show

> how they who are engaged in building industrial organisations for the practical purposes of to-day are at the same time preparing the framework for society of the future ...
>
> Every fresh shop or factory organised under its banner [of industrial unionism] is a fort wrenched from control of the capitalist class and manned with the soldiers of the Revolution to be held by them for the workers.[42]

Connolly was arguing here that the framework of the industrial republic could be built up inside the shell of capitalism. It was a matter of workers organising through their industrial unions to encroach gradually on the powers of management at the workplace. In this way they would push back the 'frontiers of control' so that the employer's ownership and prerogatives became a mere formality. In the longer run the political state would be engulfed by countless workplaces that had been organised under the banner of industrial unionism.

Connolly saw industrial unionism as 'the swiftest, safest and most peaceful' way of achieving socialism.[43] In *Ballots, Bullets or ...* he dealt with the idea of a possible capitalist coup against an elected socialist government. He claimed that the hold workers had over their factories would render useless any such attempt:

In case of a Supreme Court decision rendering illegal the political activities of the socialist party ... the industrially organised workers would give the usurping government a Roland for its Oliver by refusing to recognise its officers, to transport or feed its troops, to transmit its messages, to print its notices or to chronicle its doings by working in any newspaper that upheld it.

Finally having demonstrated the helplessness of capitalist officialdom in the face of united action by the producers (by attacking said officialdom with economic paralysis instead of rifle bullets) the industrially organised working class would proceed to take possession of the industries of the country after informing the military and other coercive forces of capitalism that they could procure the necessities of life by surrendering themselves to a lawfully elected government ...

Otherwise they would have to try to feed and maintain themselves. In the face of such organisation the airships would be as helpless as pirates without a port of call and military power a broken reed.[44]

Thus Connolly envisaged a weak state facing a strong industrial union. This led him to a highly optimistic view of how the transition from capitalism might take place. He wrote, 'we will be able to estimate our capacity for the revolutionary act of Social Transformation simply by taking stock of the number of industries we control and their relative importance to the whole social system, and when we find that we control the strategic industries in society, then society must bend to our will – or break.'[45]

Connolly's vision of a socialist society was always thoroughly democratic. With his evolution into syndicalism he began to attack the notion of a political state. He argued that the form of the capitalist state, even at its most democratic, made it an unsuitable vehicle for workers' control. One of the main reasons was that it was based on electoral constituencies which were established on a territorial basis in order to disguise the real class divisions in society. Socialism demanded that the workplace be made the centre of democracy. It was the only area where representatives could be in daily contact with their constituents and hence subject to their control. He argued that 'Socialism must proceed from the *bottom upward* whereas capitalist political society is organised *from above downward.*'[46]

His notion of an all powerful industrial union which had already displaced the capitalists from real power even before a revolution meant that he saw no function for a workers' state as subsequently argued by the Bolsheviks. The political state itself is identified with capitalism. In its place Connolly argued for a trade-union state:

The socialist republic of the future will function through the unions industrially organised ... the principle of democratic control will operate through the workers correctly organised in such industrial unions and

... the political territorial state of capitalist society will have no place or function under socialism.[47]

Connolly however did not fully embrace the semi-anarchist ideas that came to dominate the IWW. One of his distinguishing marks within the syndicalist tradition was his defence of the role of political parties. He believed that the party had two functions. It had the task of producing general propaganda to educate the working class in the period when industrial unity – and therefore full political consciousness – had not been fully formed. It should also stand for elections and try to win seats, as it was possible that 'the mechanisms of the political state can be used to assist in the formation of the embryo Industrial Republic.'[48]

Connolly did not elaborate on what was meant by the latter point. It seems that what he intended was that socialist members of parliament would press for industrial legislation that made the task of organising easier in addition to certain nationalisation measures. He regarded such activities, however, as an auxiliary rather than central form of the struggle. He wrote that he did not wish to imply that 'I regard immediate action at the ballot box by the economic organisation as essential, although I regard it as advisable.'[49]

The Weakness of Syndicalism

Socialism Made Easy rests on a major theoretical weakness. There is a crude materialism – which Connolly inherited from De Leon – running through the pamphlet. There is also a misunderstanding of the role of trade unions under capitalist society. Both these weaknesses led Connolly to an erroneous view of how socialism might be achieved.

First, the crude materialism. Throughout the pamphlet Connolly argued that workers' consciousness is shaped by the form of industrial organisation they adopt. If workers are organised in industrial unions then class consciousness will permeate upwards. Connolly assumed that a trade-union view of the world and socialist consciousness were one and the same. However, this is not necessarily the case. Industrial unionism can show workers, through their own experience, the need to unite against a particular set of bosses. It does not, however, automatically clarify the role of the state or indicate the way workers should relate to other elements in society. Unfortunately, the view that socialist, indeed revolutionary socialist, consciousness follows from the correct industrial organisation is barely argued for. It is simply asserted and supported by reference to 'the very nature of things woven, so to say, in the warp and woof of fate'.[50]

This view of working-class consciousness led Connolly to a number of practical conclusions. Reformism, for example no longer needed to be dealt with by *political* struggle. It was to be defeated by union activity. In the longer run this would undermine Connolly's belief in the need for a separate revolutionary organisation. It also reinforced Connolly's view that particular issues outside the sphere of economics and trade union activity barely warranted discussion by socialists.

The second problem with the pamphlet is, paradoxically, that it is based on a misunderstanding of the position of trade unions under capitalism. Connolly took the highly optimistic view that they could wrest control from the employers. Other revolutionaries such as Gramsci, however, argued that 'the trade union is the form which labour as a commodity is bound to assume in capitalist society, when it organises to control the market.'[51]

Although many unions include in their aspirations the overthrow of capitalism, their fundamental feature is that they exist to negotiate the price of labour. They start with the existence of the wage labour system and seek to strike the best bargain. By their very nature they are defensive and are shaped by the very system they oppose. From this arises many features which limit their use as vehicles for revolutionary change. Despite the call to solidarity, sectionalism becomes ingrained as unions mirror the capitalist marketplace. Unions under capitalism also inevitably produce a bureaucracy that arises above the membership to negotiate agreements and police them afterwards. Gramsci connected the bureaucracy to the stability the unions achieve through these agreements:

> The office becomes divorced from the masses it has regimented and removes itself from the eddies and currents of fickle whims and foolish ambitions that are to be expected in the excitable broad masses. The union thus acquires the ability to negotiate agreements and take on responsibilities. In this way it obliges the employer to acknowledge a certain legality in his dealings with the workers, a legality that is conditional on his faith in the union's *solvency* and its capacity to secure respect for contracted obligations from the working masses.
>
> The emergence of industrial legality is a great victory for the working class but it is not the ultimate and definitive victory.[52]

Bureaucracy, sectionalism, respect for agreements and negotiations are all double-edged swords. They express the acceptance by workers of the system in nonrevolutionary periods and so become an obstacle when their own consciousness changes. But these features also guarantee the permanence of the unions under capitalism.

In Connolly's view, however, it is possible to ensure the stability of the union and yet jettison all the features which make for that stability. In *Socialism Made Easy* he writes as if the revolutionary union gradually spreads its power from workplace to workplace. There is no recognition of setbacks or defeats. Once a workplace is industrially organised it becomes a fortress for the revolution.

This was completely at variance with the IWW's experience. Because of its refusal to enter into agreements and its rejection of any form of sectionalism, it was inevitably a profoundly unstable union. Typically it grew in a whirlwind of agitation and then shrank to a handful of agitators afterwards. Thus in Lawrence where the IWW fought one of its greatest battles, it had 300 members before the agitation in 1912; in September of that year it rose to 16,000 members but a year later it was back to 700.[53] In the words of Elizabeth Gurley Flynn, 'most of us were wonderful agitators but poor union organisers'.[54] The story of the IWW nationally was hardly one of stable expansion either. It began in 1905 with 60,000 members; by 1912 it had 25,000 members; the following year, 14,851; and in 1914, just 11,365 members.[55]

In addition to these major criticisms of *Socialism Made Easy* there is a number of other brief points that need to be made. Throughout there is a comparison between the way workers will achieve power under capitalism and the manner in which the bourgeoisie achieved power under feudalism. The bourgeoisie held economic power long before they took political control, and Connolly asserted that the workers' revolution would follow the same course. The comparison is false, for the bourgeoisie, an exploiting class, accumulates capital and wealth while the working class has only its organisation and politics. These cannot be accumulated gradually and uniformly but depend on the outcome of struggles.

Socialism Made Easy also underestimates the power of the political state. Like all syndicalists Connolly believed that it could be paralysed by a general strike. This has not been borne out by experience. The fact that the state is centrally organised and can command the forces of repression means that it can retain the initiative even during a general strike. Inevitably, then, the general strike functions as a means of defence rather than attack. Unless it progresses to the level of taking on the state by an appeal to the rank and file of the army and an eventual insurrection, it is the state which will paralyse the unions. Connolly's view of the revolution as a virtual stock-taking exercise of industries already under workers' control is therefore highly utopian.

Lastly, throughout the pamphlet there is an image of labour as an army with a great evenness and uniformity in the ranks where both industrial divisions and varying levels of consciousness among workers have disappeared. However the arguments for a socialist party rest precisely on the unevenness in the working class. It is for this reason that the socialist minority needed to organise independently to win over the majority of their fellow workers. By failing to recognise this, Connolly's defence of the party from within the syndicalist tradition was necessarily half-hearted.

Despite these criticisms, *Socialism Made Easy* was written with great enthusiasm and is a marvellous piece of propaganda. The first part contains basic arguments designed to recruit socialists. For its simplicity and style it has rarely been surpassed. The second part contains the more theoretical lessons learnt in America. While it clearly starts out from the revolutionary position the syndicalist politics expressed there eventually undermined Connolly's commitment to independent revolutionary organisation. The first casualty was the SLP.

The Unhappy Marriage of the SLP and the IWW

At first there seemed to be little difficulty in the relationship between the SLP and the IWW. The reason was that the IWW had induced a complete change in the politics of the SLP. Until 1905 the party had emphasised the elections and the ballot as the arena for struggle. After 1905, however, the party shifted dramatically to embrace syndicalism. The irony was that Connolly learnt his syndicalism from Daniel De Leon.

The shrinking of the SLP vote and the rise of the reformist SPA had led De Leon to revise his theories. Claiming to use a quotation from Marx, he began to argue that 'only the union can give birth to the true party of labor'. Moreover, the ballot box 'however useful and necessary, was a secondary consideration'.[56] It was De Leon who began to use the formulation that political struggle was but the 'shadow' or the 'echo' of the real struggle on the economic front. The difficulties of the SLP had given rise to an uncritical lurch in the direction of syndicalism.

The turn seemed at first to bring new success. De Leon was elected to the leadership of the IWW at its first convention and dominated the proceedings for the next three years. The SLP union organisation, the STLA, was dissolved into the IWW. A new unity was forged with the left of the SPA when its leading member, Eugene V. Debs, paid tribute to De Leon's theoretical contributions.

Connolly was in complete agreement with the SLP's turn to syndicalism. At first, however, he regarded the turn with some suspicion. He wrote to Matheson, 'I cannot help remembering that nobody in the SLP spoke of political organisation as being the "shadow" of the economic until the vote began to decline.'[57] He believed that the SLP had a tremendous future provided that 'SLP men [*sic*] do not fly off the handle and neglect the political organisation in favour of the economic'.[58]

These reservations were soon overcome as Connolly set about building the IWW in Newark, New Jersey. He tried to organise the 8,000 workers of the Singer factory where he worked, but was dismissed. He entered into discussions with the Italian *Il Proletario* group to win them over to the IWW and the SLP. When the Wobbly organisers, Haywood and Moyer, were framed and dragged before the courts in 1906, Connolly led the defence campaign in Newark. He was also instrumental in setting up the United Labor Council in New Jersey to forge solidarity among workers.

Like many other SLP members Connolly found that this type of agitation brought him out of the self-imposed limits of a sect. Increasingly he worked closely with the members of the SPA. One result of this was the New

Jersey Convention in 1906, which discussed merger between the two parties in the area. The basis for unity was felt to be the new-found agreement on syndicalism. The major issues dominating the socialist movement internationally – colonialism, militarism, the nature of the state – were, as Greaves points out, not even mentioned at the unity convention. It was dominated by the supreme issue of 'what type of union'.[59]

Connolly had by now embraced the syndicalists' supreme disregard of politics. He argued that championing industrial unionism was the sole way to win reformist workers to the banner of the SLP. After the unity convention he wrote that the SLP's unity agitation around the issue of industrial unionism would, 'bring in an influx to the SLP of the honest elements of the SPA' while the rest would be pulled towards Gompers.[60]

This optimistic scenario was to put the marriage of syndicalism and the SLP under considerable strain. The simple fact was that the SLP showed no signs of growing via the IWW. In Paterson, New Jersey, Connolly reported that the IWW had recruited 1,000 members in 1906. The SLP branch did not gain a single member.[61] Workers joined the IWW for militant trade unionism but this still left them a long way from the SLP's politics. The left-wingers in the SPA also remained in their own party. Connolly's own reduction of the argument between reform and revolution to one of what type of union meant that the issue of party membership was secondary.

The strain between Connolly's syndicalism and his membership of the SLP now blew up. The occasion was another internal row between De Leon and Connolly. The opening out of the SLP towards the class struggle through the IWW contributed to the rise of Connolly's stature in the party. By 1907 he had recovered much of the ground that had been lost during his disagreement with De Leon in 1904 and he was elected to the executive of the SLP as a delegate from New Jersey.

At its first meeting in January a dispute arose among a number of its members, including Connolly and De Leon. De Leon believed that a subcommittee of the National Executive Committee had not rejected sufficiently strongly an appeal for funds from the ILP in South Africa. The South African ILP had called for the defence of white workers. De Leon refused to print the NEC's statement in the *Weekly People*. In reality, whatever the merits of De Leon's points, the dispute was about his dominance of the party and his style of leadership.

The upshot of the dispute was twofold. The pro-De Leon element in the party ran a campaign to have Connolly recalled from the NEC for supposedly misreporting the minutes of the NEC meeting. In this they succeeded. But the new pressures building up in the party from its contact with syndicalist politics also meant that Connolly was not alone on this occasion. A number of key party cadre also saw the gap between the SLP's stagnation and the growth of the IWW. They put this down to De Leon's style of leadership. This group included Julius Ebert, the *Weekly*

People's assistant editor, and Ben Williams, a prominent member in New York.

Connolly, in common with these dissidents, was to develop not only a criticism of the SLP practice but of the very idea of a 'clear-cut' party which he had defended since 1896. Connolly, Williams and Ebert's criticism was explicitly non-theoretical. Neither the weakness of syndicalist politics nor De Leon's sectarianism was examined. Instead they tended to use their experience in the IWW against De Leon. This failure to grapple with theoretical problems meant that they fell back upon charges of 'bossism'. This extremely nonpolitical term was used to characterise the SLP's behaviour inside the IWW and also the internal regime of the SLP itself.

After the third convention of the IWW, which saw a new dispute between the politicals and anti-politicals, Connolly wrote that the election of so many SLP members to the executive board was a 'criminal mistake' as it tended to foster the suspicion that the SLP controlled and 'bossed' the IWW.[62] Inside the SLP Connolly was to find more examples of 'bossism' in the behaviour of De Leon. He put this down to the middle-class origins of the leader. Thus instead of seeking to raise the political level throughout the organisation so that members could challenge De Leon's arguments, Connolly retreated into a workerist position. He claimed that there should never be a candidate for the post of general secretary who was not from the working class. He wrote that

> the working class contains within itself all the material requisite for its own emancipation and that the place of all other sections of the population in the movement is a subordinate one, not only in theory but in fact ...
>
> To place anyone not of the working class in a position of leadership is an admission of the inferiority of our class and a perpetual source of danger.[63]

Echoes of the class struggle were now to be found in the SLP. The issue for workers in the SLP was whether 'they were able to run the party or whether they needed someone from above to guide and direct them'.[64] The question Connolly and the others now posed was why did these middle-class elements come to dominate the party? Why was it that in almost every country a working-class socialist found that his leader 'comes from a class above him'? He came to believe that the emphasis on theory inside the socialist movement lay at the heart of the problem. Theory involved socialists in discussing issues that were extraneous to the class struggle. And it was here that middle-class socialists used their knowledge and education to their advantage.

Connolly began to see his traditional opposition to these 'faddist' discussions inside the party in sharper terms. The experience of class struggle was enough. When theoreticians were deprived of their access to these areas of discussion they would find that their dominance of the party ceased. That at least was the experience of the IWW.

The IWW is not a body of 'theorickers'. It can never degenerate into a mere sect as the SLP has done. It palpitates with the daily and hourly pulsation of the class struggle as it manifests itself in the workplaces and when it moves onto the political field, as move it will, its campaigns will indeed be an expression of the necessities of the working class and not the result of the theories of a few unselfish enthusiasts. The IWW has brought a revolution in the socialist situation in America – the proletariat has at last come into his own in 'his' movement.[65]

This view was to lead to a complete break with the politics he held up to then. His attacks on the middle-class leadership and the emphasis on theory was to undermine his belief in the need for a 'clear-cut' party. For without a high level of theory that was to some extent abstracted from the immediate class struggle no party could claim to be particularly clear-cut. Connolly's criticism of the SLP sectarian legacy forced him to choose either 'the clearness of a sect' or involvement in the immediate class struggle.

Connolly had been pulled entirely into the syndicalist camp as a reaction to De Leon. The economic organisation was now primary. The 'clearness' of the party was now unnecessary. Its sole purpose was to issue the most general of propaganda. He wrote that 'since the political party was not to accomplish the revolution but only to lead the attack upon the citadel of capitalism there no longer existed the same danger in the unclearness of its membership.'[66]

Connolly also addressed the problem of how such a party with its more limited ambitions could be built. His primary concern was that a working-class leadership would develop. Put more crudely, he was determined to prevent the likes of De Leon turning it into a sect. 'Our loathing for De Leon did not turn us to anti-ballotism but did set our mind to work to discover the method by which the working class could control its own political party and put the non-working class elements where they belong.'[67]

The answer was that the party must emanate from the ranks of organised labour and be its expression. As long as labour was organised correctly it would produce revolutionary rather than reformist politics. In other words if trade unionists were organised on craft or sectional lines it was pointless calling on them to build a party since it would inevitably become reformist. But if they built up industrial unions they would be in a position to launch a revolutionary party. This was a return to a new version of Keir Hardie's approach to party building. The new theory of the party was spelt out in a letter in 1908:

I have come to believe that Hardie was wise in his generation to form the Labour Representation Council and that he showed a nearer approximation to the spirit of the much quoted phrase of Marx about the trade unions alone being able to form the political party of labour better than any of our revolutionaries ... ever did or do.

What we want to do is to show that the same method can be utilized in building a revolutionary party free from the faults and shunning the compromises of the LRC.

If that body was dominated by industrial unionists instead of pure and simplers; if it was elected by Industrial Unions and controlled entirely by them ... and also had its mandate directly from the rank and file organised in the workshops, it would be just the party we want.[68]

Connolly Moves Right

From 1908 onwards, Connolly's politics moved rightwards. This may seem a paradox. Syndicalism has been associated with the extreme left in its rejection of parliamentary and reformist politics but we have already seen that it carries within it a reduction of the political debate to one of what type of union is required. This could only mean blurring the distinction between reformist and revolutionary politics. Connolly was led by his syndicalist views to a new tolerance of reformist politics.

By October 1907, Connolly had decided to resign from the SLP. This coincided with his acceptance of a post as organiser for the IWW. He was in charge of a loosely named 'Building Section of the IWW' in New York. This provided him with an opportunity to press forward his project of an IWW-sponsored party. As a first step Connolly formed the IWW Propaganda Leagues in New York. Their purpose was to organise open-air meetings that promoted the political philosophy of the IWW. Among the prominent speakers on his soapbox circuit was Elizabeth Gurley Flynn.

However it soon became clear that Connolly's project was doomed to failure. The antipolitical wing of the IWW was by now in the ascendant. One indication of this was the political trajectory of the ex-SLP group to which Connolly was closest. These had moved further in the direction of pure syndicalism than had Connolly. Julius Ebert argued that the IWW's growth had been hampered by the SLP and therefore it should have no political affiliation of any sort. Ben Williams, now editor of *Solidarity*, the IWW's principal paper, argued against a labour party and the use of the ballot.

At the fourth IWW convention the antipolitical faction won a complete majority. An ambiguous clause in the preamble to the IWW's constitution referring to 'unity on the political field' was dropped. De Leon was expelled and took with him the remainder of the SLP to set up a rival IWW. Whereas Connolly had previously welcomed the 'squelching of the antipolitical crowd'[69] he now went along with the general drift. He was forced to conclude that an IWW-sponsored party had become an impossibility.

His political perspective had now reached a dead end. Against his former associates in the SLP he continued to argue for a looser party. Yet he could see no vehicle by which this could be built. The context in which these problems arose also sharpened the dilemma.

In the last week of October 1907, the New York stock exchange crashed and several banks closed. The depression of 1907/8 was to have an appalling effect on the labour movement. In New York, where Connolly had become an organiser, there were 184,000 men out of work. Wages were cut by between 15 and 20 per cent. The effect on the IWW was catastrophic.[70] Branches were dissolved by the dozen. The headquarters in Chicago was maintained with extreme difficulty. The industrial panic seemed to be concentrated in the very areas in which the IWW was strongest. It was forced to suspend strike activity and even the recruitment of workers to the union. On the East Coast it was to survive mainly as an organisation of the unemployed.

This turn of events severely disorientated Connolly's politics. His syndicalism had stressed the all-conquering power of the industrial union. Not only would it produce a revolutionary consciousness among workers but it would do so by demonstrating *practically* their power within the existing system. The factories could be wrested from managerial control as the industrial republic was built up gradually within the shell of the old society. Yet now as an organiser for the IWW he was acutely aware of how weak the union was. It was the IWW which was on the defensive. The notion of a gradual accumulation of industrial power looked like just a pious hope. Instead of wresting power from management, the IWW was being driven out of the factories and without this secure industrial organisation, there seemed little likelihood of a proper revolutionary party being launched.

These considerations help to explain Connolly's decision to join the Socialist Party of America. Undoubtedly this was the correct tactic for revolutionaries, as the SLP had degenerated to a sect. There was also a strong left in the SPA around Eugene V. Debs. Connolly could have joined with a clear perspective of working alongside these forces to drive the right out of the party. However, this was not the way he conceived his membership of the SPA. He joined at a time when the right-wing apparatus had been strengthened inside the party. Despite this he was appointed an organiser within six months of joining. Connolly had in fact moved to a new concept of a party that showed a drift rightwards in his politics.

He accepted the social democratic notion of the party as a 'broad church'. For Connolly the important feature about the SPA was not just that it contained a large left wing – it was rather that this section could happily coexist with the right wing. In a letter to Matheson he wrote:

In the SPA there are revolutionary clear cut elements and there are also compromising elements. I have read SP papers which branded Berger, Carl Thompson et al [the right] as tricksters and compromisers and other papers which sneered at their opponents as impossibilists, but both are loyal members of the party and fight out their differences at their convention. Neither attempts to expel the other.[71]

Connolly had in fact mistaken a temporary truce for a permanent peace. In 1912 after he had left America the right wing would sack the left-winger Haywood from the executive and begin an expulsion of the left.

Connolly's new-found political tolerance had arisen directly from his syndicalist positions. He believed that both the SPA and the SLP would eventually be overtaken by a party that emanated from the unions. Until such a real workers' party existed politics and political debate were not particularly serious. In *Socialism Made Easy* he described the political party that had been built before the economic organisations had been fully constructed as merely 'propagandist agencies' or 'John the Baptists of the New Redemption'.[72]

Connolly's description of contemporary working-class politics as 'preliminary skirmishes'[73] led to some unusual conclusions. Not only did it further undervalue politics, but it also led Connolly to avoid taking stances on particular issues. This occurred on two important occasions. In 1907 the Second International met in congress in Stuttgart. Among the main issues for debate was that of war and antimilitarism. The differing attitude of socialists to the question was expressed most sharply in the contributions of the French socialist Hervé and the German SPD member Vollmar. Hervé argued for an instruction to all socialist organisations to meet any declaration of war with a call for a general strike. Vollmar requested that the congress not tie the SPD down to any particular methods of struggle. The debate was widely reported in the socialist press. Connolly, however, took up an extraordinary position. The difference between Hervé and Vollmar, he claimed, arose from a difference in temperament. The Germans were 'cool, cautious and patient' while the French tended to be 'ardent, enthusiastic and optimistic'.[74]

A more serious consequence of Connolly's debasing of politics arose on the question of immigration to the United States. The leader of the SPA were thoroughly racist. Victor Berger, for example, claimed that 'the free contact with whites has led to further negro degeneration'.[75] Another leader, Morris Hillquit, sponsored a resolution at the 1904 congress of the Second International calling for restrictions on the immigration of the 'yellow race'.[76] In 1908 Hillquit stood for election in New York and invoked some of these racist anti-immigrant positions. For this he was criticised by De Leon. Connolly, despite his marvellous record in organising immigrants into the IWW, took a very different view. He wrote, 'he [De Leon] really is purposely doing the work of the capitalist class. It is hard to believe that any socialist really thinks that the immigration question is serious enough to justify a Socialist doing the dirty work of the capitalists as De Leon has done in his campaign against Morris Hillquit.[77] This is not to suggest that Connolly had also taken an anti-immigrant stance. His whole record proves otherwise. But his playing down of politics had led him seriously to underestimate the racist current in the SPA.

Throughout this period, Connolly's main vehicle for political expression was *The Harp*. This was a paper he founded in January 1908 to represent the views of the Irish Socialist Federation. This was a tiny organisation of Irish socialists set up by Connolly because he had come to believe that special propaganda was needed for each ethnic community to bring its members to socialism.

The paper reflected the unclarity and lack of political direction that Connolly was experiencing. It chastised socialists for turning their back on their own communities once they joined political organisations. It claimed that they dropped out of Irish clubs and societies and thus created barriers between themselves and their own people. They abjured 'all ties of kinship and tradition that throughout the world make the heart of one Celt go out to another, no matter how unknown'.[78] *The Harp* aimed to reverse this trend. These were highly spurious reasons for setting up the Irish Socialist Federation. In reality this development reflected Connolly's disillusion with American socialism. The paper, for example, promised not to take part in 'the campaigns of slander' which were the stock and trade of American socialists.[79]

In its efforts to reach the Irish community in terms of its own culture, it tended to adapt to the ideas of its environment. It reprinted many articles from the semi-republican journal *The Irish Peasant*. It opened its columns to Sinn Fein representatives and, as we shall see in Chapter 6, it took a very unclear position on this organisation. It devoted considerable space to discussing religion but adopted an extremely contradictory approach to it.

It could attack the growing power of the Catholic Church in Irish society. On one occasion it denounced Cardinal Logue for closing down the *The Irish Peasant*. The article, however, was written in the language of a loyal Catholic. Readers were informed that 'we may still kneel to the Servant of God' but not when he spoke as the 'Servant of our Oppressors'.[80] In its efforts fully to stress its own immersion in an Irish culture, it could go to extreme lengths. Lest anyone suspect it of atheism, it ran articles such as one on the 'Spiritual Side of Socialism' in which one contributor quoted a Fr. Hughes, claiming 'it must not be forgotten that the test points of Socialism were really borrowed from the Catholic Church'.[81] Connolly also indulged in some appalling rhetoric:

It is not socialism but capitalism which is opposed to religion ... When the organised Socialist Working Class trample upon the capitalist class, it will not trample upon a pillar of God's Church but upon a blasphemous defiler of the Sanctuary, it will be rescuing the faith from the impious vermin who make it noisome to really religious men and women.'[82]

The paper combined such rhetoric with reasonably clear articles. This was inevitable given the framework within which *The Harp* was working. Connolly's own embarrassment by Irish socialists who were assimilating into American society and cutting their ethnic roots led to an extreme form of moralism. They were blamed for the hostility shown by the Irish to the socialist movement. In contrast, Connolly overcompensated, going to great lengths to show that his paper had real roots in Irish culture. In reality he was succumbing to the pressures of the ethnic ghetto.

The Harp had none of the directness of Connolly's earlier or later papers. It stressed its tolerance of all political ideas. It operated under the motto, 'In things essential, Unity; in things doubtful, Liberty; in all things, Charity'. Aiming to be open to all shades of politics, it lacked a sharpness of style which resulted from Connolly's new-found conviction that working-class politics was only preliminary skirmishes until an industrial union was built.

The tragedy of Connolly's American experience was that the combination of sectarian politics and syndicalism led him into a political retreat. He had been among the tiny handful of socialists who strained at the limits of the Second International and sought to build revolutionary organisations independent of reformist currents. But the project was premature. Now when the first stirrings of a more widespread socialist discontent with the traditions of the Second International were emerging, Connolly was in full retreat to a 'broad church' approach to organising. This would make for extreme difficulties when he set about political activity in Ireland in the heady period between 1910 and 1916.

In the meantime, America produced one positive result. The articles and researches on Irish history that he had been working on for some time were at last gathered together into a book, *Labour and Irish History*. It was to become his most influential work.

5. *Labour in Irish History*

Connolly's major work, *Labour in Irish History*, was published in November 1910. It had taken twelve years to complete. The book began as a series of articles in the *Workers Republic* in 1898. After a lengthy break owing to political activity in America, these were resumed with the publication of *The Harp*. The book emerged as a compilation of these articles.

He was fully aware of the limitations of this short book. It was not a history of the Irish working-class movement, nor was it a Marxist interpretation of Irish history. Connolly left it to 'abler pens' to develop an analysis of how economic conditions had shaped and dominated Irish history.[1] The focus of the book was entirely on the relationship between the working class and the nationalist movement.

For all that, it is a marvellous piece of socialist propaganda. The style is direct and passionate. It is packed with research on political issues that were virtually unknown in his day. It was to become tremendously influential among many subsequent left-wingers in Ireland. The book is written as a polemic directed at the advanced nationalists with whom Connolly was later to fight in the 1916 rising. The Irish nationalist movement prided itself on representing the broad spread of the nation. Both its constitutional and military wings, and even its more left-wing adherents, accepted the need for class unity in the fight for Irish freedom. The example of James Stephens illustrates this.

Stephens was one of the cofounders of the Fenians in 1858. He devoted his life to organising secret cells of the movement to prepare for insurrection against British rule. He was slandered and despised by the Catholic Church and the middle classes. He was also a socialist who joined the First International. But he considered his socialism a matter of personal preference. He regarded any attempt to raise social issues – even the land question – inside the Fenian movement as the action of a 'Bedlamite' – a lunatic.[2] The need to keep the door open to win over Irish men and women of all classes took first place.

Connolly argued that the fight against the British Empire would never succeed as long as it sought to construct an alliance of classes. The upper classes saw the English garrison as a security for their wealth and property.

They had disagreements with the London administration but they feared their own people more than they hated the Empire. The attempt to conciliate the upper classes had the effect of restricting the national movement to purely constitutional questions. Its leaders had repeatedly insisted that there would be no social change. But this also meant alienating the mass of workers and peasants, because

> being explicitly told by their leaders that they must *not expect any change in their conditions of social subjection, even if successful,* they as a body shrank from the contest leaving only the purest-minded and most chivalrous of their class to face the odds and glut the vengeance of the tyrant.[3]

The nationalist movement had thus become the 'idealised expressions of middle-class interests'.[4] It produced poets and romanticists who compensated for their own weakness by a floweriness of language. But it could not mobilise. Instead its historians produced a picture of a unilinear struggle that lasted more than 700 years, transcending all class divisions. The nationalist heroes of one generation are replaced by those of the next; the only foil to their bravery being either the apathy of the masses or the intrigues of traitors.

The merit of *Labour and Irish History* is that it tears this, still powerful, image apart. The Jacobite hero, Sarsfield, is shown to be a feudal lord who did not fight for the freedom of Ireland but 'rather to secure that the class who then enjoyed the privilege of robbing the Irish people should not be compelled to give way in their turn to a fresh horde of land thieves'.[5] The Wild Geese, the mercenary soldiers drawn from the ranks of the Gaelic chiefs, who became the subject of so many ballads, are depicted as fallen aristocrats, who were later to take the side of the English army against the French Revolution.

Connolly reserves his special hatred for two major parliamentary figures, Henry Grattan and Daniel O'Connell. Grattan is shown to have despised the very Volunteers who were later to take his name. He denounced them as an 'armed rabble' once the limited goal of free trade and constitutional reform had been won from the Empire in 1782.[6] O'Connell personified the conservatism of the Irish bourgeoisie. He began his career as a yeoman who helped put down the Emmet rising. He broke the secular tradition of Tone to make the national movement the plaything of the Catholic Church. He denounced the 'tyrany ... exercised by trade unionists in Dublin' and attacked legislation limiting child labour.[7] In all things he sought to make Irish nationalism a provincial branch of the English Whigs.

The more militant successors to O'Connell, the Young Irelanders, Connolly treats with contempt. This pale shadow of the European-wide revolutionary movement of 1848 produced more poets than fighters. Connolly recounts how one of their leaders, William Smith O'Brien, refused to let the peasants of Mullinahone cut down the trees to make barricades because he was as 'rabidly solicitous about the rights of the landlord as were the chiefs of the English government'.[8] And this was in the midst of the great famine!

Connolly's aim, however, is not to catalogue a tale of horrors. It is to use the historical evidence to convince the most militant nationalists that a 'union of classes' leads to disaster. Central to his argument is the cowardice of the Irish bourgeoisie. With the exception of the brief period between 1798 and 1803, their record has been one of appalling betrayal. In this way he builds an argument around two central points which are outlined in the introduction to the book.

These are, first, that on an international level, 'the shifting of the economic and political forces which accompanies the development of the system of capitalist society leads inevitably to the increasing conservatism of the non-working class element and to the revolutionary vigour and power of the working class.'[9]

Secondly, and more specifically, the middle class in Ireland

have now also bowed the knee to Baal, and have a thousand economic strings in the shape of investments binding them to English capitalism as against every sentimental or historical attachment drawing them toward Irish patriotism; only the Irish working class remain as the incorruptible inheritors of the fight for freedom in Ireland.[10]

Connolly's Concept of Nationalism

There is, however, a third and less explicit argument running through *Labour and Irish History*. It relates to a clear attempt to reclaim republicanism for the socialist movement and stems from a confused concept of nationalism.

According to Connolly, at the heart of Irish nationalism was a different concept of property rights than that advocated by capitalism. The very fact that feudalism and capitalism were foreign imports meant that the propertied classes in Ireland 'were more English than the English'.[11] These classes and their middle-class supporters had tried to produce a diluted form of nationalism.

After the defeat of the Celtic clans in 1649, the social aspects of Irish nationalism, principally its demand for communal ownership of land, sank without trace. Its place was 'usurped by the mere political expression of the fight for freedom'.[12] This focussed entirely on constitutional arrangements as to who should control an Irish parliament. Connolly was under no doubt that this was an artificial form of Irish nationalism. In an article in the *Workers Republic* he claimed that, 'the nationalism of men who desire to retain the present social system is not the fruit of a natural growth but is an ugly abortion'.[13] But by contrast, 'the *real* nationalists of Ireland, the Separatists, have always been men of broad human sympathies and intense democracy'[14](emphasis added).

This distinction between 'artificial' nationalism which focussed on political and constitutional issues entirely and 'real' nationalism which was, consciously or unconsciously, attempting to reverse the original conquest which had imposed private property in Ireland, was not an academic one for Connolly. It had distinct political conclusions. For the elements of 'real' nationalism still abounded in the Irish character.

The Empire had tried to create a 'hybrid Irishman assimilating a foreign social system, a foreign speech and a foreign character'. But it found the 'Irish character ... too difficult to press into respectable foreign moulds'.[15] As a result many of the Irish people 'still mix with their dreams of liberty longings for a return to the ancient system of land tenure – now organically impossible'.[16] The task of socialists in Ireland was to relate to and develop this aspect of the Irish national character by showing that those aspirations could only be achieved by going forward to a workers' republic.

It is important to remember the specific conditions under which these ideas were formed. Connolly claimed that *Labour in Irish History* belonged to the literature of the Gaelic revival. In a sense this was a correct approach. Every colonised people needs to recover its own history and cultural identity from the propaganda of the imperialists. Connolly was absolutely correct to brand as a mark of slavery all the literature which tried to portray an Irish love of royalty and the 'gintlemen'. His recovery of a different tradition of Irish struggle was an important aspect of building a fight against the Empire.

The problem was that he assigned to these older traditions a contemporary political reality. Socialists had only to take over and develop a real Irish nationalism which was instinctively against private property. To an extent this reflected the desperately weak position in which Irish socialists found themselves in the 1890s. The working class had not yet entered the stage as a collective force; it was still tiny and weak. Connolly's revolutionary impatience led him to seek other springs of revolt. This in turn led him to imagine a far greater radical potential within Irish nationalism than actually existed.

His analysis was clearly wrong. In point of fact, Irish nationalism only arose because the clan system broke down completely and a new class, the Irish bourgeoisie, arose. It was precisely the champions of private property who established Irish nationalism. There was nothing 'artificial' about an Irish nationalist movement that accepted capitalist relationships. A cursory look at developments in the eighteenth century shows this.

According to Connolly, this century was characterised by social revolts of the peasantry. His examples – the Oakboys, the Hearts of Steel and the Steelboys – are mainly from Ulster where there was a far more vigorous resistance to the new landlords. Even here, however, these revolts were predominantly directed at tithes and rent rises. They were localised and those participating in no sense imagined they were fighting as part of a national movement. Aside from other localised movements such as the Houghar movement, which attacked cattle in Connaught from 1710 to 1720, and the Whiteboys in Tipperary and parts of Munster in the 1760s, the country was essentially pacified by Britain.

The force which ultimately built a nationalist movement stemmed from the growth of the Irish economy after the 1750s. The relaxation of some of the Navigation Acts, allowing Irish trade with America after 1731, and the start of the Industrial Revolution in Britain made for an expansion of Irish industry. Ireland was one of the main suppliers of linen to the British market. The Irish provisions trade grew immensely between the 1770s and 1800 as demand for beef and pork in Britain increased by four and eight times, respectively. By the 1770s, Irish exports amounted to more than 10 per cent of British trade.[17]

This expansion benefited both the Protestant and Catholic sections of the capitalist class. The penal laws had the effect of forcing the Catholic rich out of landed property and some became merchants. After 1747 the number of Catholic merchants increased although Catholics never exceeded one-third of the Dublin merchants or a quarter of the Cork merchants. While the capital at their disposal was often limited they had a reputation for 'business durability'.[18]

In 1778, a major economic crisis threatened to destroy this prosperity. A number of banks went to the wall and the linen trade was in turmoil. Under the impact of the American Revolution the most enlightened elements of the capitalist class began to demand a complete removal of the Navigation Acts which still prohibited Ireland from exporting directly to the colonies. They were particularly incensed by an embargo placed on Irish provisions in 1774 prohibiting their export to any country but Britain. This agitation became associated with a demand for the removal of the Poynings Act, which had made the Irish parliament subordinate to the English parliament.

These demands were won from a weakened Empire by a Volunteer force originally set up by the gentry to defend Ireland against invasion by France. Grattan's Parliament, named after Henry Grattan, one of the MPs who supported the Volunteers, was won by the threat of armed power in the streets. The Volunteers did not yet represent the rising bourgeoisie exclusively. They were still commanded by Whig landlords, such as Lord Charlemont, Grattan's patron. But the dynamic of the movement and the impact of the ideas of the American Revolution was pushing to the fore the new language of an Irish nation.

A number of events brought this process to full fruition. Grattan's

Parliament had officially liberated itself from English control – but in fact Dublin Castle, the centre of English administration, could still dominate affairs by manipulating the electoral system based on the rotten boroughs of the landed gentry. From the Northern industrialists, in particular, came a demand, expressed at a meeting of the Volunteers in Dungannon, for universal suffrage, annual parliaments and the payment of MPs to make the parliament fully representative and therefore free of English influence.

This also coincided with new economic conflicts with the Empire. In 1784, the English premier, Pitt, proposed full commercial union between Ireland and Britain; this union would have removed all duties on Irish exports to Britain and would also have allowed the direct re-export of goods from the colonies by Irish merchants.[19] A howl of outrage from English manufacturers led to the failure of Pitt's proposal. But this only sharpened the sense of grievance from the Irish industrialists. On top of all this came the French Revolution.

Irish nationalism was born under the impact of these events. It grew out of the failure of the liberal Whig tradition to promote equality within the Empire and to wage a consistent fight against a landed aristocracy in Ireland. It pre-eminently reflected the ideology of the industrialists who sought to promote their commerce. It had nothing whatever to do with a harking back to the clan system. It had everything to do with a pride in free enterprise.

Connolly implicitly recognised the importance of these events when he devoted one-third of *Labour in Irish History* to the period from 1779 to 1803. Yet he manages to write out the birth of nationalism among the bourgeoisie by a sleight of hand. The Volunteers are identified as an exclusively bourgeois-led movement. Connolly argues that the bourgeoisie sought to disband them after they had established Grattan's Parliament. The bourgeoisie refused to carry on a fight for protectionism to build up native industry. They did so because they sought the protection of the English garrison and wished to conciliate the landed aristocracy.

In fact, Connolly drastically foreshortened the process. The most militant Volunteers were to grow over into the United Irishmen. The Volunteers' struggle and the impact of the French Revolution were to awaken the Catholic section of the bourgeoisie who had previously been prepared to suffer discrimination. In 1793, the industrialists inside the Catholic Committee, a body formed to represent the interest of respectable Catholics, threw out the gentry elements led by Lord Kenmare, appointed Wolfe Tone as their secretary and began an open campaign for their rights.[20]

After Pitt's proposals for commercial union failed, the Dublin merchants led a major campaign for protectionism. Led by Napper Tandy, the future leader of the United Irishmen, they turned to the artisans of Dublin and occupied the chambers of the Irish parliament.[21] Connolly's notion that the bourgeoisie gave up on the struggle once Grattan's Parliament was established in 1782 is, therefore, totally mistaken.

Connolly and Republicanism

The foreshortening of the period of bourgeois radicalism had an important political sequel for Connolly. It led him to ignore the class basis of the United Irishmen and thus to create a tradition where Irish republicanism is seen as the ideology of the 'men of no property'. Connolly noted a superficial 'patriotic' policy among the Irish manufacturing class but ascribed the origins of the United Irishmen to a more 'intense and aggressive policy amongst the humbler classes of Protestants in town and country'.[22] These were able to link up with the Catholic 'tenant' as the growth of industry meant that 'the times were propitious for a union of two democracies in Ireland'.[23] The union was established because of

> the activity of a revolutionist with statesmanship enough to find a common point upon which two elements could unite, and some great event dramatic enough in its character to arrest the attention of all and fire them with a common feeling.
>
> The first, the Man, revolutionist and statesman, Wolfe Tone, and the second, the event, in the French Revolution.[24]

Wolfe Tone was an impressive revolutionist. He wrote his major pamphlet, *An Argument on Behalf of Catholics*, in response to the failure of the Belfast Volunteers to come out openly for Catholic emancipation at a banquet in 1791 to celebrate the fall of the Bastille. It was extraordinarily influential. Within three years, Tone was able to move these former Whigs into an alliance with the organisation of the Catholic peasantry, the Defenders.

The impact of the French Revolution was central. Tone supported the Jacobin wing of the revolution. One of his first biographers complained that the United Irishmen's 'obstinate and frantic glorification of every new development in France brought them into disrepute even with reformers'.[25] In fact, as Connolly pointed out, it was only their thoroughgoing revolutionary policy which they learnt from the Jacobin wing that made Protestant and Catholic unity possible. But none of this negates the fact that Tone and the United Irishmen were *bourgeois* revolutionaries who sought the 'preservation of our liberty and the extension of our commerce'.[26] At no point in *Labour in Irish History* does Connolly make this simple point. Instead there is the vaguer description of their representing 'Irish democracy' as if there was no class basis to the movement. Connolly's claim that 'real' Irish nationalism contained within it a rejection of private ownership prevented him from acknowledging such a basis.

Yet the bourgeois basis of the movement was glaringly obvious. Far from coming from the humbler classes, the leadership of the United Irishmen read like a contemporary *Who's Who* of the wealthy and influential of Irish society, as the following pen picture makes clear:

In the North, there was Robert Simms, merchant and part owner of a newspaper; Thomas Russell, the genial officer home on half pay; Samuel Nielson, draper and printer; Henry Joy McCracken, a Presbyterian cotton manufacturer; the ubiquitous ideologue, Dr William Drennan ...

The Dublin leaders included Thomas Addis Emmet, son of a state physician, a lawyer; Dr Rowan Hamilton; Oliver Bond, a woollen merchant; John and Henry Sheares, lawyers; John Sweetman, brewer; and Arthur O'Connor, Trinity educated son of a merchant family.[27]

The paper of the United Irishmen, the *Northern Star*, gave militant support to the French Revolution. But it also knew where to draw the line in defence of its own class interest. When the weavers in Belfast and Antrim demonstrated for higher wages in 1792, the *Northern Star* denounced the agitation as the work of 'a handful of idle and wicked men'.[28] In December of that year it expressed the following heart-rending cry of the radical bourgeoisie: 'By liberty we never understood unlimited freedom, nor by Equality the levelling of property or the destruction of subordination.'[29]

Tone's genius as a bourgeois revolutionary lay in an understanding of the need for a link with the peasantry. But he was not for trusting the fate of Irish capitalism to the unruly mob. In his memoranda to the French Directorate, he pressed for as large a French expeditionary force as possible so that 'the men of a certain rank in life and situation as to property would in that case at once declare themselves'.[30] Without such men who could form the government the affair would degenerate more into an 'insurrection than a revolution'.[31]

He was under no doubt that the alliance with the Catholics was primarily with their merchants, manufacturers and rich. Of the doubters within the Protestant community who were unsure of the dangers of revolution to their property he asked, 'Is it to be thought that the wealthy and respectable part of the Catholics would promote or permit unspeakable confusion in property?'[32] Republicanism produced the most consistent and determined movement against the Empire, of this there is no doubt. But it grew out of a break with all previous notions of Gaelic forms of property. It represented the short-lived confidence of a united Irish bourgeoisie.

Connolly was correct to point to the subsequent history of cowardice of this class when they traded in the radical secular ideology of republicanism for Orangeism in the North and O'Connell's brand of Catholic triumphalism in the South. In the nineteenth century the tradition of republicanism was carried through history by secret societies that were staffed predominantly by workers, artisans, and peasants. But because Connolly failed to look at the true origins of the ideology, he was not in a position to assess its usefulness as a political philosophy for these classes.

Instead, *Labour and Irish History* presents republicanism as a classless capsule that floats through Irish history embodying a connection with and a yearning for a pre-conquest Ireland. There is no criticism of the tradition and its limitations. The main thrust of the book is an attack on the constitutional nationalists, the representatives of a supposedly 'artificial' nationalism, produced by the middle class.

This blind spot is not confined simply to the origins of republicanism. While Connolly makes a clear materialist analysis of O'Connell, Grattan and the Young Irelanders, this is not the case with the forerunners of modern republicanism. Instead its leaders are either claimed for socialism or else shrouded in ambiguity. Fintan Lalor, for example, is proclaimed 'an Irish apostle of revolutionary socialism'[33] because of his land policy. In fact Lalor belonged to an era of agrarian radicals who had little in common with socialism. He sought to 'found a new nation and raise up a free people ... based on the peasantry rooted like rocks in the soil of the land'.[34] His restrictions on the right of private property applied only to land since the owners could not have claimed to have produced it themselves. Even here he was not necessarily in favour of common ownership to the extent that Connolly suggests. Lalor was primarily interested in vesting the rights of ownership in the nation rather than the crown. This did not rule out private ownership as 'She [Ireland] may if she pleases, in reward for allegiance, confer new titles or confirm the old.'[35] Lalor showed the limits of his egalitarianism when he wrote:

> It must necessarily happen that great inequalities must exist in every society in relation to wealth; that in fact there must be rich and poor. This arrangement of society is just and could not be otherwise. Although some may be born poor and therefore inheriting no accumulated wealth or capital they cannot, therefore, demand that a new distribution of wealth take place – that the property of the rich should be given to them.[36]

John Mitchel is praised for his support for the February 1848 revolution in France. But when Mitchel, like his French republican counterparts, drew back in horror as workers took the initiative in July, Connolly excuses his denunciations by claiming that he had been misled by 'garbled reports'.[37] Connolly was, in fact, fully aware of Mitchel's reactionary outlook on most questions beyond the separation of Ireland from England. In an article in 1898 he noted that Mitchel wished publicly for a 'plantation full of fat niggers' so that he might teach them what slavery meant. He quoted another article by Mitchel in which he had written that nationalists would prefer rule by the aristocrats to the best form of foreign democracy.[38] Yet the general thrust of *Labour in Irish History* in rescuing republicanism for the socialist movement excluded any presentation of these points.

Finally, Connolly's description of the Fenian tradition is also ambiguous. In an early chapter, he includes the movement alongside the Young Irelanders as furnishing a classic example of middle-class policy at work.[39] Yet in his final chapter he correctly stresses its base among organised workers and points to a coincidence 'of militant class feeling and revolutionary nationalism'.[40] There is no attempt to assess the Fenian tradition in politics or to discuss whether it is an adequate outlook for the many workers who looked to those traditions even in Connolly's day.

Labour and Irish History and the Marxist Tradition

How are we to assess *Labour and Irish History* as a Marxist analysis? Despite its blind spot on republicanism, it must still be viewed as part of the literature that had begun to challenge the mechanistic and stages approach that was dominant in the Second International. In that sense it was a positive break.

The orthodox position was based on a particular reading of Marx and Engels. In his *Preface to a Contribution towards the Critique of Political Economy*, Marx had written that 'no social order ever perishes before all the productive forces for which there is room in it have developed.'[41] This statement had been taken by Kautsky and others to mean that socialism would have to await the full development of the economic conditions in each individual country. Applied to the colonialised countries, this called for unlimited patience.

The merit of *Labour and Irish History* is that it departs from this orthodoxy. Instead of the colonial working class appearing as victims of oppression they became the principal agents of liberation. Instead of having to await a revolutionary bourgeoisie, they have to replace them as leaders of the struggle for national independence. Throughout the book, the bourgeoisie appear, at best, as cowardly opponents of the Empire.

This contempt for the latter-day bourgeois revolutionary was shared by Marx and Engels. During the 1848 revolution in Germany they aligned themselves with the 'Democratic party' in Cologne and analysed how the liberal bourgeoisie fought against the monarchy. It was soon clear that this class was terrified of the working class and the banner of revolution. They deserted the struggle and went over to the side of the military bureaucratic state. Marx broke completely from the stages approach when he summarised his experience in the March Address to the German Communist League:

> While the democratic petty bourgeoisie want to bring the revolution to an end as quickly as possible … it is our interest and our task to make the revolution permanent until all the more or less propertied classes have been driven from their ruling positions, until the proletariat has conquered state power … not only in one country but in all the leading countries of the world.[42]

These points were never fully developed by Marx and had almost been forgotten inside the Marxist movement that Connolly was operating within. Yet it was to that strand of Marxism that *Labour and Irish History* was returning.

Because of its insistence that the working class must not trust any section of the bourgeoisie, Connolly's theory has been compared with Trotsky's theory of Permanent Revolution. In a sense Connolly's advocacy of a fight for a *workers'* republic did parallel Trotsky's break with orthodoxy in Russia. But there are significant differences. Most obviously, Trotsky's *Results and Prospects*[43] was written in 1906, one year after the revolution of 1905 when Russian workers displayed levels of organisation and militancy that far surpassed those found in the advanced countries. Based on this actual experience he had an immense advantage over Connolly in being able to formulate a far more explicit challenge to the stages tradition within the Marxist movement.

Trotsky's method also differed from Connolly's. Connolly has an instinctive contempt for the Irish bourgeoisie. Aside from the remark about their being tied by 'a thousand economic strings to the empire', there is little by way of an explanation of their cowardice. Instead they are written off completely as incapable of any opposition to imperialism.

Trotsky, by contrast, produced a far more detailed analysis based on the objective contradictions in Russian society at the time he was writing. He discussed how Russian capitalism was the offspring of the Russian state. He argued that the rapid industrialisation that Russia went through destroyed the basis for an artisan class that could push the bourgeoisie from below as they did during the French Revolution of 1789. He showed that the dominance of Anglo-French capital within the Russian economy made for a greater accommodation with Tsarism. Thus, while he did not rule out bourgeois opposition to Tsarism his experience of 1905 confirmed his theory that it would be cowardly and inconsistent.

Connolly's reliance on an instinctive contempt of bourgeois radicalism and his method of deducing this from a record of their history meant that he did not undertake an analysis of the contradictions in Irish society of the day. *Labour and Irish History* finished before the rise of Parnell and there is no other work by Connolly to supplement it in this regard. The result is that, as we have seen in Chapter 3, he failed to see how the changing needs of imperialism would eventually push the Irish bourgeoisie into fighting for some form of political independence. His overall instinct that this would not result from a thoroughgoing struggle that would fully liberate the country remained correct. But this gap in his analysis was to disorientate subsequent followers.

There was one other important area in which Trotsky's approach was superior to Connolly's. The central problem of the Second International – that socialism depended on the development of the productive forces – was a real one. Connolly and Trotsky challenged the mechanical application of this truth in different ways.

Trotsky's starting point was the world economy. The productive forces had long outgrown the national boundaries and on a world level had already created the conditions for socialism. Thus, while particular countries might be backward as regards their economies they could contribute to the awakening of the world's working class by their political struggle. Any victory achieved in such countries would also have to spread to the more advanced countries.

By contrast, Connolly, like most of the rest of the Second International, did not believe that capitalism on a world level had exhausted its potential. Instead, he argued for an Irish exception. The peculiar form of Irish nationalism which predated feudalism and capitalism was what made a skipping of the capitalist stage possible. In *Erin's Hope* he had adopted the method of a 'sympathetic student of history' to argue that a people could use their 'political intuition' to jump the capitalist stage of development. In *Labour and Irish History* there is the suggestion that if Irish nationalism is rescued from its false representatives, it can become the vehicle for socialist advance.

Trotsky's theory led him to seek to develop an openly Marxist outlook by challenging all other traditions. Connolly's insight into Irish history was combined with a blind spot on Irish nationalism. Instead of challenging the republican tradition from the left, he attempted to incorporate it. This meant socialists stressing what they had in common with republicanism and fostering and developing the tradition.

Left-wing activists who came after Connolly absorbed this message from *Labour and Irish History* while forgetting the book's forthright attack on the idea of a 'union of classes'. Irish republicanism was seen as the only possible native radical tradition. Cut off from any class analysis of the roots of the republican ideology, the left, after Connolly, came to rely on a mysterious historical 'dynamic' to transform the raw elements of republicanism into revolutionary socialism.

For Connolly, the ambiguity on the republican tradition expressed in *Labour and Irish History*, was one which he would never resolve. It would take the crisis of World War I and the collapse of working-class resistance in Ireland and abroad to push him into investing more fully his hopes in that tradition. Before that, however, he would try to build a socialist movement amidst the dramatic events that shook Ireland after 1910.

6. 1910–1914: The Tumultuous Years

By the middle of 1908 Connolly had begun to think of returning to Ireland. He told Mother Jones, the veteran IWW organiser, that he was tired of America. A year later he was writing to William O'Brien that his emigration was the 'greatest mistake of my life'.[1] A number of possibilities for employment in Ireland presented themselves. The Dublin Trades Council required an organiser. There was also some discussion in the Socialist Party of Ireland about making an appointment. However nothing came of these.

In January 1910 Connolly transferred *The Harp* to Dublin. It was only to survive until June as a number of libel actions were threatened against it. Meanwhile, the Socialist Party of Ireland set up a Connolly Tour Committee, on which Jim Larkin played a prominent role, to bring him over as a speaker. On 26 July 1910 Connolly landed at Derry after being guaranteed the price of a return ticket, which he would never use. Instead he was to play a prominent role for the next six years in the growing labour movement.

Connolly's political development had been conditioned by his American experience. Chastened by his involvement in small sects, he had begun a turn to a more 'tolerant' approach to political disagreements on the left. Instead of asserting the need for an independent organisation of revolutionaries, he had reverted to support for a 'broad church' concept of organising. This led him back to the politics of the Independent Labour Party from which he had broken in the 1890s.

Throughout the period 1910 to 1914 Connolly's main vehicle of political expression was the Glasgow weekly, *Forward*, the paper of the local ILP. *Forward* belonged firmly to the Labour rather than Marxist tradition. Its political line was extremely vague and it cultivated links with all manner of disparate ideas. Each week it ran a column from the Catholic Socialist Society; for a period it stressed the compatibility of syndicalism with the Labour Party and had Tom Mann writing a column; it stressed the contribution that all – reformists and revolutionaries – made to the cause.

It was a cruel irony that Connolly had turned to organising on a minimum platform when events ahead were to demand sharp political clarity from socialists. The next few years would see the rise of republicanism, the Home Rule crisis, the Orange reaction, the struggles in 1913, and the threat of partition. It is a tribute to Connolly that his analyses of these events stand out even today. His new political orientation, however, prevented him from building an effective organisation around them.

The Republicans Re-organise

One of the first issues that confronted Connolly even before he set out for Ireland was the emergence of Sinn Fein. In 1903, just after Connolly left Ireland, Arthur Griffith had organised a new movement, the National Council, to oppose the visit of King Edward VII to Ireland. It was a loose grouping that involved republicans and radical nationalists. It managed to get the Dublin Corporation to vote against the loyal address to the monarch. Encouraged by his success, Griffith kept the National Council in existence after the royal visit as a forum for discussion among nationalist societies. In 1905, a new nationalist society in the North, the 'Dungannon Clubs', was formed by Bulmer Hobson and Denis McCullough who were both members of the IRB. The Dungannon Clubs and the National Council came increasingly to work together, taking the name Sinn Fein.

One of the first pamphlets from the new organisation, *The Sinn Fein Policy*, was based on a speech delivered by Griffith. It marked a break with all previous nationalist movements in championing industrial development as a key issue facing the country. It predicted that 'with the development of her manufacturing arm will proceed the rise of a national middle class in Ireland and a trained national democracy'.[2] It urged County Councils to invite Irish-American millionaires to promote industrial development in the the country. The Sinn Fein constitution reflected the switch in the nationalist movement to the urban middle class. It called for protection for Irish industry, an Irish stock exchange, a national bank, a merchant marine, a national civil service and a policy of withdrawal from the British parliament.[3] The latter point meant that it could constitute itself as a radical constitutional alternative to the Irish Parliamentary Party.

Sinn Fein won considerable support. Griffith's book *The Resurrection of Hungary*, which advocated the abstentionist tactic, sold over 39,000 copies. By August 1909 Sinn Fein had 581 fully paid-up members. Some 1,338 people took up £1 debentures to the Sinn Fein publishing house. Despite a poor showing in the elections, Sinn Fein managed to win support from significant groups among the urban population. On the right, Sinn Fein had the active support of businessmen such as John Sweetman and Edward Shackleton. The latter owned a paper mill in Lucan and locked out his workers in 1913. The programme of reviving Irish capitalism had a clear appeal in these quarters.

But on the left, there were also those who were won over to its programme of industrial development and militant constitutional tactics. P.T. Daly, a prominent member of the Dublin Trades Council, joined the party. So did former members of the ISRP such as Tom Brady. When the party stood in elections for the Dublin Corporation it offered a social reform programme as its platform. It called for municipal ownership, slum clearances and trade-union standards on municipal employment.

Sinn Fein was thus a classic all-class nationalist alliance. It could engage in left rhetoric when appealing to a working-class audience and still hold out guarantees to its capitalist supporters. Contradictions sometimes emerged. During the 1908 carters' strike in Dublin, the Sinn Fein paper, edited by Griffith, denounced the strike although the Sinn Fein councillors supported it. P.T. Daly and others stayed with the party, believing that Griffith's hostility was directed only at *English*-based unions, like the National Union of Dock Labourers.[4]

Sinn Fein was able to launch a daily paper in August of 1908 for a short period. Its radical wing put considerable pressure on the socialists to join what at this stage seemed like a very successful movement. In 1908, W.E. Cole, a Sinn Fein representative, addressed the Dublin Trades Council on 'Sinn Fein, the Workers and the Nationalisation of Irish Trade Unions'. He argued for a break with English-based unions, and for an Irish Board of Arbitration to settle strikes. He claimed that 'Sinn Fein is wide enough and all-embracing enough to take the best in socialism', while Sean McDermott also called on socialists to join Sinn Fein so that they would not be 'tied to the tail of English socialism'.[5]

The Dublin socialists' response to these pressures was highly confused. On one side there was a syndicalist element who accused Sinn Fein of stirring up 'race hatred' between Irish and British workers. It argued that both Irish and English workers were exploited by capitalism and therefore the national question was irrelevant.[6] On the other, majority, side, there was a softness towards Sinn Fein's policy. Prominent socialists such as Fred Ryan had written for Griffith's paper, *United Irishman*.[7]

Connolly began to respond to these developments with a series of articles on Sinn Fein in *The Harp* from 1908. His criticism of their politics was hampered on two fronts. He had always endorsed 'genuine' Irish nationalism which he believed was implicitly directed at a reconquest of Ireland from capitalist relations. Yet here was a form of militant nationalism which openly proclaimed a capitalist road. His own political development in America had also led him away from sharp polemics to stressing the need for accommodation with potential allies. The result was a fudge on his attitude to Sinn Fein which pointed to its 'good' and 'bad' points without defining the socialist attitude to it.

Connolly on Sinn Fein

The first article on Sinn Fein in *The Harp* came from a Sinn Fein supporter, 'Firin'. It was prefaced with a note from Connolly that it showed a 'striking similarity of view' to his own.[8] The article contained a demand that 'Irish socialists translate their socialistic ideas into the terms of Irish thought'. Readers were left under no doubt that this meant endorsing Sinn Fein. 'Firin' argued that 'socialism in Ireland very likely will be worked out through Sinn Fein'. He recognised that 'while political independence might not necessarily mean social amelioration of the people' it was a step that might be taken before socialism could be fought for.[9]

In the following month, April 1908, Connolly wrote an ambiguous piece which praised Sinn Fein's stress on self-reliance. He wrote that with the 'spirit of Sinn Fein every thinking Irishman who knows anything about the history of his country must concur'.[10] However, he pointed to areas where a certain 'friction' might arise between Sinn Fein and socialists. These lay primarily in Griffith's support for a dual monarchy.

Connolly's second article on Sinn Fein appeared in January 1909. This was a good deal harder. In a brilliant piece he pointed to the total inability of Sinn Fein to win Protestant workers to any programme of building capitalism under a green flag:

When the Sinn Feiner speaks to men who are fighting against low wages and tells them that the Sinn Fein body has promised lots of Irish labour at low wages to any foreign capitalist who wishes to establish in Ireland, what wonder if they come to believe that a change from Toryism to Sinn Feinism would simply be a change from the devil they do know to the devil they do not know.[11]

But Connolly did not draw the conclusion from this that socialists had to challenge Sinn Fein politically and to rival constantly its politics. Instead he took up a point made by a correspondent in the *Irish Peasant*, a paper that straddled the socialist/Sinn Fein network in Dublin. This correspondent had written that a 'rapprochement between Sinn Fein and Socialism is highly desirable', to which Connolly replied: 'To this, I desire to say a fervent "Amen".'[12]

Once again he pointed to the two sides of Sinn Fein – its economic teaching and its policy of self-reliance, which were categorised, respectively, as the 'bad' and the 'good' side. Griffith's economic theories, he claimed, were an obstacle to socialists. But he ended his article by proposing a conference of socialists in order to build a united organisation and consider their attitude to Sinn Fein.

Connolly's articles did not subject Sinn Fein's politics to an overall criticism. They took the form of pointing to possible obstacles that should be removed. Implicit in this approach was the suggestion that socialists could work for an improvement in those policies. Connolly's notion that genuine nationalism was in conflict with a pro-capitalist ethos provided the basis for this hope.

One perceptive critic pointed to the weakness of Connolly's position.

J.C. Matheson had been Connolly's comrade in the Socialist Labour Party in Scotland and had kept in touch even after Connolly's break from SLP politics in America. He criticised Connolly for endorsing the *Irish Peasant*, which was a mixture of 'Sinn Feinism, Co-operativism and Municipalism'.[13] He believed that Connolly's characterisation of the relationship between socialists and Sinn Feiners as one of 'friction' rather than hostility was wrong. He argued that their represe·ntatives on the Dublin Corporation were not socialists but 'indeed just the type of bourgeois the SLP had to fight'.[14]

Connolly privately acknowledged that some of Matheson's criticisms were correct.[15] Yet the central problem remained. Connolly had come to believe that political clarity was in contradiction to, and therefore had to take second place to, the building of a working-class movement. In a situation where many workers up to 1909 were looking to Sinn Fein, it might appear counterproductive for socialists to attack its politics.

By the end of 1909, however, Sinn Fein was going into decline. The continuing working-class militancy had already caused tensions in its ranks. In Britain, the growing conflict between the Tories and the Liberals had increased the bargaining position of the Irish Parliamentary Party and they used it to press for Home Rule. This was to pull many right-wing nationalists back into its ranks. Griffith also began to propose amalgamation with the All for Ireland League – a conservative breakaway from the Home Rule Party. This led to the final disillusionment of its left, some of whom drifted over to the newly reformed Socialist Party of Ireland.

Connolly now began to call for political attacks on Sinn Fein. In a letter to O'Brien he noted that 'Sinn Fein has become smug and respectable and has nothing to win the ardent republican or the trade unionist.'[16] He saw the demise of Sinn Fein as removing a major obstacle to building a socialist organisation. He wrote that, as Sinn Fein was becoming so decidedly reactionary, the 'opportunity of asserting the revolutionary leadership which slipped out of our hand when *United Irishman* [Griffith's paper] was established is now within our reach again'.[17]

However, having recognised the dangers Griffith's organisation posed to socialists, Connolly in his advice to O'Brien repeated his call for an uncritical stance on Irish national*ism*. He advised that socialists should pursue 'the same policy we pursued towards the extreme nationalists, viz, to discriminate between the *idea* of nationalism and the organisation officially expressing it.'[18]

This was therefore a recipe for criticising republicans on a strategic and tactical basis rather than confronting them with Marxist politics. The fundamental premise that nationalism offered an adequate answer for Irish workers was not questioned. This arose because of Connolly's conception that the *idea* of nationalism or the *real* nationalist tradition that we have encountered in *Labour and Irish History* was destined to fight private property. However, by claiming to beat republicans with the stick of Irish nationalism, Connolly was leaving his own tradition open to extreme pressure from militant republicans in the future.

The confrontation with Sinn Fein politics was thus avoided. The struggle in 1913 would widen the gap between republicans and socialists still further. But by fighting shy of a political confrontation with Sinn Fein politics, Connolly was storing up problems for the future. The full extent of this was to be seen in Connolly's own life in the period immediately prior to the 1916 rebellion. But it was also seen afterwards in the total liquidation of socialist politics into republicanism during the war of independence which began in 1919.

Home Rule

The issue which dominated Irish politics before World War I was Home Rule. The issue reappeared on the agenda again as a result of a crisis in the British establishment. In 1909, the British Chancellor of the Exchequer, Lloyd George, formulated a budget to meet an enormous deficit. It included an increase in death duties, a duty on undeveloped land, and coal and mineral royalties. Their lordships and the landed aristocracy were outraged. Defying constitutional precedent, the House of Lords threw out the budget by 300 votes to 75.

The Liberal Prime Minister, Asquith, called a general election in January 1910. The Liberals were returned but were dependent on the support of the Irish Parliamentary Party for a majority. Asquith promised that Home Rule would follow an assault on the power of the House of Lords. Lloyd George's budget was again passed but again met with stiff resistance in the Lords.

Amidst a growing constitutional crisis, a new election was held in December 1910. The issue was who ran the country – the Commons or the Lords. When the votes were cast the Irish Parliamentary Party held the balance of power. A Parliament Bill was passed in the Commons to limit the veto of the House of Lords. Despite a rearguard action by the backwoodsmen of the landed gentry – supported by one F.E. Smith, later a prominent supporter of the Unionist cause and a friend of Edward Carson – a reluctant House of Lords accepted it.

In April 1912 Asquith introduced the third Home Rule Bill. It was an extremely mild measure. Ireland was granted a separate parliament but it could not decide on the major issues of defence, relations with the Crown, or foreign policy. Inititally it was not even to have control of its own police. Control of revenue, including customs duties, was also effectively outside its scope as an Irish parliament could add no more than 10 per cent to duties and taxes proposed at Westminster.[19]

The scale of the reaction to the Bill was explicable only in terms of the constitutional crisis in Britain in the previous year. An alliance was forged between Carson and the backwoodsmen of the Tory Party.

Determined to avenge the attack on the landed gentry and to prevent any cracks in the unity of the Empire, the Tory Party swung behind Unionist resistance to the extent of preaching sedition and armed rebellion. Its new leader Bonar Law, told the Unionists that he would back 'whatever steps you may feel compelled to take, whether they are constitutional or whether in the long run they are unconstitutional'.[20]

Lenin saw the crisis in British society in terms of the 'reactionary landlords trying to scare the Liberals'. He wrote that 'the Liberal government should have appealed to the people, to the masses, to the proletariat but that was something the "enlightened" Liberal bourgeois gentlemen feared more than anything else.'[21]

Connolly took a similar position. In an article, 'Mr John E. Redmond, M.P.' (the leader of the Irish Parliamentary Party), he began by arguing that:

> the fact that national freedom is both desirable and necessary blinds many people to the truth that the advocates of such freedom on the political field may be the most intensely conservative on the social and economic field and indeed may be purblind bigots in their opposition to all other movements making for human progress or enlightenment.[22]

He opposed the tendency of the British Labour Party to hail the fighters for Irish Home Rule as 'progressives' who should be supported. He insisted that 'the non-Socialist leaders of merely national movements should be regarded in their true light as champions of the old order and not exalted into positions of popular heroes by the aid of Socialist praise or glorification'.[23]

Nevertheless, although he detested both the Tories and the Irish Parliamentary Party, Connolly believed that socialists could not stay neutral. The Tories were tied to the most die-hard landed elements who regarded any weakening of the British state as a blow against the Empire. When it came to a conflict between the two, 'It is our business to help the latter against the former only when we can do so without prejudice to our own integrity as a movement.'[24]

This meant arguing for Home Rule in very different terms from those of the nationalists. He was primarily concerned with how Home Rule would affect class politics in Ireland. After the Home Rule Bill was introduced Connolly organised a major meeting in St Mary's Hall in Belfast to press the working-class case on the issue. It welcomed the establishment of an Irish parliament as opening the way for the 're-union of Irish democracy hitherto divided upon antiquated sectarian lines'.[25] In his article, 'Sweatshops behind the Orange Flag', he wrote that 'the question of Home Rule, the professional advocacy of it, and the professional opposition to it, is the greatest asset in the hands of reaction in Ireland, the never-failing decoy to lure the workers into the bogs of religious hatred and social stagnation.'[26]

Thus Connolly's central reason for supporting the measure was that it would usher in an era of class politics. The two major blocs in Irish politics, the unionists and the nationalists, would fragment as the constitutional issue was pushed to the background. The prospect of a mass political labour movement was on the cards.

Sometimes this led to an exaggerated perspective. Speaking at a rally to celebrate the release of Walter Carpenter, an SPI member, imprisoned for protesting at the coronation of King George, he pointed to the coincidence of the great industrial struggles of 1911 with the Home Rule crisis and told the crowd, 'you are not only living in an age of progress, but an age of revolution.'[27] The success of the Dublin Labour candidates in the corporation elections of January 1912 fuelled the new expectations. In what the *Irish Times* described as a 'remarkable success' six out of seven candidates were elected. One of Connolly's associates, Tom Johnson, believed that a Labour party would take a quarter of the seats after Home Rule.

The prospect of heightened class conflict after Home Rule led Connolly into ferocious attacks on the nationalists while still supporting Home Rule. They were a 'slimy capitalist organisation ... fighting to maintain every kind of reaction and obscuranticism in our Irish cities'.[28] When the Irish Parliamentary Party called for unity in the fight for Home Rule, Connolly replied that

> every oppressor of the poor, every heartless sweater, every enemy of progress and champion of reaction feels perfectly safe in Ireland as long as the cry of 'national unity' paralyses the hand of the friend of progress and forbids open warfare against the Irish oppressor and reactionist who shelters behind Green or Orange Flag.[29]

The Home Rulers were denounced for opposing the extension of the National Insurance Act and the Bill providing for the feeding of school children in Ireland. Connolly also pressed for democratic reforms in the Home Rule Bill. He denounced the bias in representation of rural areas over the cities. He demanded full suffrage for women, the abolition of a second chamber in the senate and the payment of election expenses for working-class candidates.

Connolly's attacks on nationalist politics were not just confined to the Irish Parliamentary Party. Sinn Fein had taken a decidely reactionary position on the working-class upsurge in 1911. Even William T. Cosgrove, the future Free State prime minister, distanced himself from the official line of the party in its attacks on strikes.[30] Now the *Irish Worker*, the paper of the Irish Transport and General Workers Union edited by Larkin in Dublin, began to echo Connolly's line of breaking with the nationalists.

In 1911 it ran a series of articles attacking Sinn Fein and denouncing Griffith as a 'would-be dictator of Ireland.[31] Connolly, however, still had to win support for his view on Home Rule from socialists.

In March 1911 he moved to Belfast. The majority of socialists in Belfast were Protestants. According to William McMullen it had been their practice to avoid the question of Home Rule in the hope of concentrating on economic issues. They argued that a person could hold any view they wished on the subject and still be a socialist.[32] Connolly immediately attacked this attidude. They had to be 'brutally blunt' about their support for Home Rule. It was absolutely inconsistent with socialism to deny the right of Irish independence. His principled position was crystal-clear:

> A real Socialist movement cannot be built by temporising in front of a dying cause of Orange ascendancy ...
>
> Therefore we declare to the Orange workers of Belfast that we stand for the right of the people of Ireland to rule as well as to own Ireland, and cannot conceive of a separation of the two ideas, and to all and sundry we announce that as Socialists we are Home Rulers, but that on the day the Home Rule Government goes in to power, the Socialist movement in Ireland will go into opposition.[33]

On one point, however, Connolly's perspective was wrong. His political direction until 1914 was premised on the fact that 'Home Rule is almost a certainty of the future'.[34] This was a view held by virtually all nationalists and republicans. Connolly, however, in *Labour and Irish History* had stressed the cowardice of the Irish bourgeoisie and their inability to put up any consistent fight with the Empire. One might have expected therefore that he would have avoided the facile optimism of the nationalists. Connolly's inability to see the scale of opposition from the Orange forces and the weakness of the Liberal administration resulted from two factors.

First, he regarded the principal opposition in the North as coming from the landed element. In Connolly's Second International outlook, reaction would only be led by those elements identified with a feudal order. He did not see the scale of opposition from Northern capital arguing that 'there is no economic class in Ireland today whose interests as a class are bound up with the Union'.[35] In fact the principal markets of Northern industry lay not in the South but throughout the Empire. They feared the prospect of an all Ireland government dominated at best by the petty capitalists of the South or at worst a more radical government that arose from a weakening of the British garrison.

Second, Connolly's syndicalism meant that he did not see the depth of Orange ideology within the Protestant working class. There is little in his writings about Orangeism which recognised it as an ideology justifying discrimination and marginal privilege in the comtemporary period.

It is seen as the hangover of a settler community. Its persistence in the twentieth century was seen as entirely the result of manipulation by the landed element.

Thus while Connolly's general analysis on Home Rule, and on how socialists had to fight on the issue, was sharp and clear, his belief in its inevitable advance was to have consequences for how he built a party around his ideas.

Building the Party

The prospect of a Home Rule parliament where Irish politics would finally be fought along class lines, spurred Connolly to build the socialist party. In fact in his new model based on the American experience, he argued for *two* parties. There was the socialist party proper which took the form of a volunteer detachment which went ahead of the main movement to make propaganda. As the propaganda was of a highly general kind and not tied to particular agitations or issues, even this party was broadly based. Then there was a a general Labour Party based on industrial unions. This particular base would act as a guarantee against reformist tendencies.

The Socialist Party of Ireland provided a vehicle for the first wing of Connolly's strategy. Its first meetings in 1909 evinced tremendous enthusiasm with up to 400 people in attendance.[36] When Connolly arrived back from America in July 1910, he threw himself into organising for the SPI. His first port of call was Belfast. A meeting was organised there on 7 August by ILP supporters. Connolly used the occasion to recruit members to a branch of the SPI. Amongst the new members were D.R. Campbell, president of the Belfast Trades Council; Tom Johnson a future president of the Irish Trades Union Congress (ITUC); and Sean McEntee, a future Fianna Fail government minister.[37]

Two weeks later Connolly was in Cork, speaking at a public meeting of 2,000 workers. Twenty-four people joined, to form a Cork branch of the SPI. Two hundred copies of Connolly's new pamphlet *Labour, Nationality and Religion* were sold. This burst of activity also encouraged prominent republicans to desert Sinn Fein for the SPI. In September the former Sinn Fein councillor P.T. Daly, joined the party. Sometime later Helena O'Mahony, an active member of the nationalist women's organisation Innighe na hEireann, joined.

By mid-September 1910, the party was strong enough to hold its first annual conference. Strangely, it appears that Connolly was not present. But what surfaced now was an extreme unclarity in the organisation's politics. The conference was billed only as an 'informal one' where no votes would be taken. There was no discussion of political perspectives, the only items for debate being the methods of propaganda and organisation and the formation of an executive committee. The latter point and the role of Connolly as an organiser dominated proceedings.[38]

This playing down of politics within the SPI was built into Connolly's and William O'Brien's new conception of party building. In a letter to O'Brien the previous year. Connolly had argued that 'all that is necessary ... is a spirit of tolerance among members and a resolve to subordinate all purely individual opinions to the general welfare'. Reacting to the existence of a number of small parties, Connolly argued for unity around the 'ultimate goal' of socialism. Once this goal was formulated in precise and definite terms the party could 'allow for differences of opinion to exist as to the manner of realising it'.[39]

In practice this meant a compromise between reformist and revolutionary politics. The SPI manifesto was a retreat in terms of socialist strategy. Its aim was 'political organisation at the ballot box ... to gradually transfer the political power of the State into the hands of those who will use it to further and extend the principle of common or public ownership'.[40] There was no mention of the role of workers in their unions and workplaces. The party predicted a smooth transition to a Home Rule Ireland where the 'old party rallying cries and watchwords are destined to become obsolete and meaningless'.[41] The national question would be removed from Irish politics. As a result the SPI sought to avoid a split among socialists by not discussing in detail their attitude to the national question.

The vague, propagandist orientation of the party led to confusion and decline. Shortly after the SPI conference attendance at Dublin branch meetings began to fall off to an average of only 15.[42] A visiting committee had to be established to meet absent members. As an organiser for the party Connolly pushed for weekly as against fortnightly meetings and for the organisation to 'take up a more militant part in public life'.[43] He argued for participation in the municipal elections in 1911 but this was not taken up.

The real problem was a lack of direction. The organisation had not built up a shared political perspective. Instead members went their own way. One prominent member, Sheehy-Skeffington, was against challenging the constitutional nationalists until after Home Rule was won.[44] Another, Jack Mulray, backed a business candidate against the Dublin Labour Party in the municipal elections because he had 'a keen interest in industrial matters and without industry there was no hope for a socialist party'.[45] Connolly advised William O'Brien to concentrate on party building and to withdraw from many of his trade union positions. Instead O'Brien began to concentrate even more on the Trades Council and the ITUC.[46]

The only strategy of the SPI was to seek fusion with the ILP in Belfast. This grouping had arisen in the wake of the 1907 dock strike and had three substantial branches in the city. Connolly initiated this turn by the SPI without prior consultation with its executive.[47] He used the Glasgow paper *Forward* to reach Protestant socialists with the proposal for fusion. While in America he had made contact with a left-leaning grouping in the Belfast ILP around the Orr brothers who disagreed with the reformism of its leader, William Walker.

In one of his first articles on the need for unity Connolly actually stressed the common ground between himself and Walker in opposing the British Labour Party's support for the Irish Parliamentary Party. In his formal plea for socialist unity published in *Forward* he stressed the inevitability of Home Rule and asked the Belfast ILPers: 'What harm can come from organising on the basis of Irish political life, in view of the fact that in a few years some form of legislative independence is sure to be established in Ireland?'[48] The appeal was couched in the same mould as the SPI manifesto: unity would be on a minimum basis made possible by the removal of the constitutional issue.

Walker's political record made even this advance impossible. He belonged to that milieu of conservative skilled workers who detested any form of radicalism. In 1904 he argued that it was wiser to spend '£1000 on the return of a member to the House of Commons than to spend ten times that amount on a strike which is often not successful'.[49] The basis of his politics was appeasement of Unionism. During the election of 1905 he pandered to the sectarian vote by claiming that 'true Protestantism is synonymous with Labour'.[50]

He entered into controversy with Connolly in the pages of *Forward* to resist the unity offensive. The singular merit of Connolly's contribution was to expose the sham 'gas and water' brand of politics which paraded its 'internationalism' as a means of supporting the Empire. Connolly reduced Walker to a parochial figure who seemed more determined to uphold the achievements of the conservative-dominated corporation in Belfast over the rest of the country. However, Connolly was careful to limit the terms of the debate to who was most effective at advancing ILP-type politics in Ireland. Walker was accused of acting in 'reverse of all that the ILP stands for in Great Britain' because he opposed the formation of an Irish Labour Party.[51]

Connolly clearly had the upper hand in the debate. A number of ILP members in Belfast wrote to *Forward* afterwards supporting unity. In December 1911 Walker compounded his problems by writing an article in *Forward* attacking the calls for a general strike. In the same month Connolly was writing to O'Brien that the 'outlook is very bright' for a split in the ILP ranks.[52] He expected to pull the East Belfast branch, the largest in the town, over to unity with the SPI. In March 1912, the SPI, the ILP and the small Belfast Socialist Party met for a joint celebration of the Paris Commune. Finally in the same year Walker deserted the labour movement to take up a post as an administrator in the National Insurance Scheme.

Conditions were now ripe for the formation of a new party. On Easter Monday, 1912, a conference was held in Dublin to form the new party: the Independent Labour Party of Ireland, referred to as ILP(I). Its manifesto was extremely brief. It proclaimed that, 'the watchwords and rallying cries of the various parties led by various factions of our master class are but sound and fury ... it is no longer a question of Celt against Saxon or Catholic or Protestant but of *all workers against all exploiters*.'[53]

There was no mention of Home Rule, which was just about to be introduced in the House of Commons, nor any other reference to the national question. It was presumed that the new age opening up would render these questions obsolete. The political strategy of the new party combined a syndicalist emphasis on industrial organisation with a labour emphasis on winning seats on public bodies.

The ILP(I), like its predecessor the SPI, was organised around the most mimimum set of politics. Both parties followed Connolly's motto that unity could not be arrived at by discussing differences. In his early appeal for socialist unity Connolly had advised that 'as much as possible be left to future conditions to dictate and as little as possible to be settled now by rules or theories'.[54]

The problem was that 'the future conditions' on which he was predicating his strategy were totally contrary to his expectations. Far from the 'watchwords' of the varying factions of the master class losing their appeal, they were to grow after the introduction of the third Home Rule Bill in April 1912. Orange reaction reached an unprecedented tempo in that year and because the socialists had not attempted to formulate their theories and policies, because they had avoided discussions on their differences and virtually ignored the national question, conditions dictated that they began to split on sectarian lines.

Connolly's pragmatic arguments for an acceptance of Home Rule had settled nothing. In January 1913, the Belfast Branch of the ILP(I) overruled Connolly and insisted on joint meetings with the Walkerite rump in the old ILP. At one of these joint meetings an English speaker opposed Home Rule, claiming that the people of the North of Ireland were thrifty and industrious while the people of the South were slovenly and lazy.[55] Connolly was refused leave to reply. In July, the Walkerite faction backed the Agar-Roberts ammendment to the Home Rule Bill providing for the exclusion of four Northern and predominantly Protestant counties. They used the joint committee platform of themselves and the ILP(I) to promote this position.

Connolly now tried to retrieve the situation. He and Johnson argued that Home Rule had to be accepted as part of socialist propaganda. Three years after the SPI had tried to avoid the issue in its manifesto of 1910, it now resurfaced with a vengeance. The resolution was carried but at the height of the sectarian atmosphere of that year, it also led to the withdrawal of the 'old ILP crowd' from the party.

Connolly's party-building efforts had turned full circle. The main problem had arisen from his adoption of a 'broad church' approach. By failing to take up arguments he had ensured that socialists would be pulled by the pressures of their environment. In a period of Orange reaction this was singularly inappropriate. What had been required was a series of sharp polemics when conditions were favourable in 1910 and 1911 to clarify the main issues facing socialists. Connolly's adoption of an ILP approach to the party prevented this.

The Labour Party

The other arm of Connolly's strategy was the building of a Labour Party. While he was to win this on paper, the party was not to take flesh until well after his death.

Connolly's moment of success came at the Clonmel congress of the ITUC in 1912. Moving the resolution on behalf of the ITGWU he stressed the need for representation on all public bodies and again pointed to the new era opening after Home Rule. Unlike P.T. Daly's defeated proposal in 1902, Connolly's was not linked to support for Irish independence.

At the 1913 congress of the ITUC Connolly stressed the extent to which the Labour Party was 'above' national divisons. He claimed that in the past 'the English Labour Party was the natural ally' as it was better to appeal 'to our own class across the water than appealing to their enemies in the master class in our country'.[56] The situation had only changed because of the certain arrival of Home Rule and the establishment of an Irish parliament.

Connolly envisaged the Labour Party initially as a nonsocialist body. He insisted that they must 'keep a place for those who are not as far advanced as themselves, but whose interest would bring [them] into line'.[57] The Labour Party would be the municipal and parliamentary wing of the trade unions. Even though Connolly proposed the founding of a Labour party, he did not embrace a reformist perspective. While supporting greater state intervention, he was against 'mere government socialism'. Every extension of the functions of government should 'connote a conquest of powers by the working class instead of an invasion of our rights by the master class.'(58) This would be achieved by the increasing power of industrial unions on the factory floor. For Connolly the Labour Party had always to be tied to a militant syndicalist strategy.

Connolly wrote his pamphlet *The Re-Conquest of Ireland* for the new Labour Party. Begun in 1913, it was not published until 1915 when it became clear that the national question would not be resolved by Home Rule. It was, in fact, Connolly's worst piece of writing. Mawkish in style, it exudes a smug confidence of gradual advance in a Home Rule Ireland. There was little reference to the rise in sectarian bigotry in the North but rather the pamphlet claimed that there had been 'a marked increase in the fraternal feelings with which all classes of Labour regard each other'.[59] It was also asserted that the One Big Union would eventually encroach on the power of management until it came to administer the factories, docks, and shipyards, realising for Ireland 'the most radiant hopes of all her heroes and martyrs'.[60] Meanwhile on the electoral front an alliance of Labour with the co-operative, women's and Gaelic League movements would increasingly win electoral power.[61]

The Labour Party orientation strengthened all the worst forms of parliamentary cretinism common in the Second International. The act of voting was described in hyperbolic terms as making of the working class 'a composite whole which henceforth takes its place in history as the embodied soul of the race at that period of its development'.[62] Fortunately, such expressions were limited in Connolly's writing to only this particular pamphlet.

In any case, the Labour Party never saw the light of day during Connolly's lifetime. In 1913, D.R. Campbell was already arguing that outside Belfast and its surroundings 'any attempt to do anything in connection with the Labour Party at the moment would be a failure as matters stand'.[63] At the first meeting of the parliamentary committee, Larkin resigned the chair and Connolly refused to take it up, believing that it would not do without Larkin. Thereafter the Labour Party remained a vehicle for issuing statements and lobbying government ministers until its rebirth after World War I.

Orange Reaction

On 6 July 1912 Connolly sent a telegram to the *Irish Worker* offices in Dublin. It stated that 'the long continued and elaborately arranged attempt of the Orange Ascendancy to foment religious feeling in Belfast has at last been crowned with success'.[64]

Ever since 23 September 1911, when Carson had first arrived in Ulster as its new leader, attempts had been made to mobilise reaction. At his mass rally on that day, Carson had told the assembled ranks of the Orange Order and the Unionist Clubs that on the morning Home Rule passed they must 'become responsible for the government of the Protestant Province of Ulster'.[65]

The following February Winston Churchill, the Liberal home secretary, was prevented from speaking at the Ulster Hall. On Easter Tuesday 100,000 men marched through Balmoral in a ceremony that sealed the alliance of the Tories and the Loyalists. Accompanied by 70 other MPs, Bonar Law told them that 'once again you hold the pass – the pass for the Empire.'[66]

But it was in July, at the height of the Orange marching season, that sectarianism was fully unleashed. At the end of June skirmishes had occurred between the Ancient Order of Hibernians and some Belfast Protestant school children on an excursion in Castledawson. In response the Unionist clubs began expelling from the workplaces Catholics, socialists and even Liberals who supported Home Rule. In the second biggest shipyard, Workman Clarke, the loyalists had been drilling under the supervision of the owner's son since February.

The expulsions began on 2 July and soon 2,000 workers had been forced to leave their jobs. Later in the month the expelled workers attempted to return to work after receiving assurances by the Harland and Wolff management as to their safety. They were met by a massive assault and a new wave of expulsions began. By the end of the month, 3,000 workers had been expelled. One-fifth of them were Protestants who had socialist or Liberal sympathies.

Connolly's response to the events was sharp and courageous. The Catholic clergy along with Joe Devlin, the Home Rule MP for West Belfast, had tried to make capital out of the events by forming a vigilance committee which appealed for money and called on the Catholics of Ireland to come to the side of their persecuted brethren. By contrast, Connolly argued for fighting the expulsions on a class basis.

On 2 August the ILP(I) held a public meeting at which a call was issued for a mass labour demonstration against the expulsions. The march was called by the ITGWU. It was led by the Non-Sectarian Labour Band which had originated during the docks strike of 1911. Tragically, other union leaders made no attempt to mobilise against the expulsions. In many cases they did not even pay benefit to the expelled workers. Nor did the union headquarters throw the bigots who organised the attacks on fellow workers out of the unions. The beginnings of union appeasement of Orangeism were emerging.

The expulsions in July signalled the forward march of Orange bigotry. In September almost half a million people signed the Covenant, an oath-bound pledge to rebel in the event of Home Rule's being passed. In January 1913, the Ulster Volunteer Force was formed. Within a year Belfast businessmen had subscribed £1 million to its funds. In August a seaside excursion by the ITGWU was attacked by Orange mobs and a shot was fired at Connolly. In September an Ulster provisional government was formed.

Connolly's response to these events was hampered by the decline of the ILP(I). He had no newspaper in which to present his propaganda, the *Irish Worker* being primarily a trade-union paper which gave minimal coverage to the Northern events. His only public vehicle was the *Forward*, which circulated exclusively among socialists. Yet even here he virtually ceased writing for almost two years. Between July 1911 and May 1913 when reaction was at its height, Connolly published only two articles in *Forward*, neither directly concerned with the threat of Orangeism.

There was therefore no organised response by socialists to these events. What existed was primarily an individual response by Connolly. His reaction to Orangeism was twofold: he fought vigorously for total socialist opposition to the ideology while still trying to reach Protestant workers even when they were most under its influence.

Orangeism was primarily a right-wing and even racist creed that reacted on the Protestant working class themselves. He wrote, 'the Orange working class are slaves in spirit because they have been reared up among a people whose conditions of servitude were more slavish than their own.'[67] Orangeism's defence of marginal privilege divided the working class and left them open to Tory ideas. Connolly characterised it as follows:

> At one time in the industrial world of Great Britain and Ireland the skilled labourer looked down with contempt upon the unskilled and bitterly resented his attempt to get his children taught any of the skilled trades; the feeling of the Orangemen of Ireland towards the Catholics is but a glorified representation on a big stage of the same passions inspired by the same unworthy motives.[68]

Once the scale of the reaction became clear, Connolly launched an all-out war against those socialists who wanted to 'temporise' before Orangeism. It was not a matter of the different cultural sensibilities of individuals. All socialists – Catholic and Protestant – had to fight the reactionary movement as a matter of principle. Of the socialist who refused to resist Orangeism by standing full square for Home Rule, Connolly wrote, 'He repeats in the Labour movement the same feelings of hatred and distrust of his Catholic brothers and sisters as his exploiters have instilled into him for their own purposes from infancy.'[69]

There was to be no compromise with the poison of Orangeism. But this did not mean writing off the Protestant working class. Unlike many subsequent nationalists, Connolly did not believe that one could wait until after an independent Ireland was established before beginning the argument inside the Protestant working class. They had to be won over to the fight against Orangeism in two ways.

First, Connolly called for special propaganda for 'the conversion to Socialism of Orangemen'.[70] Part of this would mean exploding the myths about Orangeism's defence of civil and religious liberty. In a marvellous article, 'July the 12th', Connolly gave an example of the type of propaganda required. He showed that at the Battle of the Boyne, so famed in Orange mythology, William of Orange was supported by the dreaded Pope, who had a Te Deum sung in celebration of William's victory. He recounted how religious persecution had followed William's victory not just for Catholics but also for Presbyterians. The latter were forbidden to be married by their own clergymen; they had to pay tithes to Episcopalian ministers; their meeting houses were closed; and they were fined for not attending Episcopalian services. In another article on the Antrim leases, Connolly pointed to how Protestant tenants were shamefully evicted by Lord Donegal and others. He used this case as an illustration of 'the treatment of Protestant workers by Protestant exploiters.'[71] He aimed to show that historically the only difference between the Irish Catholic and the Irish Protestant was that one was 'despoiled by force' and the other by fraud.[72]

The second way of breaking Protestant workers from Orangeism was in the course of the class struggle. Connolly told Nellie Gordon, an ITGWU organiser among the textile workers, that the pogroms against Catholics could have been prevented if workers had been organised properly.[73] This was not simply a matter of words. Connolly combined his attacks on Orangeism with an open appeal to Protestant workers to fight alongside their Catholic brothers and sisters.

A particularly striking example of Connolly's unity offensive occurred in the textile industry. Many of the unskilled spinners had joined the Irish Textile Workers Union, an affiliate of the ITGWU. Connolly's efforts at organising had been opposed by Mary Galway, a trade unionist of the old Walkerite school and the skilled unions. In March 1913 the ITGWU struck and gained an increase for its members despite the violent opposition of Galway's Textile Operatives' Society and the Flax Roughers Yarn and Spinners Society, a small craft union.

A month later the same craft union was forced to strike against the dilution of its trade by cheaper unskilled labour. The ITGWU gave them full support. Connolly was invited by the Flax Roughers union onto their platform where he called for working-class unity. He also defended Mary Galway when a court had awarded damages against her.

In June 1913 workers at the Larne aluminium plant joined the ITGWU. Larne was noted as a bastion of Orangeism. Yet the militancy of the ITGWU and its willingness to fight for a reduction in the working hours had won over Protestant workers to the union. Tragically, however, the strike was broken by the Protestant clergy and the workers deserted the 'Fenian' ITGWU.

Connolly's strategy was thus limited by the scale of the reaction. Nevertheless as a political method for fighting Orangeism it left an invaluable historical legacy. He did not believe that the fight for common class demands alone would defeat Orangeism. His attacks on the 'gas and water' socialism of Walker testify to that. It was necessary to combat Orangeism from a principled socialist position. But the most favourable arena for doing so was in the thick of the class struggle. Nationalist organisations such as Sinn Fein could never win workers from Orangeism because they could only offer a capitalist alternative. Class politics based on struggle was the only way:

> In that work [of fighting sectarianism] the Socialists of Ireland know well that they can expect no help or countenance from the bigots of either Green or Orange persuasion, and while ever insisting upon the right of Ireland to control its own destinies, it allows precedence in its thoughts and plans to no interest but one, that of the working class.[74]

This, then, was Connolly's general strategy. But there were times when the scale and horror of the reaction overwhelmed him. His own concept of party building had left him without an effective organisation in Belfast that could have disciplined his perspective. One finds instead terrible ups and downs in his writings. Connolly zigzags between optimism and pessimism and subsequent demoralisation.

In March 1911 he was writing that 'Protestant workers are essentially democratic in their instincts'.[75] Two years later he was writing of them as 'servile worshippers of the aristocracy'.[76] After a number of dockers and Larne workers joined the ITGWU, he wrote an extremely optimistic article, 'The Awakening of Ulster's Democracy'.[77] Three weeks later he was claiming that the Larne strike was the first in Irish history to be broken by the clergy, implying that Protestant workers were exceptional in their reverence of the cloth.[78] This after Connolly had previously been driven out of Cobh in Cork by a mob of frenzied Catholics for speaking on socialism!

Connolly's syndicalism made for extreme difficulties in relating to the period of reaction. It was a tremendous tribute to Connolly that, by and large, he overcame them. Syndicalism sees the key problem as the type of industrial organisation workers possess rather than their varying levels of consciousness. It has real difficulties explaining why well-organised workers might have backward ideas while weaker groups of workers such as those found in Southern Ireland had better politics.

In one appalling article, 'Catholicism, Protestantism and Politics', Connolly came up with the argument that Catholicism in Ireland made for 'rebellious tendencies, zeal for democracy and intense feelings of solidarity with all strivings upward of those who toil', whereas Protestantism was a 'convertible term with Toryism, [and] lickspittle loyalty'.[79]

Subsequent history has destroyed this romantic picture of Irish Catholicism whereas the past history of the United Irishmen should have shown Connolly a different side of Protestantism. These blemishes in Connolly's writings were inevitable in a period of reaction given the political circumstances in which he found himself. Tragically, some elements on the Irish left were subsequently to elevate this weakness to a strength and ignore Connolly's central argument: that Orangeism had to be fought by Protestant workers on a class basis.

The 1913 Lockout

From August 1913 Connolly was to turn his attention to Dublin. The contrast with Belfast could not have been sharper. While that city was gripped by reaction, Dublin was participating fully in the working-class upsurge that engulfed prewar Britain.

Between 1910 and 1911 there was an upswing in trade in the British economy. By contrast the value of real wages began to decline after 1911. This provoked a period of intense class struggle. Between June and

September 1911 insurgent, violent and largely unofficial strike action occurred among seamen, the London dockers and the railwaymen. In Liverpool troops saturated the city and two workers were shot dead. Ben Tillet, the dockers' leader, argued that the strikes had done 'more for labour in the past few days than parliament would do in a century'.[80]

The ITGWU was initially drawn into these struggles through its support for the National Sailors' and Firemen's Union (NSFU). Connolly had first been appointed the Ulster organiser of the ITGWU in order to bring Belfast dockers and carters out in support of the NSFU. In Dublin Larkin tightened the union's grip on the port to back the strike.

The success of the sympathetic strike tactic during the seamen's struggle encouraged the ITGWU to use it elsewhere. After 1911 the South was convulsed in a strike wave. A mass unionisation drive was underway backed up by a policy of blacking and the sympathetic strike. The ITGWU grew from 4,000 members in 1910 to 22,000 members in 1912. Workers in many establishments won a two-shilling (10p) wage increase.

Ireland's nationalist employers were terrified. Just as they were about to win Home Rule they faced a resurgent working class. As Lenin pointed out, they decided to celebrate 'their maturity in "affairs of state" by declaring a war to the death on the Irish labour movement'.[81] The 1913 lockout arose directly from the need of the national bourgeoisie to defeat labour before an independent parliament was established.

The Dublin employers claimed that 'they were friendly to trade unionism'.[82] One of their later propagandists, Arnold Wright, claimed that they had made concessions to the 'Dictator of Liberty Hall' after 1911 in the hope of buying peace. He added that if they were dealing with an 'ordinary trade union of the English type' they might not be disappointed.[83] The problem was syndicalism.

This was rank hypocrisy. The builders' union, the United Labourers, was an 'ordinary union'. But it was still locked out in 1913 and only returned with a cut in wages. Yet in a sense there was a grain of truth in the employers' propaganda. The poverty and high levels of unemployment that characterised Dublin would always give the employers an upper hand as long as trade unionists respected the rules of collective bargaining.

The ITGWU did not. It was willing to pursue the class war above any other consideration. There was no automatic respect for contracts – working-class solidarity came first. Connolly summed up the strategy of the ITGWU as follows :

No consideration of a contract with a section of the capitalist class absolved any section of us from the duty of taking instant action to protect other sections when said sections were in danger from the capitalist enemy.

Our attitude always was that in the swiftness and unexpectedness of our action lay our chief hopes of temporary victory, and since permanent peace was an illusory hope until permanent victory was secured, temporary victories were all that need concern us.[84]

This was the philosophy of the mass revolutionary union. But no union under capitalism can fully escape the pressures of its environment. It has to operate in a contradictory fashion, responding to its members' demands in struggle and still seeking to preserve itself as a defensive organisation within capitalism. The pressures to respect contracts, and to develop a bureaucracy that disciplines workers to accept contracts, are immense. The ITGWU was not immune. On 26 May, after a period of intense class struggle, the union entered into an agreement on the docks to accept conciliation on all future disputes and to abstain from sympathetic action. In July Larkin proposed at a Dublin Trades Council meeting the formation of a National Conciliation Board to minimise strikes.[85]

The majority of the Employers Federation in Dublin were at first prepared to accept this new-found moderation of the ITGWU. But a small minority around William Martin Murphy, a prominent supporter of the nationalist Irish Parliamentary Party, believed that a decisive defeat was first necessary to tame the labour movement. After Home Rule this would produce 'ordinary unions of the English type' that could guarantee the cheap labour upon which Irish petty capitalism depended for survival. Murphy's policy won out through confrontation.

The Dublin lockout of 1913 went through four distinct phases. In the first month it was characterised by a rolling lockout. Events moved extremely rapidly. On 15 August Murphy arrived at the dispatch office of his paper, *The Irish Independent*, and ordered staff to leave the union. Forty workers were instantly sacked. Soon afterwards the authorities swore in a special constabulary and increased the number of troops in Dublin. The ITGWU stepped up efforts to win solidarity from the drivers of Murphy's Dublin Tram Company. On the 26th these staged a lightening strike. A huge open-air rally was organised the next day. The speakers at the rally, the leaders of the ITGWU and the Dublin Trades Council, were arrested and charged with sedition.

This charge was subsequently dropped but in the meanwhile Connolly was ordered to Dublin to help direct operations. A mass rally was called for Sunday the 31st. It was prohibited by Justice Swifte, a shareholder in Murphy's company. Connolly and Larkin called for defiance. For this, Connolly was given a prison sentence of three months while Larkin went into hiding. The rally went ahead on the Sunday, with Larkin making a dramatic appearance. Later that evening police took their revenge in what became known as Bloody Sunday when two workers were killed and over 600 people were taken to hospital after a baton charge.

Emboldened by the level of repression, the Employers Federation now declared a general lockout on 3 September. Connolly began a hunger strike to secure his release. Within days he and Larkin were freed. By

11 September, the lockout was complete. Over 20,000 workers found themselves out of employment.

The second phase of the dispute was characterised by an escalation in Britain. The annual meeting of the British TUC had opened the day after the Bloody Sunday police riots. It demanded free speech in Dublin, sent a delegation over to investigate and opened a fund for the Dublin strikers. On 27 September the first of the food ships to the Dublin strikers from English trade unionists arrived.

But more militant sections of the rank and file were dissatisfied with a policy of simply sending financial support. From mid-September, the railwaymen began to black goods for Dublin. When workers were sacked for this an unofficial strike movement developed. Ten thousand railwaymen came out in Liverpool, Birmingham, Derby, Sheffield and Crewe.[86] They were attacked by the railway union leader, J.H. Thomas, and eventually pressured into going back to work.

Nevertheless the escalation was sufficient to force the Liberal government to intervene. On 29 September a Board of Trade inquiry into the dispute opened. Connolly prepared the ITGWU submission. It offered a year-long suspension of the tactic of the sympathetic strike. But the employers wanted the complete humiliation of the union. On 6 October they rejected all offers of compromise.

The third phase of the strike was now one of all-out war. On 10 October Larkin launched an attack on the TUC leaders, demanding blacking and strike action. But it was the employers who were first to step up the offensive. They whipped up Catholic fears about the transportation of children to Britain for the duration of the strike. On 21 October the bishops issued a pastoral letter to denounce the scheme. Six days later Larkin was sentenced to seven months' imprisonment for incitement. On the 29th the first blacklegs were imported from Britain to break the strike.

Connolly now became acting general secretary of the union. He immediately took a series of measures to respond to the employers' offensive. He ordered mass pickets on the port of Dublin against the scabs. This meant breaking the agreement of 26 May. Using the opportunities of three bye-elections in Britain, Connolly called for a vote against the Liberals – 'the jailors of Larkin and the murderers of the Dublin workers, Byrne and Nolan', who were killed on Bloody Sunday. On 10 November he issued an appeal over the heads of the TUC leaders for sympathy stoppages. On 13 November he endorsed an appeal to form the Irish Citizen Army. The advertisement for the inaugural meeting explained:

> Let the workers keep clear of the Girondin politicians who will simply use the workers as a means to their own security and comfort. Let others who may prate about the 'rights and liberties common to all Irishmen'. We are out for the right to work and eat and live.[87]

Connolly's superb leadership brought results. The Liberals suffered ignominious defeats in the bye-elections. Working-class protest in Britain and strikes in South Wales brought the release of Larkin after seventeen days. The Citizen Army afforded a measure of protection from the scabs and the police.

As soon as Larkin was released he began a tour of England to win solidarity action. The response was tremendous; 24,000 people turned out for his first meeting in Manchester.[88] But there still remained a gap between the enthusiasm and the confidence to launch widespread action. The role of the TUC now became crucial.

The fourth and final phase of the strike resulted from the TUC decision to scab. On 9 December it met in special conference to reject a call for blacking of goods to Dublin. Instead, it tried to set itself up as a mediator. Almost immediately, the railwaymen's union, the NUR, and the NSFU began to co-operate in the transport of scabs to Dublin. The employers now sensed victory. On the 14th, the ITGWU ordered back all those who did not have to sign a declaration of leaving the union. By January the drift back to work signalled a massive defeat as workers were forced to sign a document disowning the ITGWU. Union militants were victimised and in many cases wage cuts were imposed.

The Aftermath

The lockout posed a decisive test for all sections of Irish society. The rhetoric, prejudices and pretensions of all groups were measured on the simple test: which side were they on?

One group whose response pleasantly surprised Connolly was Dublin's liberal intelligentsia. Writers such as George Russell ('AE'), W.B. Yeats, and Padraig Pearse came out openly on the side of the workers. Connolly's pamphlet, *The Re-Conquest of Ireland*, reflected a more open approach to intellectuals as a result.

The response of Protestant workers in the North was more contradictory. Under the sway of Orange reaction, many at first dismissed the strike as of no particular concern to them. In August a section of the dockers, whom Connolly had recruited into the union in Belfast, resigned in protest at his 'ungodly speech' at a Dublin rally. But the scale and courage of the struggle soon evoked a class response. As the struggle escalated after the imprisonment of Larkin, the same dockers applied to rejoin. Collections were taken up in Belfast and most support came from the shipyard workers.[89] In late November 150 dock labourers came out on strike against the importation of scabs.

However, the movement most affected by 1913 was the nationalist movement. Its argument that the workers had to await the achievement of national independence before they pursued their own class interests was contradicted by reality. Despite this an extraordinary rewriting of history has grown up to recapture 1913 for nationalist ideology. Writers such as Desmond Greaves have argued that a labour–separatist alliance was in evidence during the strike.[90] This is combined with a widespread belief that the lockout was defeated because of the refusal of *British* workers to support their Irish comrades. Nothing could be further from the truth.

On 29 November Connolly wrote an important article for the *Irish Worker* dealing with the nationalist arguments during the strike. Significantly, it has not been reprinted in any of the collections of his articles. He began by claiming that 'practically every official element in Nationalist circles has striven hard all through this struggle to make capital against Labour'.[91]

This was indeed a statement of fact. Arthur Griffith and Sinn Fein denounced Larkinism as an imported English evil. The Irish Republican Brotherhood refused to take a stand in favour of the strikers although individual members were permitted to raise solidarity and show support. On 25 November the IRB was instrumental in forming the National Volunteer Force. It invited a number of Home Rule organisations to attend the founding meeting, but the ITGWU was not invited. Worse still, the joint secretary of the Volunteers was Lawrence Kettle, a vicious opponent of the strike. As soon as he spoke there were scuffles and fights as ITGWU protesters were drowned out with the song 'God save Ireland'.[92] The IRB's all-class politics had dictated that they were more concerned with winning support from the Home Rule party than with backing the Dublin working class.

Connolly exposed a contradiction in the nationalist attitude to the strike. They opposed the sympathetic strike – but they also denounced the 'labour people in England because they send money and food instead of coming out on sympathetic strike'.[93] They insisted not only on blaming the Empire but also the English working class, who were portrayed as natural conservatives compared to the Irish rebels. Connolly countered these arguments as follows:

We are told that the English people contribute their help to our enslavement. It is true.

It is also true that the Irish people contributed soldiers to duly crush every democratic movement of the English people from the deportation of Irish soldiers to serve the cause of political despotism under Charles I to the days of Featherstone under Asquith.

Slaves themselves the English people helped to enslave others; slaves themselves the Irish people helped to enslave others. There is no room for recrimination ...

The first duty of the working class of the world is to settle accounts with the master class of the world – that of their own country at the head of the list. To that point this struggle, as all other such struggles, is converging.[94]

In February, when the strike had been defeated Connolly wrote an article, 'The Isolation of Dublin'. Here again there was no trace of the argument that British workers had let Dublin down because of their chauvinistic prejudice against the Irish. Quite the opposite. Connolly wrote of the working-class movement in Britain having 'reached its highest point of moral grandeur' during the strike.[95] He pointed to the London dock strike of 1912 as an example of how a strike in Britain had already been defeated by lack of solidarity. This had been called in conjunction with the National Transport Workers Federation but was unable to win support from the provinces. The chief culprit for Connolly, therefore, was not British workers or British-based unions but 'sectional officialism'.[96] He claimed that 'The [trade union] officials failed to grasp the opportunity offered to them to make a permanent reality of the Union of Working Class forces brought into being by the spectacle of rebellion, martyrdom and misery exhibited by the workers of Dublin.'[97]

But why did this occur? And what did it mean for Connolly's syndicalist outlook? These were issues which were addressed in a number of articles, after the strike, the most important being 'Old Wines in New Bottles'. Connolly's syndicalism had led to highly optimistic expectations at the beginning of the strike. The syndicalist sees working-class struggle as going ever onward and upward to the point of eventually encroaching completely on the employers' control. The model was the manner in which the capitalists had built up their economic power within feudalism.

Moreover, Connolly's syndicalism reduced politics to the question of the correct form of organisation. Industrial unionism was the answer not only to sectionalism within the working class but even to the problem of reformism. The role and power of the state was completely played down. The mere fact that workers were organised correctly would guarantee them an increase in economic power within capitalism.

After the strike some of these assumptions were questioned. Connolly became ever more insistent on the need to combine political and industrial action, noting that the capitalist class will 'use their political powers to hamper, penalise and if possible destroy the activities of the workers' organisation'.[98] He recognised that the mere existence of industrial unions and federations was no longer sufficient. The National Transport Workers Federation had been inspired by syndicalist politics but it was 'absolutely destitute of revolutionary spirit'.[99]

Nevertheless Connolly remained a thoroughgoing syndicalist. The key problem, he now argued, was to choose the right officials to encourage a revolutionary spirit among workers. There was no understanding of the nature of trade unionism under capitalism – or of the pressures on all trade-union officials to enforce agreements arrived at during collective bargaining and thus become divorced from their membership. Nor was there an understanding of how defeats such as that suffered in 1913 could have a temporary but devastating effect on workers' consciousness.

The syndicalists had operated on the assumption that workers' consciousness was even, progressing ever upwards. There was no need to organise
the minority who had drawn the sharpest lessons from the lockout into
a revolutionary party. The party remained a propaganda auxiliary that
did not play a role when major industrial struggles began.

This gap in Connolly's politics would make it difficult for him to understand how workers who had fought so heroically during the lockout could
join the British army nine months later when the war broke out. It also
meant that he missed a unique opportunity in 1913 to pull hundreds
of the best working-class militants into a revolutionary party.

Partition

The British House of Commons reopened on 10 February 1914 just as
the lockout was ending. Rumours abounded about partition for Ireland.
Some months previously Redmond had rejected the suggestion, declaring
that he would not be a party to 'the mutilation of the Irish nation'.[100]

But by 1914 the mobilisations of the Unionists and the timidity of
the Liberal government had put the issue firmly back on the agenda. On
7 March Lloyd George, with Redmond's agreement, proposed that each
Ulster county be given the right to opt out of a Home Rule Ireland for
a period of six years. However, as Connolly pointed out, there was every
possibility that a Tory government would be returned within that period.
It would take only a one-line bill to make the exclusion permanent.

Carson formally rejected the compromise but in reality the Unionists
were looking to widen the concessions. In response Churchill ordered
troops to the North in a show of strength. But on 19 March there was
an open mutiny among the officers in the Curragh: 58 of them resigned
their commissions rather than move against 'loyal Ulster'. They were supported by a caste of higher officers, in particular Sir Henry Wilson, the
director of military operations, who ensured that they went unpunished.

One month later, Major Frederick Hugh Crawford, of the armed loyalist
organisation, the Ulster Volunteer Force (UVF), and the commander of
the bowler-hatted Praetorian Guards who had accompanied Carson on
Covenant Day, landed 20,000 rifles at Larne. The complicity of the authorities was obvious. Crawford's ship, the *Fanny*, had spent weeks sailing
between Germany and Northern Ireland. On the night of the landing
the roads to Belfast were alive with UVF supporters who distributed the
guns without the slightest harassment by the police.

In two dreadful months, partition had become a reality. Connolly's
view of the events was clear:

My firm conviction is that the Liberal Government wish to betray the
Home Rulers, that they connive at these illegalities that they might
have an excuse for their betrayal and that the Home Rule party through

its timidity and partly through its hatred of Labour in Ireland is incapable of putting the least pressure upon its Liberal allies and must now dance to the piping of its treacherous allies.[101]

He pointed to the sharp contrast between the harsh treatment meted out to the Dublin working class in 1913 and that extended to the loyalists of the North who were allowed to organise with impunity. He advised workers to learn the lesson of the Curragh mutiny: as the officers had stood by their class, so should workers within and without the army.

His opposition to partition was total. Within a week of the scheme being mooted, he was predicting that it would produce a 'carnival of reaction.'[102] He argued that it was best to see the Home Rule Bill defeated than have it passed with partition.

There were two central reasons for his opposition. First, the position of Northern nationalists within an Orange statelet would be intolerable. The ghetto politician Joe Devlin, who dominated Catholic politics in Belfast on behalf of the Home Rulers, had put up a show of opposition but had also tried to get his supporters to accept partition as a temporary measure. In prophetic words Connolly warned Northern nationalists against this deception:

> If your lot is a difficult one even when supported by the progressive and labour forces of all Ireland, how difficult and intolerable it will be when you are cut off from all Ireland and yet are regarded as alien to Great Britain, and left at the tender mercies of a class who knows no mercy, of a mob poisoned by ignorant hatred of everything national and democratic.[103]

Second, the effects on the labour movement throughout the island would be disastrous. The optimistic scenario which saw Labour as the major opposition party in a Home Rule parliament vanished. Because of the bias against urban areas in the proposed Home Rule measures an estimated 34 out of the 128 seats would have gone to Labour – but 14 of these were in Belfast. In a parliament dominated by petty capitalists many of the measures needed by workers – the extension of medical benefits and the provision of school meals were noted as examples – would not be passed. But the disruption ran far deeper than the denial of these measures. Partition would fossilise Irish politics around the two major blocs of Green and Orange capitalists. Each would stoke up the national issue in order to weld together its support. Partition, Connolly argued, would

> perpetuate in a form aggravated in evil the discords now prevalent and help the Home Rule and Orange capitalists and clerics to keep their rallying cries before the public as the political watchwords of the day.

In short, it would make division more intense and confusion of ideas and parties more confounded.[104]

Connolly turned to the British Labour Party to oppose the measure. But a fellow contributor to *Forward*, George Barnes, explained that they took their cue from the Irish Parliamentary Party. He baldly stated that 'no one defends [partition] on its merits' but he supported the measure because he presumed that the nationalists knew their business as regards practical politics.[105]

Connolly was thrown back onto a weakened Irish labour movement to oppose partition. A major protest meeting was called by the ILP(I) in St Mary's Hall in Belfast to undermine Devlin's position. The ITUC executive and the Dublin Trades Council passed resolutions against partition. In April a national labour demonstration was called against partition. On 1 June the ITUC met in Dublin. Connolly proposed the resolution against partition, arguing that although he regarded the Home Rule Bill with contempt he wished to see it passed because of the bigotry whipped up by the Orange bosses against it. An amendment now, he argued, would mean that 'workers would not be allowed to unite on labour issues ... they would be told that they must unite with their employers on the question of inclusion or permanent exclusion'.[106] Connolly's resolution was carried overwhelmingly with Northern delegates in support.

Through Connolly's efforts the official organisations of Irish Labour took the clearest and sharpest stand against partition: their opposition was firmly based on class politics. In the midst of reaction, Connolly left a benchmark to measure all future positions on the question.

7. War and the Collapse of the Second International

On 4 August 1914 the Second International collapsed. With the outbreak of World War I socialist deputies across Europe joined in support of their own governments. Only the Russian and Serbian socialists refused to vote for war credits. The loudest antimilitarists became the worst jingoists. It was Connolly's midnight of the century. The only report of resistance to the war that he received was the unfounded rumour of the execution of the German socialist Karl Liebknecht.[1]

1914 had been an appalling year. Defeat had been piled upon defeat. In February, the ITGWU had finally been beaten in the great lockout. In March and April came the Curragh mutiny and the landing of arms for the Orange forces. In July, partition became a virtual certainty when Home Rule leaders entered into negotiations with the Unionists at a conference in Buckingham Palace. On top of all this came the war and the collapse of the Socialist International!

For Connolly there was an additional problem as his own political perspective broke down at the start of war. We have seen that after Connolly returned from America his political method rested on the twin pillars of a broad-church party and a syndicalist union. The ILP(I) was supposed to be the broad party that united reformists and revolutionaries. Connolly personally remained a revolutionary but had come to believe that the ILP(I) would gradually develop in a revolutionary direction through its links with the syndicalist movement. Connolly anticipated that the ITG-WU'S record of militant struggle would pull the whole movement to the left and thus cut off the prospects of reformism growing.

In 1914, however, both the ILP(I) and the ITGWU were severely weakened. But the crisis of 4 August was to illuminate fully the weakness in Connolly's strategy of building a broad party that was linked to a syndicalist union. Neither the party nor the syndicalist union was able to meet the demand for all-out opposition to the war.

The ILP(I) virtually collapsed with the crisis posed by the outbreak of war. The vagueness and confusion that characterised the party led to the most abject forms of political cowardice. This became clear to Connolly at the first meeting of the ILP branch in Belfast after war had been declared.

Connolly spoke at the regular street meeting. A report in the *Irish Worker* gave an account of Connolly's speech. It reported Connolly's candid remark that 'like all other parties his own was divided in opinon [on the war]. For ⁺hat reason he made it clear that his opinions were personal and did not bind others who spoke from the platform.'[2]

Connolly's daughter Nora noted that leading members of the branch refused to attend the meeting. In fact, they had taken a prowar position. Tom Johnson, the future leader of the Irish Labour Party, favoured a victory for the Allies as 'being better for the growth of liberty and democratic ideals'.[3] D.R. Campbell, the party's most prominent trade unionist, shared this position. This pair moved to stop all public meetings in Belfast on the war under the pretext that there would be violent opposition to them.

Connolly was outraged. He argued against the party allowing itself to be intimidated by 'Orange hooligans'. He demanded that it campaign on the Irish Trade Union Congress antiwar manifesto that Johnson had actually signed. He was totally isolated in his views and received only three votes for his resolution.[4] He was forced to issue his own antiwar manifesto under the name of a fictional body: the Belfast section of the Irish Citizen Army.

He encountered similiar problems in his links with the Scottish ILP. Since 1911 he had contributed regularly to *Forward*, the paper of the Glasgow ILP. By the end of 1914 these articles were voluntarily suspended lest their antiwar stance lead to the suppression of the paper. The suspension of Connolly's articles reflected the deep divisions inside the ILP despite its official pacifist position. In Glasgow, only two of the city's 17 councillors opposed the war.[5] Connolly's 'extremism' was an obstacle to those who wished to maintain the unity of the party.

The second major element in Connolly's politics – the syndicalist strand – fared a little better in its opposition to the war. His old comrades in the Wobblies in America took up a courageous antiwar and antipatriotic position. The *Irish Worker* under Larkin's editorship also took an antiwar stand and for a period was the only outlet for Connolly's magnificient journalism. But it also carried prowar articles on its front page. One of its leading columnists, 'Shellback', was allowed to write in support of the 'war against German militarism'.[6] His particular column only disappeared when Connolly took over editorship in October 1914.

Some of the major syndicalist figures in Britain came out unashamedly in support of the war. Ben Tillet, the leader of the gas workers, 'took up a constant job on the recruiting platform'. Those who had been 'the greatest of internationalists' inside the syndicalist movement before the war had, according to Connolly, become 'raving jingos howling for the blood of every rival of the British capitalist class'.[7]

The fact that individuals such as Johnson and Tillet with whom Connolly had worked closely were, no matter how reluctantly, now supporting the war was a terrible shock. It signified that the strategy of harnessing a broad-based party to the motor of syndicalism was in tatters. Faced with the war and the outbreak of chauvinism, neither syndicalism nor labourism could confront the crisis. The results were to be devastating for Connolly's politics.

The first consequence was that he was effectively deprived of a political organisation. He resigned from the Belfast ILP(I) and maintained only loose connections with its Dublin branch. The primary vehicles for his revolutionary activities were the paper of the ITGWU, the *Irish Worker* (later renamed *Workers Republic*), and the Irish Citizen Army, numbering less than 200 members. A tiny number of collaborators existed in his own union and the Dublin Trades Council. But the more Connolly rose to prominence in his opposition to the war and British imperialism, the fewer connections he had with a real socialist organisation. Quite simply his world had collapsed around him.

The Second International, which hitherto had been interconnected with Connolly's whole political life, was dead. Nevertheless, Connolly could not merely discard its ideas and traditions. Not surprising, he still used the framework of the Marxism of the Second International to examine the crisis posed by the war. He would do this in virtual isolation, having experienced so many defeats as a socialist even before the war broke out. His view of the war was to have a particular impact on his participation in the 1916 rebellion. It therefore deserves examination in some detail.

A Revolutionary Internationalist

The singular fact about Connolly in these years was that he remained a revolutionary socialist. He stood alongside a tiny handful of individuals, such as Lenin in Russia, McClean in Scotland, and Luxemburg in Germany in defending the best traditions of the Second International. In 1912 the Second International had mobilised effectively against the first Balkans war. It warned its affiliates then that if war did break out socialists 'were to utilise the economic and political crisis created by war to rouse the masses and thereby hasten the downfall of capitalist rule'.[8] It was a position that Connolly expected to be fully implemented in 1914. His internationalism was elementary. He wrote, 'To me the socialist of another country is a fellow patriot as the capitalist of my own is a natural enemy.'[9] Elementary – but uncommon throughout the socialist parties.

Once war broke out Connolly directed his special contempt at those who claimed that they had done all they could to prevent war but once it was declared they should arm to defend their own countries. This argument, which Connolly had encountered with Tom Johnson, was a common excuse among social democrats. He derided it with sarcasm:

What then becomes of all our resolutions; all our protests of fraternisa-

tion; all our threats of general strikes; all our carefully built machinery
of internationalism; all our hope for the future? Were they all as sound
and fury, signifying nothing?

When the German artilleryman, a socialist serving in the German
army of invasion, sends a shell into the ranks of the French army, blowing
off their heads, tearing out their bowels and mangling the limbs of
dozens of socialist comrades in that force, will the fact that he, before
leaving for the front, 'demonstrated' against the war be of any value
to the widows and orphans made by the shell he sent upon its mission
of murder?

Or when the French rifleman pours his murderous rifle fire into the
ranks of the German line of attack, will he be able to derive any comfort
from the probability that his bullets are murdering or maiming comrades
who last year joined in thundering 'hochs' and cheers of greeting to
the eloquent Jaurès, when in Berlin he pleaded for international solidarity?[10]

This profound antiwar position, which refused to tolerate any excuses
from socialists who 'reluctantly' supported their own government,
would lead Connolly far beyond the ILP tradition with which he had
formed links. The ILP, in Britain and Ireland, saw their main duty as
pressing for the alleviation of the distress caused by war. The pressure
and lobbying for reform continued but in different circumstances. There
was no recognition of a crisis in the methods that socialists had hitherto
pursued.

Connolly would also fight against the privations caused by war. For
example he led the ITGWU in a series of strikes to seek wage rises after
the 1915 budget. But he understood that the key issue now was preparing
for revolution. 'The signal of war', he wrote, 'ought to have been the
signal of rebellion ... when the bugle sounded the first note for actual
war, their notes should have been taken as the tocsin for social revolution.'[11]

This was by no means an abstract declaration. It meant striking first
and foremost at the enemy at home. Here Connolly quoted the motto
of the German socialist leader, Wilhelm Liebknecht, that socialists had
only one enemy – the capitalist class of the world, *those of their own country
at the head of the list.*[12] This practical call for revolution placed Connolly
far to the left of others who also refused to support the war.

A section of the Second International had opposed the war on a 'centrist'
basis. Prominent figures such as Kautsky argued for international peace
conferences and international solidarity as the means to end the war. But
when this international action was not forthcoming, they contented themselves with pressuring governments to declare the aims of their war policy.
In practice, this emphasis led to passivity and moral outrage. A variant
of this approach was the pacifist line adopted by the ILP's Keir Hardie.
Hardie called for a moral refusal to serve with the forces and an emphasis

on humanitarian appeals. What Kautsky and Hardie shared was a notion that war could be opposed without fighting capitalism itself.

Connolly had nothing in common with these positions. His view that the revolutionary struggle at home was the key to internationalism placed him closer to the position of the Russian Bolsheviks despite the very different analysis he held on the war. On the central argument that distinguished the revolutionary camp from the centrists Connolly stood with the former. He understood that capitalism led to war and that no moral protests could end it. 'We have held,' he wrote, 'and do hold that war is a relic of barbarism only possible because we are governed by a ruling class with barbaric ideas; we have held and do hold that the working class of all countries cannot hope to escape the horrors of war until in all countries the barbarous ruling class is thrown from power.'[13]

He rejected Hardie's and Kautsky's antiwar pacifism for a further reason: he believed that an oppressed nation or the working class itself would have to engage in 'war' to free itself. In this revolutionary war, there would be no humbug or cant about 'humane and civilised methods'. It would have to be waged 'thoroughly and relentlessly but with no delusions as to its elevating nature, or civilising methods'.[14]

Connolly's perspective was not a purely Irish one. He was determined to seize the opportunity to strike a blow for Irish freedom. But he believed that this would have a worldwide significance. Here he understood the tactical advantage that Irish revolutionaries held. This was a position that Lenin would also recognise subsequently in his analysis of the 1916 rebellion. Ireland lay closest to the heart of the greatest imperial power of the day. A blow struck in Ireland would therefore be a hundred times more effective than elsewhere. It would give encouragement to the struggles of colonial people throughout the Empire. By weakening the most aggressive empire in the world, an Irish rebellion could set off a wider chain reaction: 'Starting thus, Ireland may yet set a torch to a European conflagration that will not burn out until the last throne and last capitalist bond and debenture will be shrivelled on the funeral pyre of the last warlord.'(15)

It was from this clear perspective that Connolly took up the attack against the brutality and hypocrisy of the capitalist war. Each week his articles in the *Irish Worker* and the *Workers Republic* set out to destroy the propaganda of the Empire and its Home Rule supporters. He exposed the pact between the employers and the military to enforce economic conscription. He pointed to the growth of a massive state apparatus during the war and the endorsement given to it by the British TUC. He described the horrors of British colonialism in India and Egypt as a means of showing the hypocrisy of their claims to be concerned about the small nations. All the time his aim was to foment revolution.

Connolly's Pessimism

Reviewing a short pamphlet by a Swiss socialist, Paul Golay, who showed a certain hostility to Marxism, Lenin wrote: 'One who understands the necessity for an uprising, who advocates it and is capable of seriously preparing himself and others for it, is *indeed*, a thousand times closer to Marxism than the gentlemen who know all the "texts" by heart and are now busy ... justifying social chauvinism of every kind.'[16] Lenin's view of the 'real' Marxist could have been a pen picture of James Connolly.

This definition of the revolutionary camp, however, was only the starting point for Lenin. Within that camp he was to engage in many polemics on the precise slogans to raise against the war. His arguments on revolutionary defeatism or on the continued relevance of the demand for national self-determination were cases in point. He turned all his energies to winning these positions rather than simply calling for a general agreement among revolutionaries. The reason was that the crisis produced by the war would magnify all the confusions, hesitations and ambivalence amongst revolutionaries. This also applied to Connolly.

His general antiwar stance was sharp and clear. But his analysis of the war and the socialist response to it was also highly pessimistic. The tragedy was that this analysis was based on the methods he had learnt from the Second International, methods which underpinned the belief that there was little to do as a socialist as long as the war was in progress. Thus, Connolly's own instincts called for revolution while his theory led to pessimism about the possibility of working-class action. When we examine Connolly's views on the nature and causes of the war, on the reasons for the collapse of the socialist parties, and on the methods to be used to fight the war, we can begin to understand the connections between his flawed analysis and the manner in which he participated in the 1916 rebellion.

The Causes of War

One month after the war began Connolly produced an analysis of its causes in a short article, 'The War upon the German Nation'. This argued that England had established an industrial overlordship in Europe by forcing the European nations to accept English manufactured goods in exchange for raw materials. 'Self-respecting nations', he added, had come to realise that this was a 'most humiliating condition of affairs'. Germany was the first to challenge England's monopoly of the industrial market. German capitalism, Connolly argued, was more scientific and efficient. When it could not be beaten by Britain 'in fair competition industrially' it had to be 'beaten unfairly by organising a military and naval conspiracy' against it. England insisted on her monopoly of the seas so that 'peaceful trade built up by peaceful methods is to be struck out of the hands of its owners by the sword of an armed pirate'.[17]

The article showed a certain tenderness for the 'peaceful methods' of German imperialism. Yet this is not the crucial point. Connolly's main battle was with his 'own' empire. His softness on Germany, in practice, helped him sharpen his arguments against the prowar propagandists at home.

Far more important were the underlying assumptions in Connolly's argument. Nowhere is there a recognition that the war arose from the crisis of capitalism as a whole. He focussed on the rapaciousness of one country rather than the contradictions within the world system. A comparison with Lenin's analysis of the causes of war is useful here not as a means of measuring Connolly's stature against Lenin's but to show the practical conclusions of their divergent views.

In *Imperialism: The Highest Stage of Capitalism* Lenin sought the causes of war in the growth of monopoly capital in advanced countries; in the monopolies' ever closer interpenetration within their own national states; and in the competitive pressures to find more profitable outlets for the monopolies and the corresponding necessity to redivide the world into colonies of the major powers. Even though Lenin favoured the defeat of his own ruling class in Russia, this did not imply that he considered the Germans any less bloodthirsty or imperialist. The war was not produced by the crimes of one nation but from the general crisis of monopoly capitalism.

Lenin's focus on the contradictions of the world system resulted from, and subsequently reinforced, his understanding of the dialectical process at work. The crisis meant that the old reformist organisations of the working class, built up in an era of peace and stability, were in decay. But behind this decay the contradictions that had led to the war were also preparing the way for new revolutionary possibilities where socialism would be placed more immediately on the agenda. This view eventually led Lenin to abandon the notion that the democratic and socialist stages of the revolution would be separate and distinct in Russia and to launch an all-out assault for workers' power.

By contrast Connolly's stress on 'peaceful trade' that was violated, on 'fair' and 'unfair' methods of competition, suggested that an era of capitalist development lay ahead once the blockage of the British Empire had been removed. This explains why Connolly advanced the argument that a German victory was to be favoured because it would open the 'freedom of the seas', which in turn would allow the peaceful progress of capitalism to resume. It also explains why in 1915 he was still arguing that 'every socialist anxiously awaits and prays for the *full* development of the capitalist system which alone makes Socialism possible, but can only come into being by virtue of the efforts of the capitalists inspired by selfish reasons.'[18]

In arguing thus, Connolly proved that he was still a prisoner of the very tradition that had collapsed so pathetically during the war. The

Second International had stressed the long and gradual development of capitalism before the inevitable arrival of socialism. If horrors such as war were thrown up, then it must be because capitalism had not fully developed towards its final maturity. Connolly's inability to break from this viewpoint meant that he failed to see the prospects that were open for revolutionary socialists.

Why had the Second International collapsed?

Connolly's pessimistic conclusions were reinforced by his analysis of why the socialist parties had collapsed. An article on this subject, 'Revolutionary Unionism and War', written a year before the 1916 rebellion, showed Connolly's continued adherence to syndicalist politics. The war could have been prevented, he claimed, if the correct type of union organisation had existed. But in none of the belligerent countries was this the case. Nowhere was there a 'revolutionary industrial organisation directing the socialist vote nor a socialist political party directing a revolutionary industrial organisation'.[19]

The result was that the socialist deputies were isolated in parliament without power, whereas the working-class electorate had the industrial power but were not called to use it. No socialist party, therefore, *could* call a transport strike against the war even if they had wished to do so. Thus, having made their exclusively verbal protests, they had 'fired their last shots'.[20] Connolly concluded that the major problem to be addressed in the future was the building up of syndicalist organisations.

The article points to *one* important feature: the separation between the political and economic wings of the labour movement. But it is too simply stated. It is not related to the way in which the leaders of the socialist organisations and the trade unions had come to accept the structures of bourgeois democracy. As a result the ideological crisis in the labour movement was seriously understated. There is no mention of the growth of reformist ideology or proimperialist sentiment. Yet these ideas could coexist with the most militant of syndicalist forces. The French experience proved this. The General Confederation of Labour (CGT), the world's leading syndicalist organisation, joined the *union sacrée* to back the war effort.

In conclusion, Connolly's article once again pointed to a long period of waiting: socialists had to work to rebuild the correct form of industrial organisation. This tied in with the view of a peaceful period of expansion after the war ended.

How should socialists fight the war?

Pessimistic conclusions flowed from yet another aspect of Connolly's views on the war. He believed that the war should have been met with an immediate general strike. At the start of the war he wrote, 'I feel compelled to express the hope that ere long we may read of the paralysing of the internal transport service on the continent, even should the act of paralysing necessitate the erecting of socialist barricades and acts of rioting by socialist soldiers and sailors, as happened in Russia in 1905.'[21]

This call for a continent-wide general strike was accompanied by a specific call for strikes in Ireland to prevent the export of food. Connolly aimed at moving the protest against war out of the confines of parliament and towards working-class action. He quite clearly appreciated the tremendous power of the working class, noting that 'a great continental uprising of the working class would stop the war; a universal protest at public meetings would not save a single life from being wantonly destroyed.'[22]

There was, however, a problem with this approach. Paradoxically, calls for an immediate general strike once war was declared came from the more vacillating elements of the Second International. Georges Hervé, who later became a fanatical chauvinist, demanded that a general strike be used to stop the war.[23] Keir Hardie, who normally stood on the right of the socialist movement, proposed a general strike in the utopian hope that it would render pacifism possible. By contrast these calls were opposed by Lenin and Luxemburg in favour of the more concrete and 'modest' strategy of preparing for socialist revolution.

The arguments against reliance on a general strike were overwhelming. A strike alone, under conditions of full mobilisation and martial law, would not stop the war. That would require socialist insurrection. Nor could a general strike have been called simply by passing a resolution. It could only arise from the ever growing mobilisation of workers. The start of war was, however, accompanied by an outbreak of chauvinism and a decline in strike activity.

The greatest danger with Connolly's approach was that it put forward an ultimatum. Either there was a general strike or everything was lost. When an immediate stoppage failed to materialise there was no other socialist strategy available. The most militant calls for strikes could easily turn into despair and demoralisation. This is precisely what happened to Connolly.

Two weeks after the war broke out, reports filtered through of the extent of betrayal in the socialist camp, The first signs of Connolly's extreme pessimism were now in evidence. He wrote, 'Now if all this is true, what does it mean? It means that the socialist parties of the various countries cancel each other, and that as a consequence socialism ceases to exist as a world force, and drops out of the history of the world.'[24]

He castigated those who sought 'Marxism on credit', and refused to mobilise and act against the war. The first signs of moralism and despair began to creep into his writings. He argued that 'there is no moratorium to postpone payment of the debt that socialists owe to the cause; it can only be paid now. Paid it may be in martyrdom, but a few hundred such martyrdoms would be but a small price to pay to avert the slaughter of hundreds of thousands.'[25]

Ultimately, this call for a 'few hundred martyrdoms' reflected the crisis in Connolly's political perspectives.

Act, Act, Act

For Connolly there were two monumental problems that demanded immediate action: the Irish working class were being corrupted and Irish nationalism was being destroyed. Drastic measures were necessary to rescue both.

The leading bodies in the Irish labour movement had come out strongly against the war. The ITUC, the ITGWU, the Dublin Trades Council, and the Irish Citizen Army all issued manifestos against the war. In the months immediately after the outbreak of the war republicans were entirely occupied in recovering from a split in the Irish Volunteers. It fell to organised labour to lead the fight against the war. On 25 September, the British prime minister, Asquith, came to address a recruiting rally in the Mansion House. The ITGWU and the Dublin Trades Council organised a magnificent antiwar demonstration. Connolly, Larkin and Markievicz spoke, guarded by a large body of Citizen Army members with rifles. Nevertheless this courageous stand could not overcome the prowar hysteria that broke out.

Redmond and the Home Rule leaders stomped the recruiting platforms, looking for men, and many enlisted. A number came from the ranks of those who had fought during the 1913 lockout. In 1915, Labour stood candidates for the municipal elections and while they did not poll badly, the *Irish Worker* was forced to admit that 'its anti-war stand has damaged labour's political appeal.'[26]

By 1916 the scale of the corruption of the working class sunk in. In an editorial in the *Workers Republic*, Connolly noted that while the leaders of labour had stood firm, 'the same could not be said about the working class as a whole.' The ties of self-interest were binding a section of the population to the Empire. 'It would be impossible', he claimed, 'to name a single class or section of the population not heavily affected by this social, political and moral leprosy.'[27]

On another occasion, Connolly turned his sarcasm on the 'angelic and forgiving spirit of the Dublin workers'. They had 'volunteered to fight for an Empire that batoned them and for the class that degraded and robbed them'.[28] As the war progressed, the working class appeared in Connolly's writings mainly as the victims of chauvinism. No collective action seemed possible save industrial action to win wage increases.

What applied to the working class also applied to the nation as a whole. In many respects it was the weakening of the national sentiment that most concerned Connolly. Irish nationalism was not only anti-imperialist, it also contained within it, as we have seen, a collectivist instinct that could be directed against capitalism itself. The involvement of the Irish in a war for the British Empire was therefore disastrous.

Redmond's real crime in calling for recruits and in advising the British that they could withdraw their garrison from Ireland for use elsewhere was that it announced to all the world that Ireland had at last accepted its status as a British province. If the war ended with Ireland linked to the Empire, Irish nationalism would be doomed. It would be relegated to the status of a gallant tradition that had as little use as the Jacobite tradition in Scotland.

A related problem was Connolly's growing concern over the fate of Ulster. A month after the war broke out, the Home Rule Bill received the Royal Assent and was placed on the Statute Book. Its implementation was postponed until after the war. Significantly, the Bill, however, carried a proviso excluding the province of Ulster. Connolly noted the increasingly powerful role that loyalist leaders were playing in the British establishment. Their demands that the UVF be recognised as a separate division within the British Army were effectively met when the 36th (Ulster) Division was established. Edward Carson, who preached armed rebellion before the war, became an attorney general.

All of this meant that partition would become a reality once the war ended. The concessions that the Home Rulers had already made would be magnified as the Unionists claimed their reward for service for the Empire. The optimistic scenario that Connolly had predicted in 1911 of Home Rule doing away with the ancient sectarian divisions was now a pipe dream. Unless something was done, partition would bring a 'carnival of reaction'.

In these circumstances Connolly's press became more vociferous in demanding exemplary action by the minority to awaken the nation and the working class.

8. The Road to 1916

Connolly's analysis of war had led to the central conclusion that the normal methods of the Second International were appropriate only to peace time: during the war, socialists would have to employ very different methods. The disdain for 'insurrectionism' disappeared. Connolly's pessimism, however, ruled out the possibility of a *mass* insurrection and pointed in the direction of action by a minority. The only question was where that minority might come from.

At first Connolly saw this minority as coming exclusively from working-class militants. His first article after the outbreak of war, 'Our Duty in this Crisis', was addressed to 'working class democracy'.[1] The republicans were dismissed as ineffectual because they were still buried deep inside the Irish Volunteers, the broad nationalist force that had been taken over by the Home Rulers. In Connolly's view they had allowed themselves to be outmanoeuvred by Redmond. The article was contemptuous of the political confusion of the republicans, who had already misrepresented the nature of Carson's loyalist forces by seeing them as 'fearless Irishmen who had refused to take dictation from England'. Since 1907 the republicans had been expressing a sympathy with the Russian Tsar. Now this enthusiasm was being replaced 'by as blatant a propaganda in favour of the German War Lord'. This confusion would make them at best ambiguous participants in the antiwar movement: the working class would have to fight alone.[2]

Connolly's dismissal of the republicans was premature. Their leadership was intent on breaking from Redmond and was awaiting a suitable opportunity. On 20 September 1914 Redmond made a speech at Woodenbridge which was to provide them with the necessary opportunity. Prior to this speech Redmond had sought to maintain the Irish Volunteers as a distinct force for the defence of Ireland allied to the British Empire. But Redmond was told bluntly by Lord Kitchener that the Empire would not trust the Irish with rifles.[3] They would have to be integrated into the overall command structure of the British army. Under this pressure, Redmond capitulated and during his speech at Woodenbridge he appeared openly as a recruiting sergeant for the British army, calling for the volunteers to fight 'wherever the firing line extends'.[4]

The republicans seized this moment to engineer a split with Redmond. On 25 September Redmond appeared with Asquith at a recruiting meeting in the Mansion House. While the meeting was in progress IRB supporters occupied the Volunteer headquarters and dismissed its prowar executive. Immediately Redmond left to form the National Volunteers, which soon claimed 130,000 members. Just over 10,000 stayed loyal to the Irish Volunteers.

Connolly Looks to the Republicans

These developments led to a dramatic shift in Connolly's orientation. The republicans were now seen as holding the key to insurrection. Previous criticism of their record was dropped and henceforth Connolly was to work for the insurrection by smoothing over differences with them.

Connolly's accommodation to republican politics derived from the stark contrast between his desire for insurrection and the tiny forces available to him. His political organisation had collapsed. The Irish Citizen Army numbered fewer than 200 and was badly equipped. Moreover, the working-class movement generally was infected with prowar chauvinism. In this situation the prospect for insurrection demanded unity with the republicans *on republican terms*.

Connolly's change of orientation was sharp and swift. He seemed to have received prior information of the republicans' aim of splitting with Redmond. As a result, only a week after the publication of 'Our Duty in the Present Crisis', the new change was in evidence. He informed his readers that he was happy to state that 'we are not as isolated as I first thought'. Criticism of the republicans' politics was dropped completely. Indeed, Griffith came in for some praise when Connolly remarked that his paper 'was adopting a perfectly correct and sane note upon the crisis'.[5] Griffith, on the other hand, was less reserved in his attacks on socialists. He claimed, for example, that Karl Liebknecht had urged Belgian workers to fight for the Kaiser.[6]

A further sign of this new approach by Connolly occurred just before the departure of Larkin for America. Larkin had considered nominating a former Sinn Fein member, P.T. Daly, to replace him as general secretary of the union. Connolly objected vigorously on the grounds that not only was Daly incompetent but, more significantly that he would 'jeopardise our understanding with the nationalists'.[7]

From early in September the IRB adopted a policy of building broad fronts. They convened a meeting of prominent nationalists in Dublin. Pearse, Griffith and Connolly were included. The result was the formation of the Irish Neutrality League. Connolly saw the League as a vehicle for open propaganda for insurrection. But the type of unity involved reflected the pressure on Connolly to dilute his politics. At the inaugural public

meeting of the Irish Neutrality League Connolly made a number of unchar-
acteristic remarks. He praised the broad all-class unity by announcing
that 'they had on the platform men drawn from all classes. There were
labour men there and men who by no stretch of the imagination could
be called labour men. They had Home Rulers, Republicans, Socialists
and Sinn Feiners ... All had agreed that the interests of Ireland was more
dear than the British Empire.'[8]

From October onwards Connolly directed his propaganda to proposing
what he termed a 'forward policy' for the newly formed Irish Volunteers.
He praised their 'Napoleon-like stroke' in seizing the headquarters. He
advised them to counter Redmond's efforts to win adherents with a set
of proposals designed to cement unity inside the ranks of nationalists.
The Volunteers should demand the repeal of all clauses which limited
Ireland's self-governing status. This would mean arguing for a form of
dominion status that fell far short of a republic. The Volunteers should
set as their model a country such as Canada. He wrote, 'The only sane
and safe stance for the Nationalists to take is to demand the immediate
establishment of a parliament in Ireland on Canadian, South African or
Australian lines.'[9]

Greaves has claimed that Connolly proposed the affiliation of the Citizen
Army to the Irish Volunteers at its first reformed convention.[10] This is
quite possible. Greaves' praise for the tactic is, however, misplaced. It
is one thing to join with a nationalist movement in fighting imperialism.
It is quite another to liquidate one's politics into a nationalist alliance.
Connolly's overriding goal of a minority-led insurrection led him towards
pandering to nationalist politics. The proposal, for example, that the
Volunteers fight for dominion status, showed that he could even be pulled
temporarily by the right wing of that movement. At no stage in his orientation to the Volunteers did he argue for the raising of working-class issues
or for a break from all-class nationalist alliances as he had done in the
past.

Connolly's overtures to the republicans were, however, repulsed at this
early stage in the war. There was a number of reasons for this. The IRB
was primarily concerned to maintain the unity of the Irish Volunteers.
This movement was composed of two strands. The IRB supporters within
it favoured an insurrection during the war but one that would be prepared
by the traditional conspiratorial methods of a secret society. The other,
more right-wing group around Eoin McNeill and Bulmer Hobson, sought
to preserve the Volunteers as a fighting force until the war ended and
to use it then to pressure a weakened Empire into granting full Home
Rule. This latter group despised the Irish Citizen Army. Thus any overtures
by the IRB to Connolly would have jeopardised their alliance with right-
wing nationalists.

The IRB itself, however, also disliked Connolly's open methods of political agitation. When a leading military instructor of the Irish Volunteers,

Captain Montheith, was deported, Connolly proposed a full turn out of the Dublin Volunteers. The IRB regarded these methods as adventurist and a danger to their secret manoeuvres. This difference with Connolly was exacerbated when open repression against republicans and the left began in December 1914.

Subversive papers were banned and offices were raided. Increased use was made of the Defence of the Realm Act, which conferred Draconian powers on the government. The new level of repression led the IRB to retreat to more clandestine methods of operation. The broad-front groups were abandoned and their policy shifted to placing their members in key positions in the Irish Volunteers. Connolly's continuing public agitation for insurrection was considered highly dangerous to those accustomed only to the methods of a secret society.

Rebuilding

The failure to establish unity with the IRB at this stage was a blow to Connolly's hopes. He saw the new shift in the IRB policy as a move towards a more moderate position. He was unaware of the leadership's plans to carry out an insurrection during the war.

He still believed, however, that insurrection was a possibility. Early in 1915 he travelled to Glasgow and Liverpool to arrange the printing of his paper by his former comrades in the Socialist Labour Party. While there, he argued with Tom Bell, a future leader of the British Communist Party, on the course ahead. It became evident that Connolly believed the objective conditions were not the key factors in determining the possibility of insurrection. He claimed that, 'you never know if the time is ripe till you try. If you succeed the time is ripe, if not, then it was not ripe.'[11]

Yet his acute lack of forces meant that it was not a practical possibility in the short term. Forced back on his own resources, Connolly began to rebuild inside the Labour movement. The manner in which this was undertaken reflected his priorities.

One area that was entirely neglected was the political party. The last period of Connolly's life coincided with a complete retreat from any type of openly socialist organisation. Formally he remained a member of the ILP (Ireland). But there is no evidence from any of his writings in this period that he even considered it a factor in the political situation. Its Dublin branch had taken a strong antiwar position in contrast to the wavering that occurred in Belfast. Despite this Connolly made no effort to rebuild the organisation. He did not try, for example, to drive the prowar elements such as Tom Johnson out of the party. He seemed totally uninterested in the matter. This neglect of the party ran parallel to his overall analysis of the war, which he saw as an exceptional episode to which normal Second International politics did not apply.

Connolly continued, however, to maintain contact with the international socialist movement. Tragically, contacts were with the more moderate antiwar socialists. In July 1915, he reprinted an article from the *Socialistiche Auslandplatz* with which Bernstein and Kautsky were associated. This argued for an honourable peace and for popular pressure on governments to declare their war policy formally.[12]

In November 1915 he praised a pamphlet from the ILP written by Bruce Glasier, who was on the right of the party. There was no discussion of Glasier's pacifist strategy against the war. Connolly merely stated that he did not agree with Glasier's 'estimate of England's greatness' but still regarded him as 'someone who stood nobly by socialist principles'.[13] In December Connolly published a report on the Zimmerwald Conference in Switzerland. Here Lenin was to begin his fight for a break from the Second International. Connolly's report was based on that of the more right-wing delegates. He reported the impressions of two French socialists, Bourderon and Merrheim, who argued for 'international common and simultaneous action of the working class in all countries' to pressure their rulers for a just peace.[14] Despite its rhetoric, there was no call to turn the crisis of war into action against the rulers in individual countries.

What all the reports from the international socialist movement shared was a sense of extraordinary passivity and impotence. They must have confirmed Connolly in his view that socialist organisation belonged to a different era when normal capitalist development resumed. The sentiment against war was still there but the proposals for action amounted to waiting for the impossible – simultaneous action by workers across warring nations. Connolly shared the sentiments but his revolutionary instincts strove for far more. In the absence of a socialist strategy during the war he turned his energies elsewhere.

Instead of rebuilding the socialist party, then, Connolly concentrated on two organisations that fitted in with his current perspectives – the Irish Citizen Army and his own union, the ITGWU. Here, he was to operate simultaneously as a military and trade-union leader. While certain tensions arose in the ITWGU about his role in the ICA, the striking fact is how he managed to operate in two virtually distinct spheres of influence.

The Irish Citizen Army (ICA)

The Citizen Army was clearly his main priority. In times of war, he believed that militarism had to be met with military force. The political methods appropriate to peacetime, principally electoral activity, were rendered obsolete by the power of the well-armed state. Only the armed minority could challenge the state. Basic civil liberties could only be defended by mobilising the citizen militias. At the end of 1915 he was writing that 'The British government could have been halted in its inroads upon public liberties by a flat refusal on the part of the majority of its armed citizens to allow their rights as citizens to be interfered with.'[15] There was no mention of action from the wider workers' movement.

The stress on armed citizens as distinct from the organised power of workers led Connolly to the building of the Irish Citizen Army along conventional lines. Members wore uniforms and saluted their officers. These were mainly drawn from men who had served with the British army. Connolly appointed Michael Mallin as its commanding officer. He emphasised strict discipline, tidiness and drilling. Lectures were held regularly on the tactics of street fighting. Mallin also entered the ICA in several rifle competitions where they distinguished themselves by their marksmanship.

Political discussion in the ICA, however, was kept to a minimum. At the end of training sessions, Connolly or Mallin might give an address. But the level of politics in the address was very general and there was no discussion afterwards. Drilling and mock battles were the stock in trade of the ICA. One of its members, Frank Robbins, has described some of their main activities. 'On Sunday evenings in the summer the Citizen army held *aeriochta* [concerts] in Croydon Park. An aeriocht never finished without a mock attack on a lonely post by supposed red Indians with all the war-paint, feathers and tomahawks.'[16]

Once the reorganisation of the Citizen Army was achieved Connolly turned increasingly to practising attacks on key buildings. These were carried out on Dublin Castle, the centre of British administration in Ireland. Similar exercises were repeated on the Magazine Fort in Phoenix Park. A small number of weapons was removed from the army barracks at Inchicore by a soldier who was sympathetic to the ICA. On one occasion the ICA was called out during a strike. A number of scabs had been passing dockers' pickets during a wage dispute. The Citizen Army was mobilised to strengthen the picket line and deal with the scabs. This type of intervention was, however, extremely rare.

The stress on building the ICA on conventional military lines meant that they would always be overshadowed by the larger republican forces. Many of Connolly's speeches in this period ended with an appeal to join the Citizen Army. But despite the reorganisation its numbers remained very small, never exceeding 200. The Irish Volunteer force in Dublin in 1915 numbered 2,100 according to the police.[17] It was far better equipped in both weapons and uniforms. It also controlled a network of halls for training.

Clearly the Irish Citizen Army was in a poor position to compete militarily with the Volunteers. Connolly's emphasis on military training rather than politics meant that there was no reason for workers to join the former rather than the latter. Even inside the organised working class, the ICA could not assert itself. Thus a meeting of the Dublin Trades Council supported a resolution calling on workers to join *either* the Citizen Army or the Volunteers to avoid conscription.[18] There was no attempt by the Trades Council to give the ICA priority as the workers' army.

Despite Connolly's best efforts to rebuild after being repulsed by the republicans, the balance of forces still remained the same: he possessed no independent organisation capable of carrying out an insurrection. He was still totally dependent on the republicans for his plans.

The Irish Transport and General Workers Union

The other major area of activity for Connolly was the union movement. He was general secretary of the ITGWU, a member of the executive of the 100,000-strong ITUC and a prominent member of the Dublin Trades Council. In all these areas he championed a clear antiwar, anti-imperialist stance. Under his influence the ITUC became the only leading trade-union body in Europe to oppose the war.

His own union campaigned vigorously to shift the costs of the war from the shoulders of the working class. In this he laboured under considerable strain. The defeat of 1913 had left the union virtually bankrupt. In January 1915, Connolly was forced to advise members to avoid industrial action because of the union's financial situation. But as the war drew on, conditions became more favourable to workers. The shortage of labour meant a shortage of scabs. The budget in October led directly to a wage push by the ITGWU. A long strike resulted in the Dublin Steam Packet Company, continuing to the eve of the 1916 rebellion. In other industries workers made gains more quickly. By 1916 the ITGWU was putting on the first spurt of growth that would increase sizeably after the war. New branches were formed in Kerry and Galway while militancy increased over wages.[19]

In all of this Connolly functioned as a model general secretary. He organised the first union conference of the ITGWU in 1915. He broke from the personal style of leadership associated with Larkin by proposing an elected executive. He tied an increase in officials' wages to their members' wage increases. Despite the financial chaos in the union, he responded to calls from the rank and file for action. On every possible occasion he sought to link the fight against the deprivations caused by war to a struggle against capitalism itself.

His activities were not confined to his own union. He followed up the 1912 resolution at the ITUC calling for the establishment of a Labour Party by setting up a Labour Representation Conference in Dublin in May. In June Connolly pressed the Trades Council into running a candidate in the College Green constituency against the Home Ruler, Nanetti. He saw a particular need to oppose this individual and did not advocate a general policy of contesting elections during the war. His accommodation to nationalist politics was starkly apparent in his drawing up of the manifesto for the College Green election. This called on 'all who stood for the best and holiest interests of Ireland, whatever their attitude to a British Parliament' to vote for Labour.[20] Furthermore, these sentiments could coexist with his syndicalism. In August, for example, Connolly was proposing to bring all unions together to form one great Irish organisation of Labour with 'One Card, One Badge, One Executive'.[21]

Connolly had none of the narrow minded perspective of a trade-union official. Refusing to magnify gains made at the negotiating table and to indulge in resolution-mongering, Connolly encouraged a constant stream of antiwar and socialist propaganda. A typical example of this approach was shown at the Labour Day rally in June. After listening to the usual trade-union resolutions, Connolly rose to reply.

> His complaint with the resolutions was that they did not go far enough. They asked the government to re-build the slums, but there was more spent every day on the continent than would re-build all of Ireland. All governments were doing this, and would continue doing it until the workers took over the world into their own hands and ran it for the benefit of those alone who did the world's work – the workers.[22]

Such statements belie the oversimplistic claims of one recent biographer that Connolly had ceased to be a socialist in 1914 and had become a 'national revolutionary'.[23] The shortcomings in Connolly's politics lay elsewhere. His own traditions, which were derived from the Second International, offered him no way of working to involve the mass of workers in the struggle against war and imperialism. He had no perspective for seeing that the corruption of the workers' movement by the war was temporary and he believed that only exemplary action by the minority could salvage the situation. As a result, Connolly's strong antiwar stance in the unions was confined to a propaganda level. His activities in the Irish Citizen Army and in the union were two discrete areas that hardly overlapped. The ICA was the vehicle for insurrection – the unions would furnish protection from the deprivations of war.

This separation sometimes took extreme forms. One of Connolly's last articles before the rising in 1916 concerned the forthcoming congress of the ITUC in Sligo in that year. It merely noted that the ITUC had deferred its congress of the previous year 'because the feelings generated by the war' might inject difficulties such that 'in the heat of passion things might be said and done that would cause irreparable breaches in the ranks of labour'. There was no indication that the prowar elements in the workers' movement should be confronted or that the ITUC's failure to campaign actively against the war should be criticised. Connolly's advice for the forthcoming congress was that 'timidity and rashness will alike be out of place'.[24]

It is ironic that this paltry advice could be written literally days before the 1916 rebellion. Connolly's syndicalism had led him to place a premium on preserving union organisation at all costs. Neither the unity nor the structures of the unions were to be endangered by any association with the rebellion. They would resume their central role in working-class struggles only after the war was ended.

Conscription

Throughout 1915 Connolly had concentrated on building up the ICA and the ITGWU. But by November of that year a new note appeared in his writings. The general propaganda for insurrection was replaced by a sharper and more immediate demand for its organisation. The new shift was caused by the threat of conscription.

Expectations of an early Allied victory had not been met. Preparations therefore went ahead for the enlistment of all available manpower reserves. In March the British Trade Union Congress had entered into the Treasury Agreements. These promised new levels of co-operation with the civilian and military authorities. A National Registration Act followed. Asquith and the Labour Party began a campaign to get men of military age to 'attest' their willingness to serve. But even this did not stem the demand for conscription from the Tories. Towards the end of 1915 new divisions rose in the War Cabinet on the issue.

The threat of conscription gave the revolutionaries in Ireland a new lease of life. Police reports indicated that the Irish Volunteers began to grow. They had increased from 10,000 members to 13,000 members. In particular areas, the weakening of the prowar forces was more dramatic. In Cork, for example, The Irish Volunteers numbered only 30 members in 1914. By 1916 they had grown to 653. The circulation of the subversive press also rose. Republican and socialist papers were selling 20,000 on a weekly basis.[25]

In Dublin the Trades Council proposed a joint anticonscription meeting with the republicans. The meeting was held in December in the Mansion House with a capacity audience and an overflow attendance of 500 outside. Such was the strength of the anticonscription feeling that the Irish Parliamentary Party was forced to pledge a campaign of vigorous resistance.

The conscription crisis lasted from November until 18 January 1916 when the British Parliament finally agreed to the conscription of single men between 18 and 41 years of age. Ireland was excluded owing to the vigorous campaign of opposition. An attempt to impose conscription on Ireland would have broken the Irish Parliamentary Party. A police report at the time confirmed that 'a planned rising in the event of conscription being introduced was perhaps the one project in which many Redmondites would be in agreement with them'.[26]

This first dent in the prowar sentiment led Connolly to renew his practical calls for insurrection. He was acutely aware of the revolutionary possibilities but his interpretation of the events ruled out the possibility of mass participation. He knew the conscription threat would arise again. At that point the anger shown in this first crisis could intensify to a point where revolutionaries might win a mass audience. Connolly's views did not allow him to wait for this possibility and to build in the meantime a strong socialist force that could compete with the republicans for the leadership. Instead, his whole strategy was based on the fact that there had to be a pre-emptive strike before the British state tried to impose conscription on Ireland.

He took this view for two reasons. First, he saw conscription as the final militarisation of society. The all-powerful state would push it through ruthlessly. He argued that those who opposed conscription should 'not delude themselves into the belief that they are simply embarking upon a new form of political agitation'. Once the British ruling class had decided on the issue, they would enforce it 'though every river in Ireland ran red with blood'.[27] There was no mention of the possibility of workers' action to fight the threat. Connolly had already come to believe that the armed militias in the Irish Volunteers and the Irish Citizen Army represented the only possible opposition to wartime measures. But even these would be destroyed once the British state turned its energies to imposing conscription.

Second, once conscription was imposed, Ireland would be so bound to the Empire that Irish nationalism would die out completely. There was already a conflict between the 'soul' and the 'body' of the nation. Conscription would complete the reduction of Ireland to a province of the Empire. Hence the key thing was not to wait to win over the majority of workers to insurrection but rather to strike before the state was ready.

Even a minority-led insurrection demands some forces. Connolly contemplated the possibility of an insurrection by the ICA alone. But this was more in the hope of bringing out the republican forces with him. He tried to use the Trades Council to pressure the Volunteers into insurrection. During the negotiations prior to the anticonscription protest meeting in December, he demanded that the Volunteers be prepared to move. This was rejected totally by Eoin McNeill, its titular commander.

Despite this rejection, the republicans, through their influence within the Irish Volunteers, remained the only force capable of launching the pre-emptive strike. If the leadership was not prepared to move, it was necessary to appeal over their heads to the rank and file. From November 1915 until January 1916 Connolly ran a series of articles with this purpose in mind. Their major theme was to warn against revolutionaries 'who shrink from giving the blow'.[28]

Connolly's appeal to the rank and file of the republican organisations reflected a further retreat in his politics. Because there was no strong socialist organisation in existence, he was forced to appeal to them entirely on republican terms. This meant using the traditions and legends of republicanism against its own leadership. Throughout the articles Connolly openly embraced the Fenian conception of insurrection. The *unsuccessful* Fenian uprisings of 1867 were used to claim that there simply could be no talk of a 'premature revolution'. Such caution only came from the 'paraders and strutters [who] had lost the confidence and destroyed the hopes of the nation'.[29] The Manchester Martyrs were held up as the ideal. They had fought in 'a hostile city, surrounded by a hostile population'.[30] The audacity of their actions, their willingness to endanger carefully constructed organisations by their deeds, the fact that they did not wait on foreign help – all of these characteristics were presented to the rank and file of the Irish Volunteers as the supreme revolutionary qualities.

Connolly also dealt with the possible outcomes of insurrection in true Fenian terms. The justification for revolution might not lie in what was achieved immediately but in the example and the ideals left behind. Referring to the Manchester Martyrs again, he claimed that 'the echo of those blows has for a generation been as a baptismal dedication to the soul and life of thousands of Irish men and women, consecrating them to the services of freedom'.[31]

This notion of insurrection represented a crisis in his overall politics. In the past he had on occasion praised the 'abandonment of the unfortunate insurrectionism of the early Socialists'.[32] These criticisms were in line with the dominant views within the Second International. As part of that tradition, Connolly had developed in certain periods a naive respect for the ballot box. But all of that was now seen as only appropriate to normal periods of capitalist rule. In this series of articles he was returning to an earlier tradition whose origins lay in the extreme left of the Jacobin wing of the French Revolution. Here it was the revolutionaries who made the revolution. The power of their organisation and, above all, their audacity would substitute for the weakness of the masses. In place of an objective assessment of the insurrection and its effects on working-class consciousness, there was an appeal to future generations.

Connolly was driven to this method of insurrection by the gulf between the horrors of war and the weakness of working-class organisation. In a key article, 'What is Our Programme?', written at the same time that he finally sealed his pact with the republicans, he indicated that he would have greatly preferred a different way of taking on the Empire during the war. He argued that if labour had not been attacked by many of the 'fervent advanced patriots',

> it would now be in our power at a word to crumple up and demoralise every offensive of the enemy against the champions of Irish freedom. Had we been able to carry out all our plans, as such an Irish organisation of Labour alone could carry them out, we could at a word have created all the conditions necessary to the striking of a successful blow whenever the military arm of Ireland wished to move.[33]

Here the insurrection was seen as springing from the organised power of the workers' movement. But it was not to be. The defeats suffered by the working class and the terrible future which Connolly foresaw when conscription would be imposed on Ireland, led him to take the different road. He would join with the republicans to launch an insurrection on republican terms. To those who doubted his choice he replied, 'the European battlefields of today provide the one all-sufficient answer.'[34]

Plans for the Rising

Connolly's campaign for an insurrection was highly successful. It would be wrong to believe that he alone was responsible for initiating the rising, but his role was decisive. Sean T. O'Kelly, a member of the IRB, later wrote that if it had not been for Connolly the rising would not have occurred when it did.[35]

The Irish Republican Brotherhood had in fact decided on insurrection *in principle* the moment the war broke out. Its most prominent right-winger, Bulmer Hobson, had been expelled from the organisation for accepting Redmond's dominance of the Volunteers. The IRB leadership then fell into the hands of militants such as Sean McDermott and Tom Clarke. These men were determined not to let the war pass without an insurrection. But they made it conditional on German support and on a political crisis around the issue of conscription.

Once the conscription crisis broke in 1915, the prospect of a rising without German assistance began to receive active consideration. There had been some earlier signs of a change in tactics when a separate military council had been established in May 1915. This lay outside the existing command structure of the IRB and it began to make general plans for an insurrection. Connolly's propaganda during the conscription crisis helped to translate these discussions into a concrete proposal. Quite simply, his thrusts against those who 'conduct revolutionary movements with a due regard to law and order' struck home.[36] Late in December, the military council finally fixed Easter Sunday, 23 April 1916 as the date for the rising.

This proposal went before a full meeting of the IRB supreme Council on 16 January, two days before the conscription crisis was resolved with the exclusion of Ireland. It ratified the plans for the rising at Easter. It dispatched a courier to America to request the old Fenian, John Devoy, to reopen contact with the German embassy there. The setting of a definite date and the commencement of military preparations were sufficient to change the mind of the German High Command. But instead of consenting to Devoy's request for 100,000 rifles, they dispatched only 20,000, which were to land in the week before Easter.

Three days after the IRB decision on insurrection, Connolly 'disappeared'. The rumours of a planned insurrection by the Citizen Army and Connolly's public campaign worried the IRB leadership. He had previously met with Eoin McNeill and Padraig Pearse only to be counselled to act with moderation. This time he was to spend three days at an IRB safe house discussing the detailed plans for insurrection. He was warned against any attempt to lead out the Citizen Army prematurely.

The length of time Connolly spent there suggests that there was a considerable dispute about the nature of the insurrection. The nature of that disagreement is not hard to discern. Greaves has claimed that Connolly was forced to give up on a revolution led by the working class and on involving the unions in these discussions.[37] However Connolly had already abandoned this strategy long before the IRB meeting. Throughout 1915 he had continued to issue general antiwar propaganda inside the unions but this was never tied to any specific suggestions for action. Likewise during the conscription crisis when he campaigned openly for insurrection, there was not a single reference to the organised working class.

The real disagreement lay elsewhere. The IRB envisaged an insurrection along the lines of a classic secret society. It was to be an operation directed solely by the military council of the IRB. The mobilisation of the men and women who would take part in the rising would be brought about through the manipulation of the Irish Volunteer command structure by the IRB. Ceannt, Pearse and Plunkett, key members of the IRB military council joined the Irish Volunteers Headquarters Staff. From here they were to develop a chain of command that was to ignore the moderate elements in the Volunteers. Hobson and McNeill were simply to be kept in the dark about the preparations.

There were obvious practical difficulties about these arrangements. Connolly had already been arguing that McNeill be deposed as head of the Irish Volunteers. Concealing a landing of 20,000 weapons from the police was difficult enough – but keeping leading members of one's own organisation ignorant would prove impossible. Nevertheless Connolly had little choice but to accept this plan for insurrection. A week after his discussions with the IRB he wrote:

> The issue is clear and we have done our part to clear it. Nothing we can say now can add to the arguments we have put before our readers in the past few months nor shall we continue to labour the point.
>
> In the solemn acceptance of our duty and the great responsibility attached thereto, we have planted the seed in the hope that ere many of us are much older, it will ripen into action. For the moment and hour of that ripening, that fruitful blessed day of days, we are ready. Will it find you ready too?[38]

He joined the military council planning the rising. It also seems that he became a member of the IRB – or at least a 'member at large'.[39] His closest associates in the unions – Partridge, Daly, O'Shannon – were all 'old IRB members'. His decision to join brought a new and sharper turn towards nationalist politics in the months before the rising.

Connolly's Nationalism

One sign of this was a new acceptance of the mystical notion of the nation. An early example of this occurred in his comments on O'Donovan Rossa's funeral in the August issue of the *Workers Republic*. There were several references to the 'soul of a race' and the 'holiest aspirations' of the Irish. The breadth of unity at the funeral – stretching from Redmondites to socialist republicans – was praised in glowing terms. The revival of nationalist ideas was taken almost as a sign of divine intervention:

> Old medieval legends tell us how in critical moments of the struggle of an army, or the travail of a nation, some angel or deliverer was sent from above to save those favoured by the Most High.
>
> To many people today it seems that the funeral of O'Donovan Rossa came to Ireland in such a moment of national agony – came on such a mission of divine uplifting and deliverance. The mists and doubts, the corruption and poisons, the distrust and treacheries, were blown away, and the true men and women of Ireland saw with pleasure the rally of the nation to the olden ideas.[40]

This pandering to republican ideas grew in his last months. Increasingly there was a defence of Irish industry in the pages of the *Workers Republic*. William Partridge, an organiser for the ITGWU, pressed an avowedly Sinn Fein line in his speeches, arguing that 'the policy of Sinn Fein in practice meant Irishmen supporting Irish industry and helping Irishmen and Ireland'.[41] Connolly did not go this far. Instead he produced an inversion of Griffith's claim that English unions were encouraging Irish workers to destroy Irish industry. Commenting on a strike at the Irish-owned Dublin Steam Packet Company, he argued that Irish capital was being urged on by the British to cause strikes so that they could grab the trade. Irish industries were being lost because the Irish bosses were accepting the advice from their British counterparts who 'gloried in their fight and exulted in their downfall'.[42] This was a novel explanation of the behaviour of William Martin Murphy

Another aspect of this reconciliation with nationalism was Connolly's attitude to religion. As we have already seen, Connolly never advanced a materialist approach to religion. But now he appeared to retreat from even the most minimum secular position. On St Patrick's Day 1916, he wrote a special article which concluded with a prayer to 'honour St Patrick, the *Irish* apostle' because he was an 'emblem to typify that spiritual conception for which the Irish race laboured in vain'.[43]

In January 1916, Connolly proposed a vote of thanks to a Fr. Lawrence who had addressed a meeting of the Dublin Trades Council. In *Workers Republic* he hailed the occasion as 'a great meeting of working men and women, overwhelmingly Catholic in their faith ... with a priest they held in affection'. He claimed that 'there were no differences between Fr Lawrence and the Editor [Connolly] – except definitions'. The sympathetic strike, for example, he felt was an 'affirmation of Christian principles'. He concluded that the type of friendly meeting between the Trades Council and the priest provided 'safer guarantees for Ireland against the growth of anticlericalism of the French type than all the pamphlets of the Catholic Truth Society'.[44]

The increasing nationalist strain in his politics also affected the way he regarded the working class of the belligerent nations. During periods of heightened class struggle Connolly was among the best exponents of international working-class solidarity. He reported repeatedly on the activities of the Clyde Workers Committee who led many strikes in Glasgow. He was fulsome and enthusiastic in his praise of the South Wales miners when they were on strike. He claimed that the victory of their strike would directly benefit the 'measure of liberty in Ireland'.[45] His talk at the Trades Council on the strike drew sharp political lessons.

> It showed that labour already possessed the power; all that was needed was the united will to exercise it. But we have been cursed with leaders without faith in their own class, without vision, without moral courage – leaders who were always preaching our weakness instead of teaching us to rely on our strength. Had we the right kind of leaders, the war would never have taken place.[46]

This international solidarity towards British workers did not survive the divisions caused by the war. A particularly unpleasant incident, which occurred in Liverpool, shook Connolly. During the conscription crisis of 1915, a number of Irish men of military age attempted to leave Britain for America. They were met by jeering mobs. The stokers on the ship *Saxonia* came out on strike to stop them from departing. Connolly's bitterness was immense.

Some months later he replied with a proposal to ban from employment British workers who fled to Ireland to avoid conscription. Throughout an article on the subject he referred to them as 'Brit-Huns', 'British shirkers' who had declined to fight in their own country.[47] He argued that there had been no British organisation willing to champion national freedom for Ireland – despite the fact that the SLP had printed copies of the banned *Irish Worker* in 1915. His attitude to British workers was summarised in the bitter statement that 'we are sick of the canting talk of those who tell us that we must not blame the British people for the crimes of their rulers against Ireland. We do blame them.'[48] This view, of course, was completely different from that of the articles Connolly wrote during the 1913 strike when he attacked nationalist attempts to create divisions between Irish and British workers.

By way of contrast, Connolly's paper carried statements about the leaders of the working-class organisations in Germany who had collaborated with the war machine, which were mild in the extreme. He reprinted a number of articles in the *Workers Republic* at the end of 1915 which expressed the most pathetic illusions about German social democracy.

A reprint from the *New York Times* in his paper argued that Germany's success during the war stemmed from its system of 'state socialism'.[49] Readers were later informed that Germany was well-fed because the socialist movement had succeeded in breaking up the landed estates. An English newspaper was quoted to prove that 'there are no poor rates and there is very little poverty in the country'.[50]

An article headlined 'the Triumph of German Socialists' insisted that they only supported a 'defensive war'. It concluded that those socialists who had expected a 'reward for their support [for the war] were not mistaken'.[51] A Polish member of the Reichstag was quoted in praise of the German Empire's support for national freedom.[52] Finally in an extraordinary article reprinted from the *San Francisco Call*, there was a report of the first meeting between a social democrat and the Kaiser. Readers learnt about how the Kaiser had come to regard the socialists as 'splendid fellows'.[53]

How are we to assess these concessions that Connolly undoubtedly made to nationalism? It would be easy, taking these statements in isolation, to draw the relatively simple conclusion that Connolly had ceased to be a socialist revolutionary. This would be absurd because side by side with these comments there continues Connolly's burning attack on capitalism and his hatred of reformism. Moreover, even while reprinting nonsense on German social democracy Connolly was insisting to Pearse that 'the Germans are as bad as the English'.[54] At the slightest signs of working-class revival, such as the South Wales miners' strike, Connolly's internationalism resurfaced.

In his actions, Connolly still towered over many other socialists who opposed the war. His aim was revolution: his fight was first and foremost with the ruling class at home. His tragedy was that he was caught in the decaying traditions of the Second International. He saw no way out of the deep pessimism it encouraged about the war. Yet rather than retreat into passivity and despair he remained determined to strike a blow. An alliance with the republicans – in which his politics were subordinated – seemed the only way he could do so.

It is undeniable that his politics wavered under the pressure for unity with the republicans. But ultimately these waverings sprung from his isolation as a revolutionary and from the manner in which he tried to deal with that isolation from within a flawed perspective. His desire for insurrection clashed against the passivity that arose from Second International Marxism. An immense gulf separated him as a revolutionary from a working class that went along with the war. His concessions to nationalism grew with his determination to push through an insurrection, for the alliance with the IRB, where he commanded tiny forces, was the only way to achieve it.

Insurrection

From the end of January 1916, Connolly threw himself into preparing for insurrection. Liberty Hall became one of the main planning centres as arms and ammunition were stored there. An improvised bomb factory was established in the basement. An armed guard was posted permanently at the door. A police raid was met with a swift mobilisation of Citizen Army volunteers from all over Dublin. On 16 April, Connolly had the Green Flag hoisted over Liberty Hall, despite objections from some union members.

On the same evening Connolly informed members of the Irish Citizen Army about the plans for the uprising. He also added a note of warning for the future after the rising: 'In the event of victory, hold onto your rifles, as those with whom we are fighting may stop before our goal is reached. We are for economic as well as political liberty.'[55] This statement has sometimes been taken as confirmation that Connolly had by now worked out a clear stages approach to the Irish revolution. This is hardly likely. It simply expressed a certain political distrust of his own allies. It was also a recognition that during the war the socialists found themselves fighting for more limited aims. But by no means did Connolly envisage this as the end of the matter.

The rising was planned for Easter Sunday. Much has been made of the date. It has been taken as a confirmation of the blood sacrifice ideology that was supposed to inform the Rising. In this view, the leaders of the rising were mystical Catholics determined to atone for the loss of Irish nationalism and so achieve a 'redemption'.[56]

Paradoxically, the image of the 1916 rebellion as a 'blood sacrifice' is promoted assiduously by both revisionist and traditional nationalist historians. The revisionists have tried to dismiss the rising in order to elevate the status of the constitutional nationalists who, they claim, were about to win Home Rule. In this context it is useful to portray the rising as an irrational event so that the true 'blood sacrifice' – the horrors of the capitalist war – and the Home Rulers' complicity in it, can be ignored. The traditionalists are also at home with the image, as all nationalists prefer to shroud the origins of their movement in mysticism. The more it is enveloped in semi-religious imagery the less connection it has with the more mundane struggle been fought in the working-class ghettos of Northern Ireland today.

It is, however, a particularly false picture of Connolly's motivation. Padraig Pearse may, on occasion, have conceived of the rising in these terms. There is no evidence that Connolly did. The only reference he made to 'the shedding of blood' and 'redemption' was in an article written in February 1916.[57] This was a highly pessimistic piece about the working class being bought off by the Empire. In general, though, his hard-headed socialism rejected this nonsense. When Pearse once spoke of how World War I showed that 'the old earth needed to be warmed with the red wine of battlefields', Connolly replied that 'we are sick and the world is sick of this teaching'.[58] On another occasion he denounced talk of the blood sacrifice as that of a 'blithering idiot'.[59]

Disproving the blood-sacrifice concept is not just a matter of Connolly's individual statements. The military strategy for the rising was premised on a chance of success. The British war effort was stretched. War-weariness was beginning to affect the population, especially with the threat of conscription still in the air. There were only 6,000 combat troops in the country, supported by 9,500 members of the Royal Irish Constabulary.

The rising aimed – optimistically – at mobilising the bulk of the 16,000 Irish Volunteers. A landing of 20,000 rifles from a German ship, the *Aud*, was to be followed by capture of trains to distribute weapons to the Volunteer strongholds in Cork and Kerry. Inside Dublin the insurgents were to seize a series of buildings and positions along a continuous line that formed a loop around the city. It was so drawn that all military barracks fell outside it. According to Connolly it would not require very large forces to hold such a line and maintain communications. The line was also to extend out to the country to enable a withdrawal from the city, if necessary.[60] Volunteers outside Dublin were to seize neighbouring towns and either press for an advance on Dublin or allow the Dublin insurgents to retreat. A provisional government was set up and rudimentary administrative machinery was planned.

Such a plan could not have been conceived simply to produce martyrs determined on making a glorious stand. It was a serious nationalist rebellion that was drawn up within a limited political framework that did not rely on popular mobilisation. In terms of the balance of forces involved – or at least the forces the rebels originally thought they had – it was no more or less effective than many subsequent nationalist revolts in China, Cuba or Algeria.

Two events however struck a body blow to these plans and so made the rising a less impressive affair as a military episode. Two days before it was due to begin, its main military supplier, the *Aud*, was sighted by the British navy off the coast of Cork. The ship was scuttled to prevent the capture of its arms.

The second failure stemmed directly from the conspiratorial tactics of the IRB. It distributed a forged letter purporting to come from the British authorities. This announced a plan to intern the executive members of all republican organisations and to place a curfew on the city. McDermott of the IRB used the document to stampede McNeill into ordering a defensive mobilisation of the Irish Volunteers on the date of the planned rising. However on the Thursday before the rising, McNeill learnt about the full extent of the IRB manoeuvres and issued a countermand to call off the mobilisation.

The republican tactic of operating behind respectable fronts had back-fired badly. The moderate elements in the Irish Volunteers – whom they had never challenged – had very different objectives and were prepared to endanger the security of the insurgents. Connolly's warning on the need to depose right-wing leaders such as McNeill and Hobson had been prophetic.

The capture of the *Aud* and the evidence of preparations for an uprising now presented the revolutionaries with a dilemma. The British authorities had enough evidence to place them indefinitely behind bars or, more likely, sanction their legal murder. By Easter Sunday the British military authorities had already drawn up a plan for the arrest of the conspirators.

When Connolly's daughter Nora alerted him to McNeill's treachery he immediately called a meeting of the military council. He had always favoured an insurrection with or without German help. Now the majority of the military council came around to this view as a result of the circumstances. It was a case of either going ahead or facing the tender mercies of British justice. The rising was postponed for just one day.

On Easter Monday Connolly led the Citizen Army out of Liberty Hall to join the rising. He was the commander in chief of all the republican forces in Dublin. His statement to William O'Brien that 'we are going out to be slaughtered' has been misread as a confirmation of the blood sacrifice ideology.[61] It was in fact the statement of a revolutionary who was, as a consequence of his earlier decisions, forced into a rising in the most unfortunate of circumstances.

The rising lasted one week. Approximately 1,300 insurgents took part. Of them, 152 belonged to the Citizen Army which turned out nearly a full complement. The Citizen Army and the Volunteers were merged into one force and shared the defence of the various positions. Connolly took time during the rising to settle one old score: the Starry Plough, the flag of Irish labour, was raised over William Martin Murphy's Imperial Hotel in the centre of Dublin.

The British authorities replied with ferocity. The centre of Dublin was bombarded to rubble. 318 civilians lost their lives, mainly at the hands of the military. The famous pacifist Francis Sheehy-Skeffington was murdered in cold blood. Afterwards 3,500 men and 80 women were interned. 92 death sentences were passed, most of which were commuted to life sentences. A reign of terror was imposed on the country by General Maxwell. But in military terms the rising had inflicted a blow on the British war machine. In terms of damage caused to the British army it was more successful than many previous rebellions.

The rich and powerful in Irish society were enthusiastic in support of the British authorities. In Cork the employers' federation met to denounce the 'shameful outrage' of the rising.[62] In Galway the urban council called a special meeting to form a 'committee for public safety' to condemn the insurgents and encourage enlistment in a special constabulary.[63] It included the leading businessmen of the city. In the House of Commons there was cheering when the execution of the leaders of the rising was announced. A Dublin street ballad, 'Ye'll not forget the members cheering', told of the Nationalist MPs who joined in.

The executions began in May. They were to last nine days. Connolly had been wounded during the rising and this led to the postponement of his execution. At one stage there appeared to be a small chance of saving his life. William Martin Murphy's press, however, threw itself into a campaign for his murder. It argued that if Connolly and McDermott, who were among the key ringleaders, 'were treated with too great a leniency, they would take it as an indication of weakness on the part of the government'.[64]

On 12 May Connolly was executed while strapped to a chair. According to a Franciscan priest he reconciled himself with the Catholic Church by receiving communion. Ireland's foremost socialist revolutionary was dead.

Marxists and the 1916 Rebellion

The immediate reaction to the rising from socialists outside Ireland was not favourable. Connolly had contributed regularly to *Forward*, the paper of the Glasgow ILP. Yet it was to comment after the rising that, 'in no way do we approve of armed rebellion any more than any other form of militarism or war'.[65] Its editor, Tom Johnson, wrote that 'the psychology of it is a mystery to me'. George Lansbury, another leading figure of the ILP, argued that the rising was a crime against the British people. The British Socialist Party damned the rising as 'foolish'.[66]

The revolutionary left by and large welcomed the rising and defended its leaders against the lies of British imperialism. But there was also a sharp debate on what the rising meant for revolutionaries. As part of this debate, Lenin produced the most enthusiastic and accurate analysis of the event. Throughout the war he had conducted a polemic with fellow revolutionaries on the relevance of the demand for national self determination. His assessment of the 1916 rebellion originated as part of this polemic.

In April 1916, Karl Radek and a number of Polish revolutionaries had drafted a thesis on 'Imperialism and National Oppression'. Here they argued that the slogan of national self-determination could not be realised under capitalism and was undesirable under socialism. This position was supported by Bukharin and a number of other Bolsheviks. They claimed that revolutionaries should not raise 'minimum' demands such as that for national self-determination when the world was being convulsed by an imperialist war. Instead they should simply call for a socialist revolution. Both Radek and Bukharin had a tendency completely to write off the possibility of nationalist struggles in the smaller states of Europe.

The Easter Rising provided a test for these opposing views. Radek regarded its failure as confirmation of his general arguments. The Irish national question was played out. Its social basis had been the peasantry who demanded land reform. But these had been bought off by the concessions granted under the various Land Acts. By the beginning of the twentieth century the Irish nationalist movement was carried by an urban petty bourgeoisie who had originated among the peasantry. Lacking any social base, the rising they launched in 1916 had to be regarded as a mere *Putsch*.[67]

Trotsky disagreed with Radek's general opposition to the slogan of national self-determination. But he agreed that 1916 showed that 'the historical basis for a national revolution had disappeared even in backward Ireland.' The class agency of the national movement had become the tiny urban petty bourgeoisie. But unlike Radek he did not believe that they were totally isolated. They had managed to bring about the 'ascendancy of the green flag over the red in the Labour movement'. Trotsky believed that this was only a short-term and unstable development. What was termed the national revolution therefore 'amounted in practice to a workers' revolt'.[68]

Both Radek and Trotsky reduced the national movement to a particular class – the peasantry – who had deserted it. Both limited the role that their late substitute – the urban petty bourgeoisie – could play. In Radek's view they could not achieve anything more than the organisation of a *Putsch*. In Trotsky's view they became sideline players in a movement that was going in the direction of workers' revolution. The notion that workers would more or less automatically come to the fore was connected with Trotsky's failure at this point to recognise the key role of a party in fighting for such a leadership.

Lenin agreed with Trotsky's view that the rising had been conducted by 'the urban petty bourgeoisie and a section of workers'.[69] But it could not be reduced to that bald fact. The rising was part of 'the centuries-old Irish national independence movement ... [which had] passed through various stages and combinations of class interests'.[70] There was therefore a political demand for Irish independence, a sentiment for national freedom that revolutionaries had to relate to. This movement may have been weakened by the desertion of the peasantry but the crisis of imperialism that was manifest during the war would reawaken it. The significance of the Easter rebellion was that it proved that 'owing to the crisis of imperialism the flames of national revolt have flared up *both* in the colonies and in Europe and that national sympathies and antipathies have manifested themselves in spite of the Draconian threats and measures of repression. All this before the crisis of imperialism hits its peak.'[71]

Lenin's prime concern was that revolutionaries should not 'allow the war to oppress [their] thinking'.[72] A symptom of this would be a sectarian attitude to these nationalist revolts. Such an attitude would be disastrous because the dialectic of history meant that although the small nations of Europe were 'powerless as *independent* factors in the struggle against imperialism' their revolts could act as a spur to the most powerful anti-imperialist force – the international working class.[73]

Lenin noted that revolts like that of 1916 would be accompanied by all the 'prejudices and reactionary fantasies' of the petty bourgeoisie.[74] Socialists, however, should not start from the subjective intentions of those leading the rising but rather from the fact that they were striking a blow against imperialism. Thus, Lenin's polemic was directed at those in the revolutionary camp who did not know how to relate to movements of the oppressed. It was in this context that he issued his famous warning:

> To imagine that social revolution is *conceivable* without revolts of small nations in the colonies and in Europe, without revolutionary outbursts by a section of the petty bourgeoisie *with all its prejudices*, without a movement of the politically non-conscious proletarian and semi-proletarian masses against oppression by landowners, the church, and the monarchy, against national oppression, etc – to imagine all this is to *repudiate social revolution*.
>
> So one army lines up in one place and says 'We are for socialism' and another, somewhere else, says 'we are for imperialism' and that will be a social revolution. Only those who hold such a ridiculously pedantic view could vilify the Irish rebellion by calling it a 'putsch'.[75]

Lenin's article on 1916 was a brilliant polemic against the remnants of the ideas of the Second International. In place of passivity it argued that revolutionaries must use every popular movement against imperialism. It remains relevant today as an antidote to those who use the 'blood sacrifice' notions of Pearse as a means of dismissing the rising. It vindicates Connolly's general strategy of fighting alongside republicans.

Connolly's Role in 1916

But Lenin's article was not an endorsement of Connolly's specific tactics. For one thing there is no mention of Connolly or the Citizen Army despite the fact that the article was published in October 1916, six months after the rising took place. The article was not meant as an assessment of the tactics of socialists in Ireland. The focus of the article was primarily on how the Easter rebellion would affect the coming European-wide revolution.

His comment that the rising was 'premature' was meant neither as a criticism nor an endorsement of individuals such as Connolly who had pressed so vigorously for it. Lenin simply took as given the fact that the rising was dominated by the politics of the radical petty bourgeoisie and argued that socialist revolutionaries had still to support it with enthusiasm. Quoting Lenin to put Connolly's action beyond criticism is, therefore, absurd.

How, then, are we to assess Connolly's specific involvement in the rising as a Marxist? Two biographers have given diametrically opposing views. Austen Morgan has argued that Connolly ceased to be a socialist in August 1914 once the war broke out and became a national revolutionary. In 1916 he became a Germanophile and 'collaborated with a wartime imperialist state'.[76] He was fighting British domination and *not* the havoc that capitalism had created. If he had survived the rising he would most probably have emerged as the leader of Sinn Fein. This, Morgan contends, was a complete break with what he stood for up to this point.

Morgan can only argue that such a radical break occurred in Connolly's politics because he defines Connolly's early socialism in labourist terms. Indeed, Connolly initially 'imported a British conception of socialist strategy'.[77] There is little doubt where Morgan's own preference lies. Socialism, for Morgan, means utilising the ballot box in order to reform the state. Connolly's break is therefore a matter of some regret.

This ignores the obvious fact that while Connolly supported electoral activity as a tactic, he also stood on the revolutionary wing of the Second International. His break from reformism, and with it from any loyalty to his own state, enabled him to argue for a socialist leadership of the national struggle. Morgan dismisses this aspect of Connolly's politics entirely. He claims that his early statements that economic and *national* freedom could only be won in a workers' republic were purely 'rhetorical'.[78]

Not surprisingly, therefore, Morgan is totally unable to understand why Connolly worked with republicans at all. At times one gets the impression that the republicans represented a far greater threat than the British state. He claims, for example, that the 1916 rebellion had 'the ring of a militarized state about it'.[79] His charge that Connolly *either* had to fight British domination or capitalism shows a classic social-democratic conception of socialism. The possibility that the British state with all its supposedly 'civilised' traditions might be tied to the most brutal forms of imperialist exploitation is barely countenanced. Ultimately Morgan's dismissal of the 1916 rising and Connolly's role within it springs from a form of pacifism which abhors revolutionary violence.

Connolly towered over the pacifist tradition even with all his shortcomings. He understood that to fight war it was not sufficient to issue proclamations and wait for the ruling classes to make peace. He maintained the best traditions of the Second International in recognising that one's own ruling class was the main enemy in war. Instead of joining in the chauvinist chorus of abuse against the Kaiser, Connolly focussed on the crimes of the British Empire. Accusing Connolly of collaborating with imperialist Germany misses the point entirely. It makes as much sense as the accusation that Lenin was a German agent simply because he took a train ride to Russia with the help of the German general staff.

Morgan dismisses Connolly from a social-democratic tradition. By contrast Desmond Greaves wrote from an orthodox Stalinist position to portray him as an Irish Lenin. According to Greaves, Connolly matured to a full understanding of the theory of the popular front and the stages view of history after January 1916. He advanced far beyond the formulations of *Labour in Irish History* where he had seen the working class as the sole inheritor of the fight for Irish freedom. Instead he came to see the existence of a 'national' bourgeoisie with whom he could ally in a 'national front'.[80]

Greaves argues that in his last months Connolly believed that the aim of the first stage of the fight for freedom would be a republic where loyal capitalists would be left in possession of their wealth. Thus, he broke from the idea that a republic could only be realised as a socialist republic. The struggle for socialism would only begin in a free Irish state after a period in which the working class restrained itself for the benefit of the overall alliance.

There are obvious difficulties with this account. At no stage did Connolly make an open political declaration in favour of the stages theory and the alliance with the 'national bourgeoisie'. Neither did he explicitly break from the positions of *Labour in Irish History*. Moreover, Connolly was not in fact in alliance with the 'national bourgeoise' in 1916. Greaves is conflating the opposition of native capital to imperialism as it developed after the conscription crisis of 1918 with the position before 1916 when the bourgeoisie, in the main, supported the Empire. Greaves attempts to impose a popular-front model on Connolly's activities in order to lend a certain legitimacy to the subsequent strategy of the Irish Communist Party. This party has, on numerous occasions, sought alliances with the 'progressive' sections of Irish capital.

Greaves' more general support for the manner in which Connolly allied himself with the republicans leads him to glorify all of Connolly's actions throughout 1916 as the height of tactical sophistication. Connolly's pandering to nationalist sentiment is held up as praiseworthy. His embracing of a Jacobin concept of insurrection is excused by the false claim that Connolly had originally worked for a mass working-class insurrection. Connolly's analysis of the war is not critically examined; rather it is equated with Lenin's. Connolly's failure to maintain an independent political presence during the 1916 rising is completely ignored.

The result is that Connolly comes across as performing a superhuman feat. Politically isolated, lacking any substantial organisation, depressed at the socialist response to the war, he nevertheless succeeds in imposing his strategy on 1916. The real situation was quite the reverse. The balance of forces alone ensured that it was Connolly who had to accommodate his politics to his republican allies.

The question remains, therefore why did Connolly make such

concessions to republican politics during 1916? We have pointed to a number of reasons throughout this book.

First, from his earliest days in Ireland, Connolly's insight into the necessity of a working-class leadership of the national struggle was not matched by an understanding of the nature of republicanism. He saw it as a tradition that could be won over to socialism. This view stemmed from his belief that Irish nationalism could be pushed to undo the conquest which had imposed private property on Ireland. So believing, he failed to see that radical nationalism could, in fact, offer a new opening for Irish capitalism rather than sound the death knell of private property. His neglect of Griffith's ideas was one consequence of this perspective.

He therefore directed his criticisms exclusively at the constitutional nationalists and never subjected republicanism to a sustained political critique. He operated as an adviser to the republicans rather than challenging their tradition in its entirety. As a result not only did republican influence grow among the best workers and socialists, it was ultimately to force Connolly to make increasing concessions to its principles. Connolly's acceptance of the republican method of insurrection therefore had its roots in the ambiguities of his earlier analysis of the national question in the 1890s.

Second, it took a series of defeats to bring these ambiguities in his earlier positions to the fore. Between 1912 and 1916, Connolly witnessed an unparalleled series of defeats. In 1912 he saw the power of Orange reaction. In 1913 he entered the great battle that led to the defeat of the ITGWU in the lockout. His high hopes for industrial unionism were dashed. In 1914 he had to confront the possibility of partition as well as the miserable collapse of the Second International with the outbreak of war.

It was a tribute to Connolly that he held firm to his revolutionary socialist politics throughout this period up to his death. At all times he sought to combine a fight for Irish freedom with the reawakening of the working class. But his own political development made him singularly unable to resist the pressures of those defeats. His belief in syndicalism – in the all-conquering power of industrial unionism – combined with his negative experience of socialist sects in America, led him to argue against building independent revolutionary socialist organisations. Such a party could have forced Connolly to argue and clarify his politics, and better prepared him to meet this period of defeat.

In a period of working-class advance, Connolly, like the syndicalist movement generally, displayed tremendous militancy. But in periods of defeat, his reluctance to build a separate organisation led to confusion and vacillation. The crisis of the war was to expose these confusions to intense pressure. Moreover, the absence of a political organisation meant that Connolly was forced to call on others to act. In times of war, it meant a turn to the republican movement to achieve the insurrection.

Pressuring other forces to act entailed for Connolly an adaption to their politics.

Third, Connolly's inability to break from the traditions of the Second International meant that there was no strategy available to him as a socialist during World War I. The Second International's politics was premised on normal capitalist development. The emphasis on the ballot box reflected this.

Unable to see that the war expressed the maturing of the contradictions within the world system, Connolly became increasingly pessimistic about the prospects for socialism in the short term. He viewed developments in one-sided rather than dialectical terms. He feared, for example, that the introduction of conscription to Ireland would strengthen the state to an immeasurable degree and destroy all working-class traditions. The prospect of massive resistance developing played no part in his calculations. Increasingly, his concern became one of 'striking a blow' to reawaken the working class and the Irish nation. In trying to compensate for the weakness of the working class, he was forced to make more concessions to nationalist politics.

The 1916 rebellion needs to be defended by socialists today from the increasing attacks on it. But the manner in which Connolly joined the rebellion revealed the full extent of the concessions. Quite simply, the red flag was lowered beneath the green. There was no separate propaganda from the ICA. There was no call to the unions he represented as general secretary. Instead Connolly uncritically penned his name to the most general of documents, the Proclamation of an Irish Republic. In practice he liquidated his politics into the general nationalist movement.

Was there an alternative? In all probability this could only have rested on a very different approach than the one adopted by Connolly in the decades before 1916. It would have meant supporting the rising by agitating for working-class activity. That would have entailed a need for specific socialist propaganda that distinguished itself from the nationalism of the rising's leaders. It would have meant marching alongside the republican fighters while arguing for more limited military objectives. It would have meant some preparation to preserve socialist political organisation after the inevitable crackdown. All of this would have required a perspective which held that socialists could fight alongside republicans – and still compete with their politics.

It has been argued that, for all that, Connolly achieved *something* – the awakening of the Irish national movement. Undoubtedly, the rising was a major factor in this. But the question also remains, which class came to the fore in that movement and whether there was inevitability about this. Quite clearly, it was the Irish bourgeoisie who reaped the gains of the national struggle – even though their representatives played no part in the 1916 rebellion. Symbolically, the man who played the most decisive role in influencing both the Cumman na nGaedheal and Fianna

Fail governments in a post-rising Ireland, Arthur Griffith, took absolutely no part in the rising.

The lesson of 1916 for socialists is an old one: the working class can only intervene in history to its advantage as a *conscious* political force. Every time it simply 'plays its part', or provides the 'backbone', it loses out to classes above it. That was a point made by Connolly himself. It need only be added that the working class requires a political organisation that articulates its specific interests against all ideologies that contend with revolutionary socialism.

9. The Socialist Movement after Connolly

The 1916 rebellion was the prelude to one of the first successful nationalist revolts against the British Empire in this century. It was a revolt led by the most conservative of revolutionaries. At its root, however, the anger against the British Empire meshed with new demands for a redivision of land, for workers' rights and for a very different type of state from the one that eventually emerged. The speed with which Connolly's specifically socialist message was marginalised after his death therefore deserves brief examination.

The broad picture of events in the immediate aftermath of 1916 is beyond dispute. Within months of the 1916 rebellion the mood in Ireland changed decisively. The heroism of the republican fighters, the brutal imposition of martial law in Dublin and the growing disgust with the war throughout the whole of Europe all contributed to this change. The first indication of the new mood came in January 1917 when Count Plunkett, the father of the executed leader of the 1916 rising, Joseph Plunkett, won the North Roscommon bye-election for Sinn Fein.

At the time of the rising, Sinn Fein had declined to one central branch in Dublin. It held the decisive advantage, though, of being an open republican party. By April 1917, the number of Sinn Fein Clubs had grown to 166, with a membership of 11,000. In October, the party held a re-organised convention in the Mansion House in Dublin where Griffith symbolically stepped aside as president of the organisation in favour of the 1916 rising hero, Eamonn De Valera. But although open discussion on what form of a government the movement sought was brushed aside, Griffith's policy of building up native Irish capital was effectively dominant.

In April 1918, Westminster enacted a bill to introduce conscription to Ireland. Despite its efforts to put up some token opposition the Home Rule party was marginalised as a result. In December 1918, fresh from the anticonscription campaign, Sinn Fein swept the board in the general election. In January 1919, the Sinn Fein deputies boycotted Westminster and proclaimed an independent Irish parliament, Dáil Éireann.

Almost simultaneously, on 21 January the first shots of the Anglo-Irish war were fired when republicans opened fire on the police in Soloheadbeg, in Co. Tipperary. The newly reorganised Irish Republican Army (IRA), pledging allegiance to Dáil Eireann, launched a guerrilla war which lasted until the truce of July 1921. Faced with the stark choice between embarking on a near genocidal war against the Irish and seeking some settlement, the British prime minister, Lloyd George, opted for the latter course.

The treaty concluded between the Irish and British governments was described by Lionel Curtis, an adviser to Winston Churchill, as one of the 'greatest achievements of the Empire'.[1] Effectively it imposed partition on the island and limited the sovereignty of the 26 county-states. Its ratification by the Dáil in January 1922 represented a victory for the most moderate elements inside the republican camp, who were content to retain their ties to the Empire. These forces also understood that a continuation of the war might raise the the possibility of a deeper and wider social revolt.

For, contrary to the depictions of nationalist historians, the period of the Anglo-Irish conflict was one in which the Irish working class entered the stage of history in a most impressive manner. It was Connolly's misfortune to have died before the revival of Irish labour. Between 1918 and 1923 Irish workers reached unprecedented heights of militancy. Their struggles dwarfed the first great period of working-class struggle between 1911 and 1912. By 1920, 120,000 workers had joined the ITGWU. Trades Councils – or Workers' Councils, as they were known – mushroomed across the country. There were 28 local general strikes between 1917 and 1921. These occurred in small provincial towns. Charleville, for example, had five general strikes although there was no previous history of trade unionism in the town. Before 1921 no fewer than eight workplace soviets were established where workers took over the management of their enterprises.[2] In April 1920 a general strike won the release of republican prisoners from Mountjoy prison.

The opportunities for revolutionary socialists had never been as favourable. Indeed the leadership of both the socialist movement and the unions lay in the hands of two close associates of Connolly: Tom Johnson and William O'Brien. Yet in this short period they played a central role in transforming a militant movement into the puny, passive and loyal Labour opposition that has restrained left politics in Ireland ever since.

How this occurred has been a matter of considerable interest to the Irish left. Peadar O'Donnell claimed that during the war of independence 'Connolly's chair was left vacant ... the place that Connolly purchased for the organised Labour movement in the leadership of the independence was denied or reneged'.[3] O'Brien and Johnson are supposed to have backed off from the national struggle and concentrated on a syndicalist orientation. The implication drawn by many on the Irish left was that O'Brien and Johnson were *insufficiently* republican and so became conservative social democrats. Connolly, by contrast, was saved from this fate because of his willingness to become a republican in 1916.

The notion that Johnson and O'Brien broke with the Connolly tradition has much to recommend it. Johnson and O'Brien were cast as labour bureaucrats while Connolly belonged to the revolutionary socialist tradition. But this account, however, ignores one crucial point: the manner in which O'Brien and Johnson could relate to, and develop, the weaknesses in Connolly's political legacy. On paper they shared three major strategic planks with Connolly: they were thoroughgoing syndicalists; they eschewed any challenge to republican politics, and they led the broad-based party, the Socialist Party of Ireland (which they revived in 1917) along lines laid down by Connolly. More importantly it ignores the manner in which O'Brien and Johnson combined elements of syndicalism with an accommodation to republican politics. Far from being insufficiently republican, they accepted all too readily their role within the republican scheme of things.

No analysis of Connolly's politics, therefore, would be complete without an examination of how his self-professed heirs managed to latch onto the ambiguities of the Connolly legacy and distort them for their own reformist ends.

The War of Independence

The irony was that in the immediate aftermath of his execution Connolly was an embarrassment to Johnson and the other union leaders. Two months after the rising the ITUC met in congress in Sligo. Its executive reported that it had written to the British authorities expressing their concern that many who were 'innocent of any connection with the revolt will be unjustly punished'. It never demanded clemency for Connolly.[4] Johnson advised the delegates that the unions were not the place to discuss the revolt. He called for a minute's silence both for those who had fallen in 1916 and for those who had served in the British army during World War I. The Irish Citizen army were disowned as mere 'tenants' of Liberty Hall without any connection with the ITGWU.[5]

This was soon to change. As the wave of militant nationalism swept the country, the same leaders who disowned Connolly after the rising reversed their position and, once more, pledged themselves to fight for Connolly's brand of socialism. An additional factor in their considerations was the tremendous wave of enthusiasm that arose in Ireland in support of the Bolshevik revolution of October 1917. O'Brien and Johnson immediately positioned themselves inside the camp of the Irish Bolsheviks. This placed them in a certain quandary, as the hallmark of Bolshevism was its determination to confront all other political traditions in the name of an active fight for revolutionary socialism. One of the means by which the leaders of Irish Labour avoided this course was by using Connolly's decision to participate in the rising in 1916 as a rationale for hiding the Red flag behind the Green.

This was, of course, a grave distortion of the legacy of a man who

waged a determined fight against the strategy of all class alliances. Nevertheless, it was precisely this strategy that the Irish 'Bolsheviks' were determined to adopt. The pattern was set by the first major labour mobilisation
against conscription in 1918. A general strike was called to bolster the
activities of the Mansion House conference against conscription. This was
an all-class alliance which linked Home Rulers, republicans and socialists.
O'Brien had represented labour on this committee. He joined a delegation
to the Catholic hierarchy in Maynooth, pleading for their involvement.[6]
The bishops responded by using Sunday Masses to issue a prayer against
conscription and to call for public meetings to take up anticonscription
pledges. The general strike arose in this context.

By failing to fight conscription from an independent class position, based
on principles of socialism rather than nationalism, the leaders of Irish
labour could not challenge the loyalist ideas of Protestant workers. Some
months previously, 10,000 workers had backed a Belfast Trades Council
demonstration against the threat of conscription but when the general
strike was called by what amounted to a pan-Catholic bloc, it fell on
deaf ears in the North.

The liquidation of socialist politics continued as labour withdrew from
the general election in November 1918. The leaders of Irish labour decided
to put the need for national unity before their class. In a manifesto on
the elections the ITUC claimed that the workers of Ireland 'should will-
ingly sacrifice for a brief period their aspiration towards political power,
if thereby the future of the nation can be enhanced'. They added proudly
that by refusing to challenge the republicans, the Labour Party was showing
that it was the 'only party which is prepared to sacrifice party in the interest
of the nation'.[7]

Thus, it was not simply the case that the union leaders wanted to ignore
the national struggle. They saw themselves as unofficial allies of the nationalists, acting as adjuncts to the cause. They sought to advise Sinn Fein
in the hope of winning a better place as union officials in an independent
Ireland. In Peadar O'Donnell's words, they took up a position on the
'prompter's stool'.[8] They aimed to paint republicanism a little more red
– rather than challenging its politics from a revolutionary socialist, and
therefore an anti-imperialist standpoint. In this they were expanding on
weaknesses in Connolly's own position.

They did so, however, in a manner which broke with all of Connolly's
achievements. He had understood that the fight against the national
oppression of Ireland could link into a fight for a workers' republic. O'Brien
and Johnson found in the national struggle yet another obstacle to revolutionary change. In a report to the Third International, the international
organisation of revolutionary socialists formed after the Russian Revolution, the leaders of the SPI claimed that 'the preoccupation of the people
with the struggle against British imperialism has been an obstacle of
importance in preventing the spread of revolutionary socialism'.[9] Connolly

at least had understood that an anti-imperialist struggle could be pushed in the direction of a fight for the workers' republic, even though he failed to see that this would require a confrontation with republican politics. In arguing that the fight against the Empire was an obstacle to socialism, O'Brien and Johnson were adopting the mechanical politics of the Second International and, in the process, relegating themselves to the role of unofficial and subservient advisers to the republicans.

This preferred role was most sharply expressed in 1919 when Johnson was involved in writing the Democratic Programme of the first Dáil. Under the impact of the Russian Revolution, Johnson included a number of references to nationalisation and workers' control.[10] Even though his draft was cleansed of all radicalism, a fellow union leader recalled that the usually unemotional Johnson had to be prevented from standing and cheering when it was adopted.[11] The faith of a bureaucrat in resolutions passed within the corridors of power was overwhelming.

In 1921 Johnson and O'Brien again took up the role of advisers to the republicans when they joined a Dáil Éireann committee to devise a labour policy for a new Ireland. They also sought to make full use of the Sinn Fein scheme of conciliation courts for settling strikes. The illusions that the union leaders had regarding Sinn Fein were expressed in a private letter sent by another prominent leader, Thomas Foran, to Larkin. He claimed that Sinn Fein had changed completely and that 'Griffith has had to move with the times. The movement is more advanced than you seem to think, and every day becomes more infected with Bolshevik propaganda.'[12]

The illusions regarding Griffith, De Valera and the other leaders of the republican forces went hand in hand with a syndicalist view of the world. There was no contradiction here. Syndicalism postpones a political contest until the union organisation has been built up. It sees politics as a future 'echo' of its strong union organisation. In Ireland the ITUC leaders believed that as long as the republicans did not blatantly interfere with the strengthening of the unions, there was no reason why they should not be left to complete the first stage of the national struggle. The ITUC leaders expressed the connection between their syndicalist outlook and their political strategy in the period when they argued that, 'whatever part labour is destined to play in the political life of Ireland, its part in the industrial and economic life must take precedence, since in Ireland as everywhere else economic power must *precede* and make possible political power'.[13]

There was a crucial difference between Connolly's syndicalism and that of his epigones. Connolly embraced syndicalism as a revolutionary strategy; the latter saw it as a cover for building up a bureaucratic apparatus in the unions. O'Brien spent much of this period, as treasurer of the ITGWU, converting the union debt into considerable property holdings.[14] The concentration on building up the union apparatus meant that not only were the republicans given a free political hand but rank-and-file militancy was also dampened down. O'Brien and Johnson effectively sabotaged workers' struggles both for wage increases and against the British Empire.

The most blatant example of the divergence between their revolutionary rhetoric and their actions occurred in Limerick in April 1919. Limerick workers proclaimed a soviet to protest at British army restrictions. Instead of giving momentum to this protest, Johnson advised them to evacuate the town, arguing 'they did not expect to beat the British army'. He said that 'he believed that it was quite possible that it would be by the action of the Labour movement in Ireland the insurrection would some day be developed ... But Limerick was not the occasion.'[15] During the massive wage battles in the same year, the ITUC called for co-ordination of strike action – and then did nothing. In May 1920, when railway workers refused to transport armed British soldiers, the ITUC failed to escalate the blacking to the level of strike action. By November they had ordered the resumption of military transport.

These courses of action stemmed directly from the concentration on strengthening the union apparatus. But the syndicalist ideology also enabled the union leaders to abstain from concrete political arguments. This occurred specifically over the treaty. When the Anglo-Irish Treaty was being debated, *Voice of Labour*, the paper of the ITGWU, claimed that the main danger did not arise from English rights in Ireland but from 'the capitalist concentration of society prevailing in Ireland ... which no particular form of government can safeguard against'.[16] It boasted that only six branches of the union had been 'foolish' enough to discuss the issue.

Once the treaty was accepted, the union leaders found themselves with a state governed by a section of their republican allies. The formation of an Irish state apparatus brought a complete change in the outlook of the leaders of Irish labour. Preserving union organisation now meant accommodation to the new nationalist state. Over the next year the language of syndicalism was dropped in favour of a moderate labour outlook.

Rank-and-file militancy, however, was increasing as the question of wage cuts came to dominate union struggles in 1922. Eighty soviets were proclaimed in 1922. In the most serious case, 39 creameries of the Condensed Milk Company were occupied across North Munster. On the land, there was huge opposition from farm labourers to the wage cuts. In West Waterford, 15,000 workers struck both in the towns and the farms in solidarity with those facing the cuts.[17]

To safeguard their organisation, the union leaders were determined to prove their loyalty to the new republican state. Johnson informed the *Manchester Guardian* that the soviets in North Munster were 'local, spontaneous and unofficial', and were 'unconnected with any general policy of the unions'.[18] The ITUC report for 1923 informed the new state authorities that, 'were it not for the mollifying influence of Labour leaders and officials, the present position would be infinitely worse.'[19]

The combination of a conservative syndicalism with a subordination to republican politics now bore fruit in a weak form of social democracy that was loyal to its own nationalist state. The new turn was expressed sharply on the day after the treaty was accepted by the Dáil. Johnson and O'Brien led the first delegation to that body to plead for measures to reduce unemployment and to modify wage cuts. The focus had changed from rhetorical backing for struggle to pleadings inside the corridors of power.

The betrayals of O'Brien and Johnson were not isolated cases. Europe bristled with leaders such as Serratti in Italy or Cachin in France who professed Bolshevik politics but who behaved as social democrats. What was unique in Ireland was the absence of a distinct left challenge to their politics until late in 1921. Here the political traditions left by Connolly had a direct bearing.

Connolly's last position on the role of the socialist party came close to a left version of the ILP tradition in Britain. This sought to play down political differences and to stress the unity of reformists and revolutionaries. Connolly's syndicalism meant that differences inside the party were never taken seriously. Thus, Johnson's support for World War I or O'Brien's insistence on building a base in the union hierarchy were never publicly challenged. To make matters worse there was the confusion and lack of clarity on how to relate to republicanism.

After Connolly's death, the SPI was revived. Initially it had a few hundred members and was able, for example, to mobilise 10,000 people in support of the Russian Revolution in 1918. But the party was hampered by two major defects. First, the propagandist notion of a party inherited from Connolly meant that it did not seek to intervene in the rising tide of working class militancy. It did not conceive of itself as fighting for a leadership role in the struggles. It was content to issue the most general propaganda. Second, it imprisoned the left grouped around Connolly's son Roddy into a hopeless alliance with O'Brien and Johnson. The tiny forces of the left understood that their leaders were 'for the most part under the influence of Sinn Fein'.[20] But it was unable to break from these leaders. An attempted challenge to the party leadership by the left in September 1919 was condemned by the press, the church and Sinn Fein. Faced with this unholy alliance behind O'Brien and Johnson, the left retreated.

The result was that the party increasingly became a paper organisation. It dwindled in membership and became simply a vehicle through which the union leaders could both preserve their left credentials and engage in manoeuvres with both the Second and Third Internationals. It became, in brief, a debating society when the level of struggle called for real initiatives. The left opposition to O'Brien and Johnson was thus extremely slow to emerge. When it did, it, too, suffered from some of the shortcomings inherent in Connolly's politics – in particular an inability to see republicanism as an ideology of a different class.

Opposition to the existing leadership came from two fronts. The two-hundred-strong Irish Citizen Army came into conflict with O'Brien over the latter's refusal to oppose the Anglo-Irish Treaty. Yet, tragically, the ICA accepted a resolution from Countess Markievicz pledging support to De Valera. Once the Civil War had begun, it placed itself under the command of the Dublin Republican brigade led by Oscar Traynor and handed over its ammunition to the IRA.[21] They fought simply as soldiers, with no say in republican policy, during the Civil War.

The Communist Party of Ireland (CPI) was founded in October 1921 as a tiny organisation after O'Brien and Johnson had been expelled from the SPI as 'reformists'. One sign of its break with syndicalism was that it was the first organisation to condemn the treaty. But it did not break with the earlier traditions of investing republican organisations with a potential for socialism. Instead of seeking to build on the working-class upsurge of 1923, the CPI turned to the republican forces who opposed the treaty. It pressed them to launch a military offensive and offered six of the eight pages of *Workers Republic* to De Valera's party 'unconditionally and without expense'. It added, 'as long as they require our services we are at their disposal in this crisis'.[22]

The inability of the young CPI fully to grasp the Bolshevik position was evident in their views on how the Third International's theses on the national and colonial question should be applied in Ireland. Roddy Connolly interpreted their import as follows:

> The communists support the militant Republicans, the only objectively revolutionary movement ... by trying to rally to it organised labour and by endeavouring to get the republicans to adopt a programme of social revolutionary importance in such a manner as to transfer them into a subjectively revolutionary force under communist influence.[23]

In fact the Third International had stressed the provisional and limited nature of communist support for national movements in their struggle against imperialism. The Third International argued that even in this alliance the Communist Party 'must unconditionally maintain the independence of the proletarian movement, even if it is only in an embryonic stage', and not seek to tie workers to national liberation movements. It called for a struggle against the 'attempt to clothe the revolutionary liberation movements ... in communist colours'. Above all communist support for such movements was to be subordinated to the need to build an organisation that could 'fight against the bourgeois democratic trend in their own nation'.[24]

For the CPI, however, the earlier Connolly tradition of seeking to advise republicans rather than challenge their politics prevailed. The notion that the republicans could be placed 'under the influence' of socialists became an illusion that haunted the left for decades afterwards. The tragedy of the early CPI was not that it made mistakes – it was rather that it had too short a time, before the advent of Stalinist dominance, to learn the genuine Bolshevik tradition.

10. Conclusions

How, then, can Connolly's politics be assessed? Firstly, as has become clear, although Connolly cannot be claimed for any particular Marxist tradition, he belonged primarily in the revolutionary camp. This much is patently obvious from his life. His political practice was based on Marx's dictum: 'The emancipation of the working class is the task of the working class.' He saw an unbridgeable gulf between his own politics and those who identified socialism with mere state building. In an early article he had written:

> Socialism properly implies above all things the co-operative control by the workers of the machinery of production; without this co-operative control the public ownership by the State is not Socialism – it is only state capitalism.
>
> To the cry of the middle class reformers, 'make this or that the property of the government' we reply, 'Yes, in proportion as the workers are ready to make the government their property.'[21]

Socialism was impossible without workers' democracy and could never be won without workers actively struggling for it.

Secondly, he was totally opposed to the notion that capitalism could be reformed out of existence. This was particularly obvious in his writings in the period before 1910. He vigorously opposed the decision of Millerand, the first socialist to enter a coalition government in France, and afterwards began to criticise a tendency towards reformism inside the socialist organisations.[2] This led him to become a supporter of one of the few organisations in the world which excluded reformists, the American Socialist Labour Party.

Even in his disillusionment with the SLP's sectish politics, he never abandoned his belief in the need for decisive revolutionary change. What changed was simply the means by which this could be brought about. Instead of a narrow party there had to be a broad church. Instead of a focus on socialist propaganda there was the practical task of building an industrial union. The Labour Party that he founded could only clear away some of the obstacles facing the building of revolutionary unions – it was never seen as a vehicle for gradually establishing socialism.

Thirdly, on all the major issues of his day Connolly stood on the left. In the greatest test facing socialists he was one of the few national leaders to oppose the horrors of the capitalist war. Although a trade-union general secretary, he was prepared to break every rule of officialdom in calling for strikes, if necessary over the heads of established union leaders. Less well known was his stance on the question of women: while many of his contemporaries fudged the question of suffrage, Connolly was an enthusiastic supporter. Despite his own conservative views on the family, he could pen some marvellously prophetic advice:

> In its march towards freedom, the working class must cheer on the efforts of those women who, feeling on their souls and bodies the fetters of the ages, have arisen to strike them off, and cheer all the louder if in its hatred of thraldom and passion for freedom the women's army forges ahead of the militant army of labour.
>
> But whosoever carries the outworks of the citadel of oppression, the working class alone can raze it to the ground.[3]

Finally, his application of a socialist strategy to Ireland broke entirely with reformism. He despised the 'gas and water' socialism that refused to face up to issues such as Orange reaction. Most significantly, he broke from the stages approach that saw an independent capitalist Ireland as the first goal of socialists. He grasped the fundamental insight that the national question in Ireland could not be solved short of a struggle for a workers' republic.

Yet to understand Connolly fully it is necessary to see him as a revolutionary inside the tradition of the Second International. From an early stage he sensed the passivity and compromising nature of much of what passed for socialism. His own instincts rebelled against that straitjacket of the tradition. But he was in a highly unfavourable position to carry out the task of building a coherent political alternative to the failings of the Second International.

The Irish working class up to 1913 was among the weakest in Europe. By contrast in Russia, where the seeds were planted for a different type of Marxism, workers were concentrated in massive enterprises while the politial structures were dominated by a semi-feudal autocracy. The Russian workplace, thus, became the focus of political struggles when as, early as 1905, the workers were leading the fight for democracy. It was possible to build a tradition in Russia where political and economic struggles were fused; where one could not simply *imagine* a leap over stages but see the concrete possibilities in a powerful working class; where a turn to the workplace did not mean a syndicalist disregard for political struggles. By contrast, Connolly's revolutionary instincts did not immediately connect with the experience of workers. It was inevitable therefore that he would remain a rebel within the tradition of the Second International.

His politics were formed in a difficult struggle with the Marxist outlook of the day. The Second International's motto that backward countries would automatically follow the stages of development set by the advanced countries left Irish socialists with little option but to support the Home Rulers and to await the full development of Irish capitalism. Connolly never undertook a detailed study of the exact economic ties that bound the Irish bourgeoisie to the Empire – but instinctively he recognised the bourgeoisie as cowardly and incapable of carrying through the national struggle. The problem was how to reconcile this insight with the overall tradition that Connolly adhered to.

Lacking a theoretical alternative, Connolly sought exceptions. Like most other socialists of the day he clung to a strict stages view of history – but yet saw a possibility of fighting for socialism in backward Ireland. His optimism arose from the fact that Ireland had the peculiarity of having feudalism and capitalism imposed from without. There were therefore native sources of radicalism to be tapped in the fight against capitalism.

As we saw, in *Labour in Irish History* and *Erin's Hope* Connolly's arguments against constitutional nationalism were directed not only at its tendency to compromise with the Empire. He also sought to resuscitate the tradition of 'real nationalism' that was implicitly directed at a reconquest. Clearly, this led to an ambiguity about Irish republicanism. Connolly argued vehemently against their tendency to forge all class alliances, writing *Labour in Irish History* to show the terrible record that arose from this strategy. As late as the 1916 rebellion, Connolly was warning the Citizen Army to hold onto their weapons as they would come into conflict later with their republican allies. Yet republicanism was still the political tradition closest to genuine nationalism and its supposed anti-capitalist instincts.

In practice, Connolly sought to incorporate republicanism into the socialist tradition rather than challenge it. Nowhere, as we have seen, is there a fundamental critique of the tradition. At most there is tactical advice offered to the republicans about the need to engage in open political activity. Republicanism itself appears as a set of politics that belongs naturally to the Irish people. It floats through history with no class base. Its founder, Wolfe Tone, appears as a declassed revolutionary statesman rather than as a representative of the bourgeoisie, albeit of its most progressive section. Fintan Lalor's demand that the rights of property be vested in the nation rather than in the monarchy is taken as evidence that he was an apostle of revolutionary socialism. The reactionary positions taken up by republicans such as Mitchel and O'Donovan Rossa is glossed over.

The attempt to incorporate republicanism led to an extraordinary blind spot on the politics of Arthur Griffith. Here was an influential figure who preached militant nationalism – in order to build an Irish capitalist republic. In Connolly's first period in Ireland there was not a single word of criticism of Griffith although he was aware of the challenge Griffith posed to the left. Instead there was an attempt to win Griffith's backing for ISRP candidates. At a later period, when Sinn Fein had already begun to attract significant sections of the Dublin left, Connolly found himself totally on the defensive. On one hand there was a plea for a reconciliation between Sinn Fein and socialists, and suppport for the Sinn Fein strategy of import controls. On the other, the focus of the criticism was directed at Griffith's call for a return to Grattan's Parliament. It was as if Griffith's procapitalist outlook stemmed from his inconsistency as a republican.

In Connolly's own lifetime, the working-class upsurge from 1911 to 1913 clarified the nature of republican organisations. Neither Sinn Fein, the IRB nor the Irish Volunteers could jeopardise their aspirations for all-class unity by supporting the workers of Dublin. But defeats in all circumstances have a tendency to obliterate lessons that are learnt at the high point of the struggle. Tragically not even a minority of workers came to recognise the class nature of Irish republicanism through these events.

Connolly's own politics and the way they developed in conflict with the prevailing mechanistic brand of Marxism contributed to this befuddled view of republicanism. It was not *only* that the despair of World War I led Connolly to submerge himself completely in republican politics during 1916. The roots of the ambiguity go right back to his early pamphlet *Erin's Hope* where he first argued his views on Irish nationalism. Connolly had already spent nearly 20 years (except for the brief period from the point at which Home Rule seemed inevitable up to the Dublin lockout) looking to Irish nationalism as a force which could be pushed to the left. During the war, the pressure to substitute other forces for a weakened working class led him back to a completely dependent alliance with republicans. The problem was not that Connolly was prepared to fight alongside the republicans right up to the 1916 rebellion – it was that he lowered the Red Flag during that fight.

The other main strand of Connolly's politics – syndicalism – was also shaped by his conflict with the tradition of the Second International. The Second International divided the fight for socialism into a minimum programme, which guided the day-to-day activity of looking for piecemeal reform, and a maximum programme, which was increasingly relegated to the distant future. Connolly's first reaction was to look to the sectish politics of the SLP where the fight for reform was discarded entirely. But the way in which this isolated revolutionaries from the day-to-day lives of workers led Connolly towards revolutionary syndicalism.

Here was a strategy that seemed to connect the immediate struggles of workers to the goal of socialism. Each gain in workers' confidence, each increase in the membership of industrial unions was a step towards wresting factories from the control of the employers. The image for

Connolly was that of the bourgeoisie under feudalism: they had built up sufficient economic power within feudalism to guarantee the political success of their revolution. The working class, he believed, could do likewise.

In a period of rising working-class confidence, syndicalism generalised in a revolutionary direction. Its enthusiasm for struggle, its contempt for middle-class reformers, its championing of workers' self-emancipation were highly positive. It was this which led Lenin to make a special attempt to win the syndicalists to Bolshevism after the Russian Revolution.

But in a period of working-class defeat it could also lead to a pandering to the rightward drift inside the working class. Its tendency to play down political questions could mean avoiding 'difficult issues'. There are some signs that Connolly was affected by this tendency after the period when the IWW in America suffered major defeats. However, it is also striking how Connolly rose above the weakness of the tradition.

During his period as a Belfast organiser for the ITGWU, when all the pressures were on to build an industrial union by avoiding politics, Connolly took the most unsyndicalist of roads: he made the political divisions within the working class the centre of his activity. This was one of his lasting achievements. By insisting that all socialists – Protestant and Catholic – defend Home Rule, fight Orangeism and resist partition he recognised that industrial unity meant nothing if a section of the working class colluded in oppression.

In one area, however, Connolly's syndicalism led to a major weakening of his politics. The Second International had always glossed over the ideological struggle. If socialism was inevitable, then it was not absolutely necessary to fight the bourgeois ideas which many workers held. In Connolly's case this was translated from the start of his political career into an extreme distaste for any discussion on religious or sexual matters. In his eyes these issues were raised only by liberal 'faddists'.

The syndicalism he developed in America strengthened this trend to extremes. The creation of industrial unions was seen as a panacea for all political problems. Reformism only arose directly from craft unionism – industrial unions would lead to revolutionary politics. Attempts at political clarification resulted from middle-class intellectuals trying to dominate the workers' movement. The central issue was building the union.

In practical terms, this meant that Connolly could never build a party. It has been wrongly assumed that he was not interested in this. In fact, for most of his life his central commitment was to building a political organisation. In 1911 for example – at the height of the working-class upsurge – he was advising O'Brien that trade-union activity had to take second place to party building.[4]

The problem was that his own syndicalism made it impossible. There were two reasons for this. The party was seen entirely in propagandist terms. It made abstract socialist arguments but never sought to take the lead in day-to-day struggles. At no point, for example, did the ILP(I) seek to intervene in the upsurge in 1913 with a concrete strategy that could have helped win a mass of new recruits.

Connolly's syndicalism also led him to adopt a broad-church approach to party building. Since the political struggle was the mere 'echo' of the industrial battle, the division between reformists and revolutionaries was secondary. As long as both promoted the industrial union, the 'theoretical issues' would be solved in the industrial practice.

The tragic irony was that this strategy was implemented during the most turbulent period of working-class history when political clarity was absolutely essential. Connolly, who was tremendously clear in his attitude to Orangeism, could pull together a united party, the ILP(I), which made no mention of the national question. Or he could be the most serious socialist in opposing World War I – and yet not publicly denounce socialists in his own ranks, such as Tom Johnson – who supported the British war effort. The broad-church approach to party building led in fact to the political collapse of those tiny organisations he had established.

Connolly's tragedy was that he had to survive without an organisation. This meant that he often zigzagged between terrific bouts of optimism and pessimism. In 1912 he was convinced that Home Rule was an inevitability and that Labour would be the major opposition in an all-Ireland parliament. By 1916, he had begun to wonder seriously if sections of the Irish working class had not been bought off by the Empire.

It is a great tribute to Connolly that he survived this crisis as a revolutionary. The small Irish left today stand on the shoulders of a true giant. But in order to see further it will have to examine many of his positions critically and remove many of the ambiguities that derived from his isolated struggle.

Postscript

There was, thus, no one coherent 'Connolly tradition' of politics. His failure to build a party ensured this. Instead his politics was splintered and fragmented as different groupings claimed to follow in his wake.

Ever since the Southern Irish state was established the Irish left has been split into two broad camps. The first, the social-democratic tradition, looked to gradual industrialisation to introduce class politics. The second tradition straddled republicanism and socialism. Partially under Connolly's influence, partially through a fear of building open Marxist organisations, revolutionary socialists in Ireland have traditionally placed themselves inside the republican camp. Partition was seen as producing not just a 'carnival of reaction' but also an unstable arrangement that could be overthrown by a form of radical republicanism.

Despite the rapid industrialisation of the South in the 1960s and '70s – only 16 per cent now work in agriculture – the hopes of social democrats have not been realised. Despite recent gains for the Labour Party and

the Workers Party, 'normal' class politics, where the left becomes a contender for government, seem as distant as ever. Indeed the very prospect
of a majority socialist government – no matter how mild its policies –
is something which underdeveloped Irish capitalism could barely countenance. Capitalism in Ireland is highly subsidised. The state guarantees
to both native and foreign capital massive grants, minimal taxes on profits,
freedom from exchange controls and, in the words of the former US
ambassador William Shannon, a 'stability under right-wing governments'.
There is limited scope for reform, especially in a period when social democracy across the world is in retreat.

Attempts by both the Labour Party and the Workers Party to appear
responsible can only mean accepting the parameters set by this weak form
of capitalism. In practice, both parties are agreed on the need to repay
the huge debt of the Southern state, on 'planned' rather than 'unplanned'
cuts, on subsidies to industry, etc.

The other problem for social democracy is partition. Despite its own
rhetoric the Southern state has come to rely on the institutions of partition.
Tony Benn, the former British Labour minister, has revealed that the
most vociferous opponents of any consideration of a British withdrawal
from Northern Ireland are Southern politicians. Among those politicians
are representatives of the Irish Labour Party.

In all countries social democracy has come to develop a loyalty to the
state apparatus which it aims to use as a vehicle for reform. Southern
Ireland is no exception. Both Labour and the Workers Party have joined
in support of repression against republicans. Both believe that the fight
in the North is a potential danger to the institutions of parliamentary
democracy which they defend.

The social democrats also have more specific reasons for supporting
repression. They see the Northern crisis as arising from a form of 'tribalism'
which the 'fascists' of the IRA have stirred up. It is a major obstacle to
the modernisation of Irish politics which they wish for. As a result their
enthusiasm for repression on occasions outdoes the nationalists in Fianna
Fail.

Social democracy in Ireland, therefore, is caught in a cleft stick. Its
own politics has left it with a small base in Irish society. Some 85 per
cent of the Southern electorate still vote for right-wing parties. To break
such voting allegiances would demand a period of intense class struggle.
But the Labour Party and the Workers Party are terrified of initiating
such struggles. It goes completely against the project of establishing a
moderate social democratic government which a weak Irish capitalism
could sustain. Similarly, to advance a socialist solution to the problem
of Northern Ireland would mean opposing partition as Connolly did. But
that would entail standing alongside the republicans, whom it views as
a threat.

Irish social democracy has chosen to comfort itself with its own tragedy:

the Irish are viewed as 'naturally conservative', prone to the wilder forms of nationalism, capable only of salvation in a post-1992 Europe. Connolly's politics is clearly of little relevance in this scheme of things. His originality lay precisely in avoiding the passivity that postponed class politics to a future stage of development. His positions on partition and Orangeism are simply an embarrassment. Thus while symbolic references are still made to him in social-democratic circles, the views of Conor Cruise O'Brien, who charged him with ignorance of Protestant workers, have now become the orthodoxy.[5]

Connolly, however, has far more relevance to those who regard themselves as belonging to the revolutionary camp. Here the political ambitions are reflected in the hope that Ireland may become 'a Cuba on the edge of Western Europe'. When the Irish revolutionary left was reborn after 1968, many considered that in a short time the Cuba scenario could occur as the Northern struggle 'spilled over' to engulf the South. Republicanism was also understood to have a social dynamic within it that would come to the surface when it had to confront those considered to be the real masters of the South: British imperialism. Many who wore the Connolly badges in this period described themselves as 'republican socialists' to emphasise the mixture of Marxism with native traditions. Republicanism with its base in the 'men of no property' was seen as needing only a small push to force it to the left.

Twenty years after the initial upsurge and 15 years after the republican leader Jimmy Drumm decreed 1974 the 'Year of Victory', this optimism has evaporated. Yet the illusions in republicanism have not. Sections of the left – and the republican movement itself – have increasingly come to adopt a stagist approach. The cause of right-wing dominance of Irish politics, it is now claimed, is reducible to one source: partition. The republican movement is the one force that has taken on this issue and therefore can claim the allegiance of the left. This has led to a demand that all criticism of the republican struggle should be prefaced with a declaration of loyalty to the republican family.

Connolly's own ambiguities on republicanism are clearly a major source for this brand of politics. Indeed republicans themselves have shifted increasingly from a worship of Pearse to a worship of Connolly for this very reason. But the responsibility is not entirely his. The rigid stages approach finds its direct antecedent in the Stalinist tradition. The Communist Party, as early as the 1930s, was demanding that the left limit their fight to achieving an Irish republic as the only way to win over the rank and file of Fianna Fail. During the Republican Congress debates in 1934, Robert McVicar, the leader of hundreds of Northern Protestant socialists who had marched to Connolly's grave, demanded an all-out fight for a workers' republic. Peadar O'Donnell and the Communist Party told him that 'we [the left] dare not jump through a stage in the fight by raising now the slogan of a "Workers Republic" and leaving Fianna Fail to say that they are standing for one kind of Republic and we stand for a different one.'[6] It is a tradition that has been dominant ever since.

Unfortunately, the ambiguity on republican politics has not served the Irish revolutionaries well. For almost 20 years republicanism has had the allegiance of some of the best fighters in the country. Yet it has been unable to break out of the ghettos of the North.

The problem lies in the very nature of republicanism. It is not a working class ideology despite the fact that many of its adherents are drawn from the working-class. As a set of politics it does not promote the organised power of the working class. Indeed it is extremely cynical on the potential for workers' organisation in Ireland. Its more left-wing adherents may support strike action, and even play an active role in some strikes, but this sits uncomfortably alongside an overall republican outlook which denies that the working class are a political force, capable of destroying partition by entering into a fight with both native and foreign capital in Ireland.

There are therefore only two methods open to republicans – like all other nationalist movements – to advance their cause. There is the armed struggle and there is the policy of seeking to win allies from the more nationalist wing of the establishment. There are tensions between them – but they are not contradictory.

Today's republican movement has developed considerable political sophistication – but the armed struggle has to remain central to its strategy. As Connolly once pointed out, Irish republicanism is distinguished by, and united through, its worship of the 'physical force' methods above all other tactics.[7] After the Brighton bombing in 1984, when the British Tory cabinet were attacked, the philosophy of republicanism was summed up in the claim of a spokesperson of the movement that if the bomb had been successful, the course of British history would have been changed. The armed struggle is always for republicans the 'cutting edge' of the movement.

The problem with the tactic is not just that there are inevitably counter-productive incidents which arise from the communal nature of the struggle, but that the whole tactic encourages political passivity. If 300 IRA guerrillas can change the course of, presumably, Irish history, then there is little reason to mobilise 30,000 or even 3,000. Not surprisingly today mobilisations are increasingly confined to electoral campaigns and anniversary marches. In Trotsky's words, the tactic 'belittles the role of the masses in their own consciousness'.[8]

The other element of republican strategy has been to seek alliances with other nationalists. During the H Block protests in 1981, this was first mooted by Gerry Adams, the president of Sinn Fein, when he proposed a 'United Nationalist Front' to involve Fianna Fail and the Social Democratic and Labour Party, the Catholic middle-class party in Northern Ireland. In the later anti-extradition protests, republicans concentrated on winning over the grass roots of Fianna Fail. In the New Year message from Sinn Fein in 1989, there was a call for a campaigning forum of all nationalist parties to win Irish self-determination.

One could only adopt such a strategy by being blind to the class realities of Irish society. Unfortunately, republicanism is. In his recent book, *The Politics of Irish Freedom*, Adams advanced the argument that the ruling class of the South are not drawn principally from the native ruling class but are agents of Britain.[9] At the Sinn Fein Ard Fheis in 1989 he added somewhat more graphically, that 'the only difference between Ballymurphy [Belfast] and Ballymun [Dublin] was that the Brits were more visible'. The notion here is that the Southern establishment defends partition only because it is under British influence. All other elements, from the native industrialist to the urban workers, have an interest in seeing partition and Britain's influence removed.

This is clearly nonsense. Southern capital has grown in recent years. While still weak, it has found that the Irish state has done more than enough to promote its interests. No less than 40 per cent of all state grants to industry end up in the hands of native Irish capitalists. More than half of the national debt is owed to native Irish banks and capital. The state which collaborates in maintaining partition is not run by puppets of Britain – it is there to serve the interests of native capital and its multinational allies. When it supports the border, it does so not because it is told to but in order to protect the stability of capitalist rule throughout the island.

Looking for allies in Fianna Fail or 'all nationalist parties' is not just utopian, it is a recipe for disaster. Instead of building links between the oppressed Catholic minority of the North and Southern workers, the focus is placed on alliances with the supporters of Irish capitalism. Moreover, the calls for allies in these quarters lead to one inevitable consequence: demoralisation as the calls never produce results and are invariably followed by cries of betrayal.

Here Connolly clearly took a very different road. From his earliest period he railed against the 'union of classes' and the 'broad platforms' that were so broad they could accommodate the greatest charlatans, provided only that they had some nationalist credentials or were eager to acquire them. Unfortunately, however, as we have seen, Connolly did not recognise that such strategies were inevitable within the politics of Irish republicanism. Today therefore it is necessary to look beyond Connolly for perspectives on how socialists should relate to Irish republicanism.

In Ireland, socialists should take the same starting point as Connolly did; namely, that the British presence is the source of violence and bigotry in Ireland. Its support for partition must be totally opposed. In that sense, socialists should stand alongside republicans against British imperialism.

But it is also necessary to look for a strategy that makes for victory rather than continual endurance. After 20 years the republican movement has still not managed to take the struggle out of a cul-de-sac. An alternative to republicanism *has* to be built. Connolly's view that only the working class has any real interest in seeing through the struggle against imperialism remains fundamental. However unless working class leadership of every fight against oppression is promoted through an open party it will always remain just a mere aspiration. Building that party is still the challenge facing the revolutionary movement in Ireland today.

Notes

Introduction

1. O. Dudley Edwards, *James Connolly: The Mind of an Activist* (Dublin: Gill and Macmillan, 1971) p 109.
2. D. Ryan as quoted in A. Morgan, *James Connolly: A Political Biography* (Manchester: Manchester University Press, 1988) p x.
3. A. de Blacam, *What Sinn Fein Stands For* (Dublin: Talbot Mellifont Press, 1920) pp 105–6.
4. Revd Coffey, 'James Connolly's Campaign against Capitalism in the Light of Catholic Teaching' in *The Catholic Bulletin*, 1920.
5. Revd, McKenna, SJ, *The Social Teaching of James Connolly* (Dublin: The Catholic Truth Society, 1920) p 10.
6. C. Markievicz, *James Connolly's Policy and Catholic Doctrine* (Dublin: O'Brien Collection, National Library of Ireland, no date) p 7.
7. McKenna, *Social Teaching*, pp 7–8.
8. J. Connolly, 'State Monopoly versus Socialism' in O. Dudley Edwards and Bernard Ranson (eds), *James Connolly: Selected Political Writings* (London: Jonathan Cape, 1973) p 194.
9. Edwards, *The Mind of an Activist*, pp 29–30.
10. J. Connolly, *Labour, Nationality and Religion*, in Edwards and Ransom, *James Connolly*, p 75 and p 79.
11. D. Ryan, *James Connolly: His Life, Work and Writings* (Dublin: Duffy, 1924) pp 2, 27.
12. C. Desmond Greaves, *The Life and Times of James Connolly* (London: Lawrence and Wishart, 1976).
13. T.A. Jackson, in foreword to Pat Dooley, *Under the Banner of Connolly* (Connolly Association pamphlet, no date).
14. Quoted in Irish Communist Organisation, *Press Poisoners in Ireland* (Dublin, no date) p 19.
15. Greaves, *Life and Times*, p 242.
16. C.C. O'Brien, *States of Ireland* (London: Hutchinson, 1972) pp 98–100.
17. A. Morgan, *James Connolly*.
18. P. Bew, P. Gibbon, H. Patterson, *The State in Northern Ireland* (Manchester University Press, 1979) pp 1–44.
19. Ibid, p 25.
20. *Irish Times*, 12 Dec 1987.

Chapter 1

1. R. Fox, *James Connolly: The Forerunner* (Tralee: Kingdom Press, 1946) p 16.
2. J. Braunthal, *History of the International 1864–1914* (London: Nelson, 1966) pp 200–1, 209 and 221.
3. E. Hobsbawm, *Industry and Empire* (London: Penguin, 1968) p 138.
4. J. Furbes Munro, *Africa and the International Economy 1800–1960* (London: Dent, 1976) p 64.
5. T. Cliff, 'Economic Roots of Reformism' in *Neither Washington nor Moscow* (London: Bookmarks, 1982) p 114.
6. E. Hobsbawn, *Labouring Men* (London: Weidenfeld and Nicolson, 1976) p 236.
7. J. Joll, *The Second International* (London: Weidenfeld and Nicolson, 1955) pp 51–2.
8. Quoted in A. Callincos, *Marxism and Philosophy* (Oxford: OUP, 1983) p 63.
9. *The Workers Republic*, 2 Dec 1899.
10. J. Connolly, 'Labour, Nationality and Religion' in O. Dudley Edwards and Bernard Ransom (eds), *James Connolly: Selected Political Writings* (London: Jonathan Cape, 1973) p 75.
11. K. Marx, *The Civil War in France* in Marx and Engels, Selected Works, vol 2 (Moscow: Progress, 1969) p 217.
12. Quoted in M. Salvadori, *Karl Kautsky and the Social Revolution* (London: New Left Books, 1979) p 162.
13. Ibid, p 23.
14. *The Workers Republic*, 4 Nov 1899.
15. For material on Connolly's early activity in Edinburgh, see Bernard Ransom, 'James Connolly and the Scottish Left' (unpublished PhD thesis, Edinburgh, 1975) and Greaves, *Life and Times*.
16. Y. Kapp, *Eleanor Marx: The Crowded Years 1884–1898* (London: Virago, 1979) p 61.
17. Ibid, p 197.
18. Henry Collins, 'The Marxism of the SDF' in Asa Briggs, *Essays in Labour History* (London: Macmillan, 1971) p 55.
19. See L. Trotsky, *Writings on Britain,* vol I (London: New Park, 1974) pp 13–28.
20. D. Gluckstein, 'Keir Hardie – The Man Who Made the Labour Party' in *International Socialism*, No 32 (1984) p 53.
21. Ibid, p 60.
22. Ransom, *Connolly and Scottish Left*, p 6.
23. Connolly to Hardie, 8 June 1894, 19 June 1894, 3 July 1894 in William O'Brien Collection, National Library of Ireland (NLI) MS 13933.
24. H. Pelling, *The Origins of the Labour Party* (London: Macmillan, 1954) p 108.
25. J. Leslie, *The Irish Question* (Cork Workers Club, 1986) p 4.
26. Ibid, pp 12–13.
27. Greaves, *Life and Times*, p 57.
28. Ibid, p 61.

29. Ibid, p 59.
30. Ibid, p 63.
31. Ransom, *Connolly and Scottish Left*, p 32.
32. Matheson to Connolly, 7 July 1904, O'Brien Papers, National Library of Ireland (NLI), MS 13906.
33. *Labour Leader*, 15 Feb 1896.

Chapter 2

1. Greaves, *The Life and Times*, p 74.
2. M. Daly, *Dublin: The Deposed Capital* (Cork University Press, 1984) p 276.
3. Quoted ibid, p 267.
4. Ibid, p 18.
5. Ibid, p 59.
6. A. Mitchell, *Labour and Irish Politics* (Dublin: Irish University Press, 1985) p 16–17.
7. Daly, *Dublin*, p 71.
8. Quoted in D. Howell, *A Lost Left: Three Studies in Socialism and Nationalism* (Manchester University Press, 1986) p 43.
9. S. Levenson, *James Connolly, Socialist, Patriot and Martyr* (London: Quartet, 1977) p 47.
10. Greaves, *Life and Times*, p 75.
11. See ISRP Minutes Books, National Library of Ireland, MS 16264–67.
12. Ibid.
13. ISRP 'Programme', in D. Ryan (ed), *Socialism and Nationalism* (Dublin: Three Candles, 1948) pp 184–6.
14. Ibid, p 185.
15. Ibid, p 184.
16. Ibid, p 185.
17. Ibid, p 186.
18. *Workers Republic*, 27 Aug 1898.
19. Ibid, 8 Oct 1898.
20. Ibid, 19 Aug 1899.
21. Ibid, 16 Sept 1899.
22. See Howell, *A Lost Left*, pp 42–53.
23. *Workers Republic*, Feb 1901.
24. Levenson, *James Connolly*, p 98.
25. *Workers Republic*, 3 June 1899.
26. Ibid, 28 July 1900.
27. Ibid 28 July 1900.
28. Ibid 1 July 1899.
29. Connolly to Matheson, 9 March 1903, NLI, MS 13906.
30. *Workers Republic*, May 1903.
31. J. Lee, *The Modernisation of Ireland: 1848–1918* (Dublin: Gill and Macmillan, 1973) p 3.
32. P. Bew, *Land and the National Question* (Dublin: Gill and Macmillan, 1978) pp 142–3.
33. A. Morgan, *James Connolly*, p 30.

34. *Workers Republic*, 9 Sept 1899.
35. Ibid, 23 Sept 1899.
36. Ibid, May 1903.
37. Ibid, 24 Sept 1898.
38. Maud Gonne McBride, *A Servant of the Queen* (London: Gollancz, 1974) p 227.
39. *Workers Republic*, 24 Sept 1898.
40. Ryan, *The Workers Republic*, p 36.
41. R. Kee, *The Green Flag* (London: Weidenfeld and Nicolson, 1972) p 431.
42. Ibid, p 429.
43. *Workers Republic*, 1 Oct 1898.
44. Ibid.
45. *Workers Republic*, 10 Nov 1900.
46. Ryan, *Socialism and Nationalism*, p 62.
47. Ibid, p 62.
48. O'Lehane to Lyng, 29 Oct 1901, NLI, MS 15700.
49. Lee, *Modernisation*, p 11.
50. Ibid, p 17.
51. E. Strauss, *Irish Nationalism and British Democracy*, (London: Methuen, 1951) p 210.
52. T. Garvin, *The Evolution of Nationalist Politics* (Dublin: Gill and Macmillan, 1981) p 96.
53. *Workers Republic*, May 1899.
54. O'Lehane to Hogan, 5 Feb 1904, NLI, MS 15700.
55. *The Harp*, April 1909.
56. *Workers Republic*, 17 June 1899.
57. Quoted in J. Newsinger, 'As Catholic as the Pope: James Connolly and the Roman Catholic Church in Ireland', in *Saothar*, vol 1 (1986) p 8.
58. *Workers Republic*, 17 June 1899.
59. Ibid.
60. D. Ryan (ed), *The Workers Republic* (Dublin: Three Candles, 1951) pp 57–8.
61. G. Salvemini, *The French Revolution 1788–1792*, (London: Jonathan Cape, 1965) p 61.
62. Ryan, *The Workers Republic*, p 59.
63. Ibid, p 57.
64. *Workers Republic*, 17 June 1899.
65. ISRP Minutes, 6 Feb 1899.
66. Ibid, 13 March 1899.
67. Ibid, 2 Jan 1899.
68. O. Dudley Edwards and B. Ransom (eds), *James Connolly: Selected Political Writings* (London: Jonathan Cape, 1973) pp 136–7.
69. R. Luxemburg, 'Socialism and the Churches' in *Rosa Luxemburg Speaks* (New York: Pathfinder, 1970) p 132.
70. Ibid, p 152.

Chapter 3

1. F. Engels, 'Letters from London', in K. Marx and F. Engels *Ireland and the Irish Question* (Moscow: Progress, 1971) pp 306–8.
2. Marx to Meyer and Vogt, 2 April 1870, in K. Marx and F. Engels, *Ireland*, p 294.
3. Ibid, p 293.
4. Ibid, p 293–4.
5. Engels to Marx, 29 Nov 1867 in Marx and Engels, *Ireland*, p 145.
6. Quoted in I. Cummins, *Marx, Engels and National Movements* (London: Croom Helm, 1980) p 117.
7. ISRP Programme in D. Ryan (ed), *Socialism and Nationalism* (Dublin: Three Candles, 1948) p 186.
8. H.B. Davis, *Nationalism and Socialism* (New York: Monthly Review Press, 1967) p 130.
9. J. Riddell (ed), *Lenin's Struggle for a Revolutionary International: Documents 1907–1916* (New York: Monad, 1984) p 12.
10. *Workers Republic*, Oct 1901.
11. See J. Gray, *City in Revolt* (Belfast: Blackstaff, 1985) p 33; also J. Boyle, *The Irish Labour Movement in the 19th Century* (Washington: Catholic University of America Press, 1988) pp 182–91.
12. S. Cronin, *Young Connolly* (Dublin: Repsol, 1978) p 30.
13. J.F. Lalor, *The Rights of Ireland and The Faith of a Felon*, with introduction by James Connolly, National Library of Ireland, William O'Brien Collection, p 10.
14. Ibid, p 9.
15. J. Connolly, Introduction to Lalor, *The Rights of Ireland*, p 2.
16. Ryan, *Socialism and Nationalism*, p 33.
17. Ibid, p 12.
18. J. Connolly, *Erin's Hope and the New Evangel* (Dublin: New Books, 1972) p 6.
19. Ibid, p 6.
20. Ibid, p 7.
21. Ibid, pp 6–7.
22. Ibid, p 7.
23. Ibid, p 9.
24. Ibid, p 8.
25. *Workers Republic*, 13 Aug 1898.
26. Connolly, *Erin's Hope*, pp 12–13.
27. K. Simms, 'Warfare in Medieval Gaelic Lordships' in *Irish Sword*, XII, 47 (1976) pp 99–100.
28. M. O'Dowd, 'Gaelic Economy and Society' in C. Brady and R. Gillespie (eds) *Natives and Newcomers* (Dublin: Irish Academy Press, 1986) pp 125–6.
29. K. Nicholls, *Gaelic and Gaelicised Ireland* (Dublin: Gill and Macmillan, 1972) p 71.
30. G. MacNicholl, *Ireland before the Vikings* (Dublin: Gill and Macmillan, 1972) p 67.
31. R.D. Edwards, *Ireland in the Age of the Tudors* (London: Croom Helm, 1977) p 17.

32. T. Garvin, *The Evolution of Nationalist Politics*, (Dublin: Gill and Macmillan, 1981) p 106.

33. J. Connolly in O. Dudley Edwards and B. Ransom (eds) *James Connolly: Selected Writings* (London: Jonathan Cape, 1973) p 171.

34. Ryan, *Socialism and Nationalism*, p 22.

35. Edwards and Ransom, *Selected Writings*, pp 169–70.

36. Ibid, p 169.

37. Ryan, *Socialism and Nationalism*, p 31.

38. Ibid, p 23.

39. *Workers Republic*, 20 August 1898.

40. Ryan, *Socialism and Nationalism*, p 29.

41. Ibid, p 24.

42. S. Levenson, *James Connolly: Socialist, Patriot and Martyr* (London: Quartet, 1977) p 51.

43. *Workers Republic*, 12 Aug 1899.

44. *Workers Republic*, 13 Aug 1898.

45. Maud Gonne McBride, *Servant of the Queen* (London: Gollancz, 1974) p 281.

46. *Workers Republic*, 13 Aug 1898.

47. Levenson, *James Connolly*, p 56.

48. *Workers Republic*, 3 Sept 1898.

49. *Workers Republic*, 20 Aug 1898.

50. *Workers Republic*, 5 Aug 1899.

51. Ibid.

52. Quoted in Cronin, *Young Connolly*, p 55.

53. *Workers Republic*, 18 Nov 1899.

54. *Workers Republic*, 16 Dec 1899.

55. Ryan, *Socialism and Nationalism*, p 55.

56. Ibid, p 54.

57. Ryan, *Socialism and Nationalism*, p 56.

58. *Workers Republic*, 2 Sept 1899.

59. M. O'Riordan, 'Connolly Socialism and the Jewish Worker' in *Saothar*, no 13 (1988).

60. R. Kee, *The Green Flag* (London: Weidenfeld and Nicolson, 1972) p 442.

61. *Workers Republic*, 16 Sept 1899.

62. *Workers Republic*, 23 June 1900.

63. *Workers Republic*, 15 Dec 1900.

64. *Workers Republic*, March 1902.

65. R. Crotty, *Ireland in Crisis: A Study in Capitalist Colonial Underdevelopment* (Dingle: Brandon, 1986) p 42.

66. Ibid, p 48.

67. E. Strauss, *Irish Nationalism and British Democracy*, (London: Methuen, 1951) p 201–2.

68. W.B. Yeats, 'September 1913' in *Collected Poems* (London: Macmillan, 1982) p 120.

69. P. Bew, *C.S. Parnell* (Dublin: Gill and Macmillan, 1980) p 125.

70. Strauss, *Irish Nationalism*, p 220.

Chapter 4

1. D. Herreshoff, *The Origins of American Marxism* (New York: Monad, 1973) p 145.
2. R. Challinor, *The Origins of British Bolshevism* (London: Croom Helm, 1977) pp 14–15.
3. Ibid, p 16.
4. *SLP Platform, Constitution and Rules*, O'Brien Collection, NLI, MS LO p 89, p 4.
5. Ibid, p 6.
6. Ibid, p 3.
7. Quoted in Irish Communist Organisation, *Connolly in America* (Dublin: ICO Books, 1971) p 9.
8. Ibid, p 8.
9. D. De Leon, *Reform or Revolution* (New York: Labor News, no date) p 3.
10. Ibid, p 11.
11. I. Kipnis, *The American Socialist Movement* (New York: Monthly Review, 1972) p 16.
12. Cork Workers Club, *The Connolly De Leon Controversy* (Cork: CWC, 1986) p 7.
13. Ibid, p 13.
14. See K. Marx, 'The Critique of the Gotha Programme' in Karl Marx and Frederick Engels, *Selected Works,* vol 3 (Moscow: Progress, 1977) pp 22–4.
15. K. Marx, 'Wages, Price and Profit' in Karl Marx and Frederick Engels *Selected Works,* vol 2 (Moscow: Progress, 1977) pp 71–2.
16. Cork Workers Club, *Connolly De Leon,* p 27.
17. Ibid, p 29.
18. I. Kipnis, *American Socialist,* p 18.
19. Cork Workers Club, *Connolly De Leon,* p 29.
20. Ibid, p 8.
21. Ibid, p 31.
22. Ibid, p 18.
23. Ibid, p 8.
24. J. Connolly, *Labour, Nationality and Religion* in O. Dudley Edwards and Bernard Ranson (eds) *James Connolly: Selected Political Writings* (London: Jonathan Cape, 1973) p 101.
25. Matheson to Connolly, 9 Dec 1905.
26. Greaves, *The Life and Times,* p 331.
27. Cork Workers Club, *Connolly De Leon,* p 9.
28. S. Levenson, *James Connolly: Socialist, Patriot and Martyr* (London: Quartet, 1977) p 113.
29. Herreshoff, *The Origins,* p 143.
30. Ibid, p 136.
31. Ibid, p 145.
32. Connolly to Matheson, 19 Nov 1905.
33. M. Dubosky, *We Shall be All* (Chicago: Quadrangle, 1969) p 76.
34. P.S. Foner, *The Industrial Workers of the World 1905–1917* vol 4 of *History*

of Labor Movement in the United States (New York: International Publishers, 1980) p 36.

35. Ibid, p 123.
36. Ibid, p 124.
37. Ibid, pp 127–8.
38. Ibid, p 136.
39. Kipnis, *American Socialist*, p 120.
40. Ibid, p 112.
41. J. Connolly, *Socialism Made Easy* (Dublin: Plough Books, 1971) p 36.
42. Ibid, p 38 and pp 40–1.
43. Ibid, p 40.
44. D. Ryan, ed, *The Workers Republic* (Dublin: Three Candles, 1951) p 67.
45. Connolly, *Socialism Made Easy*, p 45.
46. Ibid, p 39.
47. Ibid, p 40.
48. Ibid, p 46.
49. Ibid, p 46.
50. Ibid, p 47.
51. A. Gramsci, *Selections from Political Writings 1910–1920* (London: Lawrence and Wishart, 1977) p 264.
52. Ibid, p 264.
53. T. Cliff, *Class Struggle and Women's Liberation* (London: Bookmarks, 1984) p 59.
54. E. Gurley Flynn, *Rebel Girl* (New York: International Publishers, 1976) p 150.
55. Cliff, *Class Struggle*, p 59.
56. Herreshoff, *The Origins*, p 148.
57. Connolly to Matheson, 19 Nov 1905.
58. Ibid.
59. Greaves, *Life and Times*, p 192.
60. Connolly to Matheson, 10 June 1906.
61. Connolly to Matheson, April 1907.
62. Connolly to Matheson, 27 Sept 1907.
63. Connolly to Matheson, March 1908.
64. Ibid.
65. Connolly to Matheson, March 1908.
66. Edwards and Ransom (eds), *James Connolly*, p 289.
67. Connolly to Matheson, April 1908.
68. Connolly to Matheson, 7 May 1908.
69. Connolly to Matheson, 27 Sept 1907.
70. Foner, vol 4, p 100.
71. C. Reeve and A.B. Reeve, *James Connolly and the United States* (New Jersey, Atlantic Highlands: Humanities Press, 1978) p 154.
72. Connolly, *Socialism Made Easy*, p 36.
73. Ibid, p 47.
74. *The Harp*, Jan 1908.
75. Kipnis, *American Socialist*, p 130.
76. J. Riddell, *Lenin's Struggle for a Revolutionary International* (New York: Monad, 1984) p 17.

77. Reeve and Reeve, *James Connolly*, p 103.
78. *The Harp*, Jan 1908.
79. Ibid.
80. *The Harp*, May 1908.
81. *The Harp*, Jan 1910.
82. *The Harp*, Jan 1909.

Chapter 5

1. J. Connolly, *Labour and Irish History* (London: Bookmarks, 1987) p 26.
2. P. Bew, *Land and the National Question* (Dublin: Gill and Macmillan, 1978) p 48.
3. Connolly, *Labour*, p 28.
4. Ibid, p 27.
5. Ibid, p 34.
6. Ibid, p 61.
7. Ibid, p 125.
8. Ibid, p 134.
9. Ibid, p 23.
10. Ibid, p 24.
11. Ibid, p 22.
12. Ibid, p 27.
13. *Workers Republic*, 7 Oct 1899.
14. Connolly, *Labour*, p 158.
15. Ibid, p 21.
16. Ibid, p 27.
17. L.M. Cullen, *Anglo-Irish Trade* (Manchester: Manchester University Press, 1968) p 46.
18. D. Dickson, *New Foundations: Ireland 1660–1800* (Dublin: Helicon, 1987) p 121.
19. R. Foster, *Modern Ireland 1600–1972* (London: Allen Lane, 1988) pp 253–4.
20. Dickson, *New Foundations*, p 176.
21. Ibid, p 164.
22. Connolly, *Labour*, p 78.
23. Ibid, p 79.
24. Ibid.
25. F. McDermott, *Theobald Wolfe Tone* (London: Macmillan, 1939) p 86.
26. Ibid, p 70.
27. G. O'Tuathaigh, *Ireland before the Famine* (Dublin: Gill and Macmillan, 1982) pp 11–12.
28. M. Elliot, *Partners in Revolution* (New Haven: Yale University Press, 1982) p 28.
29. Ibid, p 28.
30. P. MacAonghusa and L. Keegan eds, *The Best of Wolfe Tone* (Cork: Mercier, 1972) p 123.
31. Ibid, pp 123–4.
32. W. Tone, *An Argument on Behalf of Catholics* (Belfast: ICO Books, 1973) p 22.

33. Connolly, *Labour*, p 149.
34. J.F. Lalor, *The Rights of Ireland and The Faith of a Felon* (NLI, William O'Brien Collection) p 9.
35. Ibid, p 10.
36. Quoted in B. Purdie, 'Reconsiderations on Republicanism and Socialism' in Austen Morgan and Bob Purdie, eds, *Ireland: Divided Nation, Divided Class* (London: Inklinks, 1980) pp 87–8.
37. Connolly, *Labour*, p 144.
38. *Labour Leader*, 26 March 1898.
39. Connolly, *Labour*, p 30.
40. Ibid, p 158.
41. K. Marx, 'Preface to a Critique of Political Economy' in Karl Marx and Frederick Engels, *Selected Works,* vol 1 (Moscow: Progress, 1977) p 504.
42. K. Marx, 'The Address to the Central Committee of the Communist League' in Karl Marx, *The Revolutions of 1848* (London: Penguin, 1973) pp 323–4.
43. L. Trotsky, *The Permanent Revolution* (London: New Park, 1982) pp 161–254.

Chapter 6

1. Connolly to O'Brien, 24 May 1909, MS 13908, NLI, Dublin.
2. Cork Workers Club, *Sinn Fein and Socialism* (Cork: CWC, no date) p 26.
3. F.S.L. Lyons, *Ireland since the Famine* (London: Collins, 1982) p 257.
4. *Irish Worker*, 9 Sept 1911.
5. *The Harp*, June 1908.
6. *The Peasant*, 31 Aug 1907.
7. R. Davis, *Griffith and Non-Violent Sinn Fein* (Dublin: Anvil Books, 1974) p 137.
8. *The Harp*, March 1908.
9. Ibid.
10. *The Harp*, April 1908.
11. *Irish Nation*, 23 Jan 1909.
12. Ibid.
13. Matheson to Connolly, 8 April 1908, MS 13906, NLI, Dublin.
14. Matheson to Connolly, 27 April 1908, MS 13906, NLI, Dublin.
15. Connolly to Matheson, 7 May 1908, MS 13906, NLI, Dublin.
16. Connolly to O'Brien, undated MS 13939, NLI, Dublin.
17. Ibid.
18. Ibid
19. G. Dangerfield, *The Strange Death of Liberal England* (London: Paladin, 1983) p 100.
20. Ibid, p 119.
21. V. Lenin, *The Irish Question* (Dublin: Repsol, no date) p 13.
22. D. Ryan, ed, *Socialism and Nationalism* (Dublin: Three Candles 1948) p 75.
23. Ibid.

24. Ibid, p 76.
25. Cork Workers Club, ed, *Ireland upon the Dissecting Table* (Cork: CWC, 1983) p 21.
26. D. Ryan, ed, *The Workers Republic* (Dublin: Three Candles, 1951) p 96.
27. *Irish Worker*, 2 Sept 1911.
28. *Forward*, 14 Jan 1911.
29. *Forward*, 25 Jan 1913.
30. *Irish Worker*, 30 Sept 1911.
31. *Irish Worker*, 16 Sep 1911.
32. William McMullen, Introduction to D. Ryan (ed), *The Workers Republic*, p 5.
33. *Forward*, 23 Aug 1913.
34. *Forward*, 27 May 1911.
35. Ibid.
36. *The Harp*, Nov 1909.
37. Greaves, *The Life and Times*, p 249.
38. Minutes of the SPI Conference, MS 15674(1), NLI, Dublin.
39. Connolly, to O'Brien, 12 Sept 1909 MS 13908, NLI, Dublin.
40. SPI Manifesto in D. Ryan, ed, *Socialism and Nationalism*, p 190.
41. Ibid, p 191.
42. SPI Minutes, MS 16270, NLI, Dublin.
43. SPI Minutes, 13 Jan 1910.
44. Connolly to O'Brien, 24 May 1911.
45. SPI Minutes, 18 February 1911.
46. Connolly to O'Brien, 24 May 1911.
47. SPI Minutes, 27 June 1911.
48. *Forward*, 27 May 1911.
49. John Gray, *City in Revolt* (Belfast: Blackstaff Press, 1985) p 27.
50. Ibid, p 37.
51. *Forward*, 1 July 1911.
52. Connolly to O'Brien, 7 Dec 1911.
53. *Irish Worker*, 20 April 1912.
54. *Irish Nation*, 23 Jan 1909.
55. McMullen, Introduction to D. Ryan (ed), *The Workers Republic*, p 25.
56. Irish Trade Union Congress Report (1913), p 34.
57. ITUC Report (1914), p 43.
58. *Forward*, 16 Aug 1913.
59. J. Connolly, *The Re-Conquest of Ireland* (Dublin: New Books, 1972) p 61.
60. Ibid, p 62.
61. Ibid, pp 64–5.
62. Ibid, p 18.
63. ITUC Report (1914), p 6.
64. *Irish Worker*, 6 July 1912.
65. A.T.Q. Stewart, *The Ulster Crisis* (London: Faber, 1967) p 48.
66. Ibid, p 55.
67. *Forward*, 2 Aug 1913.
68. Ibid.

69. *Forward*, 10 May 1911.
70. *Forward*, 9 Aug 1913.
71. *Forward*, 9 Aug 1913.
72. *Forward*, 12 July 1913.
73. Neille Gordon Reminiscences, W. O'Brien Collection, NLI, Dublin, MS 13096.
74. *Forward*, 18 March 1911.
75. *Forward*, 11 March 1911.
76. *Forward*, 3 May 1913.
77. *Forward*, 7 June 1913.
78. *Forward*, 28 June 1913.
79. *Forward*, 3 May 1913.
80. B. Holton, *British Syndicalism 1900–1914* (London: Pluto, 1976) p 96.
81. Lenin, *The Irish Question*, p 4.
82. D. Nevin, *Jim Larkin and the Dublin Lockout* (Dublin: Irish Printers, 1964) p 41.
83. A. Wright, *Disturbed Dublin*, (London: Longman and Green, 1914) p 105.
84. Edwards and Ransom, *James Connolly*, p 313.
85. *Irish Worker*, 2 Aug 1913.
86. Holton, *British Syndicalism*, p 191.
87. R. Fox, *The History of the Citizen Army* (Dublin: Duffy, 1945) p 10.
88. Holton, *British Syndicalism*, p 194.
89. A. Morgan, *James Connolly: A Political Biography* (Manchester: Manchester University Press, 1988) p 120.
90. C.D. Greaves, *The ITGWU: The Formative Years* (Dublin: Gill and Macmillan, 1982) p 102.
91. *Irish Worker*, 29 Nov 1913.
92. F.X. Martin, *The Irish Volunteers* (Dublin: Duffy, 1963) p 108.
93. *Irish Worker*, 29 Nov 1913.
94. Ibid.
95. *Forward*, 7 Feb 1914.
96. Ibid.
97. *Forward*, 7 Feb 1914.
98. Edwards and Ransom, *James Connolly*, p 323.
99. Ibid, p 315.
100. Lyons, *Ireland*, p 306.
101. *Forward*, 30 May 1914.
102. *Irish Worker*, 14 March 1914.
103. *Irish Worker*, 4 April 1914.
104. *Forward*, 21 March 1914.
105. Ryan (ed), *Socialism and Nationalism*, p 124.
106. ITUC Report (1914), p 70.

Chapter 7

1. *Forward*, 22 Aug 1914.
2. *Irish Worker*, 22 Aug 1914.
3. A. Gaughan, *Tom Johnson: First Leader of the Labour Party* (Dublin: Kingdom Books, 1980) p 43.

4. Connolly to O'Brien, 22 Aug 1914, MS 13908, NLI, Dublin.
5. W. Kendal, *The Revolutionary Movement in Britain* (London: Weidenfeld and Nicolson, 1969) p 111.
6. *Irish Worker*, 5 Sept 1914.
7. *Workers Republic*, 15 April 1916.
8. 'Basel Manifesto of Second International' in J. Riddell, (ed), *Lenin's Struggle for a Revolutionary International* (New York: Monad, 1984) p 88.
9. *Forward*, 15 Aug 1914.
10. Ibid.
11. O. Dudley Edwards and B. Ransom, (eds), *James Connolly: Selected Political Writings* (London: Jonathan Cape, 1973) p 336.
12. *Forward*, 22 Aug 1914.
13. *The Worker*, 30 Jan 1915.
14. Ibid.
15. *Irish Worker*, 8 Aug 1914.
16. V. Lenin, *Collected Works,* vol 21 (Moscow: Progress, 1964) p 354.
17. *Irish Worker*, 29 Aug 1914.
18. *Workers Republic*, 18 March 1916.
19. Edwards and Ransom, *James Connolly,* p 339.
20. Ibid.
21. *Forward*, 15 Aug 1914.
22. Ibid.
23. Riddell (ed), *Lenin's Struggle,* p 23.
24. *Forward*, 22 August 1914.
25. Ibid.
26. A. Mitchell, *Labour in Irish Politics* (Dublin: Irish University Press, 1974) p 64.
27. *Workers Republic*, 5 Feb 1916.
28. *Workers Republic*, 3 July 1915.

Chapter 8

1. *Irish Worker*, 8 Aug 1914.
2. Ibid.
3. F.S.L. Lyons, *John Dillon* (London: Routledge and Kegan Paul, 1968) p 359, pp 363–4
4. F.S.L. Lyons, *Ireland Since the Famine* (London: Collins, 1982) p 329.
5. *Irish Worker*, 15 Aug 1914.
6. *Sinn Fein*, 17 Nov 1914.
7. Connolly to O'Brien, 6 Oct 1914, MS 13908, NLI, Dublin.
8. *Irish Worker*, 17 Oct 1914.
9. Ibid.
10. C.D. Greaves, *Life and Times of James Connolly* (London: Lawrence and Wishart, 1976) p 365.
11. Ibid, p 369.
12. *Workers Republic*, 10 July 1915.
13. *Workers Republic*, 13 Nov 1915.
14. *Workers Republic*, 25 Dec 1915.

15. *Workers Republic*, 4 Dec 1915.
16. F. Robbins, *Under the Starry Plough* (Dublin: Academy Press, 1977) p 43.
17. B. McGiolla Choille, *Intelligence Notes* (Dublin: Government Publications, 1966) p 221.
18. *Workers Republic*, 23 Oct 1915.
19. C.D. Greaves, *The Irish Transport and General Workers Union*, (Dublin: Gill and Macmillan, 1982) p 155.
20. *Workers Republic*, 12 June 1915.
21. *Workers Republic*, 14 Aug 1915.
22. *Workers Republic*, 5 June 1915.
23. A. Morgan, *James Connolly: A Political Biography* (Manchester: Manchester University Press, 1988) p 139.
24. *Workers Republic*, 15 April 1916.
25. McGiolla Choille, *Intelligence Notes*, p 226.
26. Ibid, p 224.
27. *Workers Republic*, 27 Nov 1915.
28. *Workers Republic*, 13 Nov 1915.
29. Ibid.
30. *Workers Republic*, 27 Nov 1915.
31. Ibid.
32. D. Ryan, *Socialism and Nationalism* (Dublin: Three Candles, 1948) p 33.
33. *Workers Republic*, 22 Jan 1916.
34. *Workers Republic*, 20 Nov 1915.
35. Greaves, *Life and Times*, p 392.
36. *Workers Republic*, 13 Nov 1915.
37. Greaves, *Life and Times*, p 392.
38. *Workers Republic*, 29 January 1916.
39. William O'Brien, Introduction to D. Ryan (ed), *Labour and Easter Week* (Dublin: Three Candles, 1966) p 10.
40. *Workers Republic*, 7 Aug 1915.
41. *Workers Republic*, 8 Jan 1916.
42. *Workers Republic*, 4 Dec 1915.
43. *Workers Republic*, 18 March 1916.
44. *Workers Republic*, 29 Jan 1916.
45. *Workers Republic*, 24 July 1915.
46. *Workers Republic*, 31 July 1915.
47. *Workers Republic*, 11 March 1916.
48. *Workers Republic*, 25 March 1916.
49. *Workers Republic*, 9 Oct 1915.
50. *Workers Republic*, 27 Nov 1915.
51. *Workers Republic*, 6 Nov 1915.
52. *Workers Republic*, 13 Sept 1913.
53. *Workers Republic*, 4 Dec 1915.
54. D. Ryan, *James Connolly: His Life, Work and Writings* (Dublin: Duffy, 1924) p 105.
55. Greaves, *Life and Times*, p 403.
56. J. Newsinger, 'Jim Larkin, Syndicalism and the 1913 Dublin Lockout'

in *International Socialism Journal*, no 25 (1984) p 61.
57. *Workers Republic*, 5 Feb 1915.
58. Ryan, *James Connolly*, p 91.
59. C. Reeve and A.B. Reeve, *James Connolly in the United States* (New Jersey, Atlantic Highlands: Humanities Press, 1978) p 274.
60. William O'Brien, Introduction to D. Ryan (ed), *Labour and Easter Week*, p 16.
61. Ibid, p 21.
62. A. Mitchell and P. O'Snodaigh, *Irish Political Documents 1916–1919* (Dublin: Irish Academy Press, 1985) p 25.
63. Ibid, p 21.
64. Ibid, p 26.
65. *Forward*, 6 May 1916.
66. Irish Communist Organisation, *The Marxism of James Connolly* (Dublin: ICO Books, undated) p 26.
67. J. Riddell, *Lenin's Struggle for a Revolutionary International* (New York: Monad, 1984) pp 374–5.
68. Ibid, pp 372–4.
69. Ibid, p 377.
70. Ibid, p 377.
71. Ibid, p 366
72. Ibid, p 365.
73. Ibid, p 378.
74. Ibid, p 378.
75. Ibid, p 377.
76. Morgan, *James Connolly*, p 199.
77. Ibid, p 45.
78. Ibid, p 45.
79. Ibid, p 182.
80. Greaves, *The Life and Times*, p 428.

Chapter 9

1. D. Mahon, *Republicans and Imperialists: Anglo-Irish Relations in the 1930s*, (New Haven: Yale University Press, 1984) p 1.
2. E. O'Connor, *Syndicalism in Ireland* (Cork: Cork University Press, 1988) p 51.
3. P. O'Donnell, *There will be Another Day*, (Dublin: Dolmen Press, 1963) p 14.
4. Irish Trade Union Congress Report (1916), p 7.
5. ITUC Report (1916), p 12.
6. A. Mitchell and P. O'Snodaigh, *Irish Political Documents 1916–1949* (Dublin: Irish Academy Press, 1985) p 42.
7. Ibid, p 52.
8. P. O'Donnell, *Another Day*, p 17.
9. Report of SPI to Third International, MS 15674(1), NLI, Dublin.
10. P. Lynch, 'The Social Revolution that Never Was' in T. Desmond Williams (ed), *The Irish Struggle 1916–1966* (London: Routledge and Kegan Paul, 1966) pp 41–54.

11. A. Mitchell, *Labour in Irish Politics* (Dublin: Irish University Press, 1974) p 110.
12. Ibid, pp 106–7.
13. Ibid, p 81.
14. D. O'Connor Lysaght, 'The Rake's Progress: The Political Career of William O'Brien' in *Saothar*, no 9 (1983) pp 48–62.
15. ITUC Report (1919), p 86.
16. Mitchell, *Labour*, p 146.
17. E. O'Connor, 'Agrarian Unrest and the Labour Movement in Co. Waterford' in *Saothar*, no 6 (1980) pp 40–58
18. O'Connor, *Syndicalism*, p 147.
19. Ibid, p 109.
20. SPI Report, MS 15674(1), NLI, Dublin.
21. R. Fox, *The History of the Irish Citizen Army* (Dublin: Duffy, 1944) p 218.
22. M. Milotte, *Communism in Modern Ireland* (Dublin: Gill and Macmillan, 1984) p 55.
23. R. Connolly, 'The Republican Struggle in Ireland' in *Communist International* (1922) p 60.
24. J. Degras, *The Communist International 1919–43,* vol 1 (Oxford: OUP, 1956) p 143.

Chapter 10

1. J. Connolly, *The New Evangel* (Dublin: New Books, 1972) pp 27–8.
2. B. Ransom, *Connolly's Marxism* (London: Pluto Press, 1980) pp 98–9.
3. J. Connolly, *The Re-Conquest of Ireland* (Dublin: New Books, 1972) p 45.
4. Connolly to O'Brien, 24 May 1911, MS 13908, NLI, Dublin.
5. C.C. O'Brien, *States of Ireland* (London: Hutchinson, 1972) pp 89–100.
6. Republican Congress, 13 Oct 1934.
7. *Workers Republic*, 22 July 1899.
8. L. Trotsky, *Against Individual Terrorism* (New York: Pathfinder, 1987) p 7.
9. G. Adams, *The Politics of Irish Freedom* (Dingle: Brandon, 1986) p 91.

Bibliography

Connolly's Writings

Most of Connolly's writings are found in newspapers, pamphlets and a number
of collections of his work. His principal works are:
Erin's Hope: The End and Means and *The New Evangel*
(Dublin: New Books, 1972).
Socialism Made Easy (Dublin: Plough Books, 1971).
Labour, Nationality and Religion (Dublin: New Books, 1972).
Labour in Irish History (London: Bookmarks, 1987).
The Re-Conquest of Ireland (Dublin: New Books, 1972).

Other articles by Connolly can be found in the following collections: Cork
Workers Club, *The Connolly–De Leon Controversy on Wages, Marriage and
the Church* (Cork: CWC, 1976).
Cork Workers Club, *The Connolly–Walker Controversy on Socialist Unity in
Ireland* (Cork: CWC, 1974).
Cork Workers Club, *Ireland upon the Dissecting Table: James Connolly on Ulster
and Partition*, (Cork: CWC, 1975).
D. Ryan (ed), *Socialism and Nationalism* (Dublin: Three Candles, 1948).
D. Ryan (ed), *Labour and Easter Week* (Dublin: Three Candles, 1949).
D. Ryan (ed), *The Workers Republic* (Dublin: Three Candles, 1951).
P. Berresford Ellis (ed), *James Connolly: Selected Writings*, (Harmondsworth:
Penguin, 1973).
O.D. Edwards and B. Ransom (eds), *James Connolly: Selected Political Writings*
(London: Jonathan Cape 1973).

Other Books, Articles, Pamphlets

G. Adams, *The Politics of Irish Freedom* (Dingle: Brandon, 1986).
B. Anderson, *Imagined Communities: Reflections on the Origins and Spread of
Nationalism* (London: Verso, 1983).
P. Bew, *Land and the National Question* (Dublin: Gill and Macmillan, 1973).
P. Bew, P. Gibbon, H. Patterson, *The State in Northern Ireland* (Manchester:
Manchester University Press, 1979).

P. Bew, *C.S. Parnell* (Dublin: Gill and Macmillan, 1980).

G. Boyce, *Nationalism in Ireland* (London: Croom Helm, 1982).

J. Boyle, *Leaders and Workers* (Cork: Mercier, 1978).

J. Boyle, *The Irish Labour Movement in the 19th Century* (Washington: Catholic University of America Press, 1988).

C. Brady and R. Gillespie (eds), *Natives and Newcomers* (Dublin: Irish Academy Press, 1986).

J. Braunthal, *History of the International 1864–1914* (London: Nelson, 1966).

A. Callincos, *Marxism and Philosophy* (Oxford: OUP, 1983).

R. Challinor, *The Origins of British Bolshevism* (London: Croom Helm, 1977).

J. D. Clarkson, *Labour and Nationalism in Ireland* (New York: Columbia University Press, 1925).

T. Cliff, 'The Economic Roots of Reformism' in *Neither Washington nor Moscow* (London: Bookmarks, 1982).

T. Cliff, *Class Struggle and Women's Liberation* (London: Bookmarks, 1984).

Rev. Coffey, 'James Connolly's Campaign against Capitalism in the Light of Catholic Teaching' in *The Catholic Bulletin* (1920).

H. Collins, 'The Marxism of the SDF' in Asa Briggs, *Essays in Labour History* (London: Macmillan, 1971).

N. Connolly O'Brien, *James Connolly: Portrait of a Rebel Father* (Dublin: Four Masters, 1975).

R. Connolly, 'The Republican Struggle in Ireland' in *Communist International* (1922) Special Congress Issue.

S. Cronin, *The Young Connolly* (Dublin: Repsol, 1978).

R. Crotty, *Ireland in Crisis: A Study in Capitalist Colonial Underdevelopment* (Dingle: Brandon, 1986).

L.M. Cullen, *Anglo-Irish Trade* (Manchester: Manchester University Press, 1968).

I. Cummins, *Marx, Engels and National Movements* (London: Croom Helm, 1980).

M. Daly, *Dublin: The Deposed Capital* (Cork: Cork University Press, 1984).

G. Dangerfield, *The Strange Death of Liberal England* (London: Paladin, 1983).

H.B. Davis, *Nationalism and Socialism* (New York: Monthly Review Press, 1967).

R. Davis, *Griffith and Non-Violent Sinn Fein* (Dublin: Anvil Books, 1974).

A. De Blacam, *What Sinn Fein Stands For* (Dublin: Talbot Mellifont Press, 1920).

D. De Leon, *Reform or Revolution* (New York: Labour News, no date).

J. Degras, *The Communist International 1919–43* (London: OUP, 1956).

D. Dickson, *New Foundations: Ireland 1660–1800* (Dublin: Helicon, 1987).

M. Dubosky, *We Shall be All* (Chicago: Quadrangle, 1969).

O.D. Edwards and K. Pyle, *1916: The Easter Rising* (London: MacGibbon and Kee, 1968).

O.D. Edwards, *James Connolly: The Mind of an Activist* (Dublin: Gill and Macmillan, 1971).

O.D. Edwards and B. Ranson ed, *James Connolly: Selected Writings* (London: Jonathan Cape, 1973).

R. D. Edwards, *Ireland in the Age of the Tudors* (London: Croom Helm, 1977).

M. Elliot, *Partners in Revolution* (New Haven: Yale University Press, 1982).

D. Fitzpatrick, 'Strikes in Ireland, 1914–21' in *Saothar*, no 6 (1980).

D. Fitzpatrick, *Politics and Irish Life, 1913–21: Provincial Experiences of War and Revolution* (Dublin: Gill and Macmillan, 1977).

E. Gurley Flynn, *Rebel Girl* (New York: International Publishers, 1976).

P.S. Foner, *The Industrial Workers of the World 1905–1917*, volume 4 of *History of the Labor Movement in the United States* (New York: International Publishers, 1980).

R. Foster, *Modern Ireland 1600–1972* (London: Allen Lane, 1988).

R. Fox, *The History of the Irish Citizen Army* (Dublin: Duffy, 1945).

R. Fox, *James Connolly: The Forerunner* (Tralee: Kingdom Press, 1966).

T. Garvin, *The Evolution of Nationalist Politics* (Dublin: Gill and Macmillan, 1981).

A. Gaughan, *Tom Johnson: First Leader of the Labour Party* (Dublin: Kingdom Books, 1980).

D. Gluckstein, 'Keir Hardie: The Man who made the Labour Party' in *International Socialism*, no 32 (1984).

A. Gramsci, *Selections from Political Writings 1910–1920* (London: Lawrence and Wishart, 1977).

J. Gray, *City in Revolt* (Belfast: Blackstaff, 1985).

C.D. Greaves, *Liam Mellows and the Irish Revolution*, (London: Lawrence and Wishart, 1971)

C.D. Greaves, *The Life and Times of James Connolly* (London: Lawrence and Wishart, 1976).

C.D. Greaves, *The ITGWU: The Formative Years* (Dublin: Gill and Macmillan, 1982).

D. Herreshoff, *The Origins of American Marxism* (New York: Monad, 1973).

J. Hinton, *The First Shop Stewards Movement* (London: Allen and Unwin, 1973).

E. Hobsbawn, *Industry and Empire* (London: Penguin, 1968).

E. Hobsbawn, *Labouring Men* (London: Weidenfeld and Nicolson, 1976).

B. Holton, *British Syndicalism 1900–1914*, (London: Pluto, 1976).

D. Howell, *A Lost Left: Three Studies in Socialism and Nationalism* (Manchester: Manchester University Press, 1986).

Irish Communist Organisation, *Connolly in America* (Dublin: ICO Books, 1971).

Irish Communist Oranisation, *The Marxism of James Connolly* (Dublin: ICO Books, no date).

W. Kendal, *The Revolutionary Movement in Britain* (London: Weidenfeld and Nicolson, 1969).

D. Keogh, *The Rise of the Irish Working Class: The Dublin Trade Union Movement and Labour Leadership 1890–1914* (Belfast: Appletree Press, 1982).

Y. Kapp, *Eleanor Marx: The Crowded Years 1884–1898* (London: Virago, 1979).

I. Kipnis, *The American Socialist Movement* (New York: Monthly Review, 1972).

J. Joll, *The Second International* (London: Weidenfeld and Nicolson, 1955).

R. Kee, *The Green Flag* (London: Weidenfeld and Nicolson, 1972).

J.F. Lalor, *The Rights of Ireland and the Faith of a Felon*, in O'Brien Collection, NLI, Dublin.

E. Larkin, *James Larkin* (London: Routledge, 1965).

J. Lee, *The Modernisation of Ireland: 1848–1918* (Dublin: Gill and Macmillan, 1973).

V. Lenin, *The Irish Question* (Dublin: Repsol, no date).

J. Leslie, *The Irish Question* (Cork: Cork Workers Club, 1986).

R. Luxemburg, 'Socialism and the Churches' in *Rosa Luxemburg Speaks* (New York: Pathfinder, 1970).

S. Levenson, *James Connolly, Socialist, Patriot and Martyr* (London: Quartet, 1977).

F.S.L. Lyons, *John Dillon* (London: Routledge and Kegan Paul, 1968).

F.S.L. Lyons, *Ireland since the Famine* (London: Collins, 1982).

D.R. O'Connor Lysaght, *The Republic of Ireland* (Cork: Mercier, 1970).

D.R. O'Connor Lysaght, 'The Rake's Progress: The Political Career of William O'Brien' in *Saothar*, no 9 (1983).

P. MacAonghusa and L. Keegan, *The Best of Wolfe Tone* (Cork: Mercier, 1972).

M. Gonne McBride, *A Servant of the Queen* (London: Gollancz, 1974).

F. McDermott, *Theabald Wolfe Tone* (London: Allen Lane, 1988).

B. McGiolla Choille, *Intelligence Notes 1913–16* (Dublin: Government Publications, 1966).

S. MacIntyre, *A Proletarian Science: Marxism in Britain 1917–33* (Cambridge: University Press, 1980).

Rev. McKenna, *The Social Teaching of James Connolly* (Dublin: Catholic Truth Society, 1920).

G. MacNicholl, *Ireland before the Vikings* (Dublin: Gill and Macmillan, 1972).

D. Mahon, *Republicans and Imperialists: Anglo-Irish Relations in the 1930s* (New Haven: Yale University Press, 1984).

C. Markievicz, *James Connolly's Policy and Catholic Doctrine* (NLI, Dublin, no date).

F.X. Martin, *The Irish Volunteers* (Dublin: Duffy, 1963).

K. Marx, *The Civil War in France* (Moscow: Progress, 1969).

K. Marx and F. Engels, *Ireland and the Irish Question* (Moscow: Progress, 1971).

K. Marx, 'The Address to the Central Committee of the Communist League' in K. Marx, *The Revolutions of 1848* (London: Penguin, 1973).

K. Marx, *The Critique of the Gotha Programme* (Moscow: Progress, 1977).

K. Marx and F. Engels, *Wages, Prices and Profit* (Moscow: Progress, 1977).

K. Marx, 'Preface to a Critique of Political Economy' in K. Marx and F. Engels *Selected Works*, vol 1 (Moscow: Progress, 1977).

M. Milotte, *Communism in Modern Ireland* (Dublin: Gill and Macmillan, 1984).

A. Mitchell and P. O'Snodaigh, *Irish Political Documents 1916–1919* (Dublin: Irish Academy Press, 1985).

A. Mitchell, *Labour in Irish Politics* (Dublin: Irish University Press, 1985).

J. Forbes Monro, *Africa and the International Economy 1800–1960* (London: Dent, 1976).

A. Morgan and B. Purdie (eds), *Ireland: Divided Nation, Divided Class* (London: Inklinks, 1980).

A. Morgan, *James Connolly: A Political Biography* (Manchester: Manchester University Press, 1988).

A. Morgan, 'Politics, The Labour Movement and the Working Class in Belfast 1905–23' (unpublished PhD thesis, Belfast: Queen's University).

P. Murray, 'Electoral Politics and the Dublin Working Class Before the First World War' in *Saothar*, no 6 (1980).

J. Newsinger, 'Jim Larkin, Syndicalism and the 1913 Lockout' in *International Socialism Journal* no 25 (1984)

J. Newsinger, 'As Catholic as the Pope: James Connoly and the Roman Catholic Church in Ireland' in *Saothar*, vol 1 (1986).

K. Nicholls, *Land, Law and Society in 16th Century Ireland* (Dublin: National University of Ireland, 1976).

K. Nicholls, *Gaelic and Gaelicised Ireland* (Dublin: Gill and Macmillan, 1981).

C.C. O'Brien, *States of Ireland* (London: Hutchinson, 1972).

W. O'Brien, *Forth The Banners Go* (Dublin: Three Candles, 1969).

S. O'Casey, *History of the Irish Citizen Army*, (London: Journeymen Press, 1980).

E. O'Connor, *Syndicalism in Ireland* (Cork: Cork University Press, 1988).

E. O'Connor, 'Agrarian Unrest and the Labour Movement in Co Waterford' in *Saothar*, no 6 (1980).

P. O'Donnell, *There will be another Day* (Dublin: Dolmen Press, 1963).

G. O'Tuathaigh, *Ireland before the Famine*, (Dublin: Gill and Macmillan, 1982).

M. O'Riordan, 'Connolly, Socialism and the Jewish Worker' in *Saothar*, no 13 (1988).

H. Patterson, *Class Conflict and Sectarianism: The Protestant Working Class and the Belfast Labour Movement 1868–1920* (Belfast: Blackstaff Press, 1980).

H. Pelling, *The Origins of the Labour Party* (London: Macmillan, 1954).

B. Ransom, 'James Connolly and the Scottish Left' (unpublished PhD thesis, Edinburgh, 1975.

B. Ransom, *Connolly's Marxism* (London: Pluto Press, 1980).

C. Reeve and A.B. Reeve, *James Connolly and the United States* (New Jersey, Atlantic Highlands: Humanities Press).

J. Riddell (ed), *Lenin's Struggle for a Revolutionary International: Documents 1907–1916* (New York: Monad, 1984).

F. Robbins, *Under the Starry Plough* (Dublin: Academy Press, 1977).

E. Rumpf and A.C. Hepburn, *Nationalism and Socialism in Twentieth Century Ireland* (Liverpool University Press, 1977).

D. Ryan, *James Connolly: His Life, Work and Writings* (Dublin: Duffy, 1924).

M. Salvadori, *Karl Kautsky and the Second International* (London: New Left Books, 1979).

G. Salvemini, *The French Revolution 1788–1792* (London: Jonathan Cape, 1965).

A.T.Q. Stewart, *The Ulster Crisis* (London: Faber, 1967).

E. Strauss, *Irish Nationalism and British Democracy*, (London: Methuen, 1951).

C. Tsuzuki, *H.M. Hyndman and British Socialism* (London: OUP, 1961).

W. Tone, *An Argument on Behalf of Catholics* (Belfast: ICO Books, 1973).

C. Townsend, *Political Violence in Ireland: Government and Resistance since 1848* (Oxford, Clarendon Press, 1983).

L. Trotsky, *Writings on Britain,* vol 1 (London: New Park, 1974).
L. Trotsky, *The Permanent Revolution* (London: New Park 1982)
L. Trotsky, *Against Individual Terrorism* (New York: Pathfinder, 1987).
D. Williams (ed), *The Irish Struggle 1916–26* (London: Routledge, 1966).
A. Wright, *Disturbed Dublin* (London: Longman and Green, 1914).

Index